RETHINKING THE COMMUNICATIVE TURN

SUNY SERIES IN SOCIAL AND POLITICAL THOUGHT

RETHINKING THE COMMUNICATIVE TURN

ADORNO, HABERMAS, AND THE PROBLEM OF COMMUNICATIVE FREEDOM

MARTIN MORRIS

State University of New York Press

Published by
State University of New York Press

For information, address State University of New York Press, 90 State Street,
Suite 700, Albany, NY 12207

Production by Kelli Williams
Marketing by Fran Keneston

Library of Congress Cataloging-in-Publication Data

Morris, Martin, 1962–
    Rethinking the communicative turn : Adorno, Habermas, and the problem of
communicative freedom / Martin Morris.
        p.   cm. — (SUNY series in social and political thought)
    Includes bibliographical references and index.
    ISBN 0-7914-4797-9 (alk. paper) — ISBN 0-7914-4798-7 (pbk. : alk. paper)
        1. Sociology—Philosophy. 2. Communication—Philosophy. 3. Habermas, Jürgen. 4.
    Adorno, Theodor W., 1903–1969. I. Title. II. Series.

HM585 .M67 2001
301'.01—dc21   00-057353

10 9 8 7 6 5 4 3 2 1

Contents

Contents

Acknowledgments

My understanding of the important questions raised and issues addressed here was assisted especially by my graduate work with Asher Horowitz in Political Science at York University and the continuing discussions that have followed. Also invaluable were my exchanges with Fredric Jameson (Wm. A. Lane, Jr. Professor of Comparative Literature and Chair of the Graduate Program in Literature) and Romand Coles (Political Science) at Duke University during my fellowship stay there. Others who read, commented, and otherwise advised on elements or earlier versions of this text were Robert Albritton, Mildred Bakan, Antonio Callari, Nadine Changfoot, Michael Hardt, Martin Jay, Alkis Kontos, Dieter Misgeld, David Shugarman, Tracy B. Strong, Kenneth Surin, and Candice M. Ward. The anonymous reviewers at the State University of New York Press provided fine recommendations for improvement of the text as a whole. I wish to make special mention of Morton Schoolman's enthusiastic reading of the manuscript during its final phases. Zina Lawrence and Michael Rinella at the State University of New York Press kindly supported the project. Drucilla Cornell, Vassilis Lambropoulos, and Lambert Zuidervaart offered welcome encouragement regarding the project and its elements during the various phases of its completion. Among the many with whom I have learned, the following deserve special mention: my early teachers with whom I have kept in touch and who have offered kind words regarding this project, Cary J. Nederman and Rob Steven, and my other teachers, friends, and colleagues with whom I have engaged, David Bell, David Denemark, Gad Horowitz, Russ Janzen, Christian Lenhardt, Graham Longford, Stephen Newman, Steve Patten, Ross Rudolph, Tim Sinclair, Michael Stevenson, Graham Todd, and William

Walters. While I take responsibility for the written words contained within, I extend my sincerest gratitude to all those above for bestowing on me the generosity of their thoughts.

A Social Sciences and Humanities Research Council of Canada Post-Doctoral Fellowship, 1996–98 took me to Duke University, which I greatly appreciate. I thank Fredric Jameson for his kind hospitality as Chair of the Graduate Program in Literature during my postdoctoral residency at Duke. I was privileged to have the opportunity to participate in such a highly stimulating environment and to come into contact with so many fine minds. This book was completed while teaching at York University and Wilfrid Laurier University.

Many people gave me their support during the course of this project in countless ways through their friendship and love, for which I am deeply grateful. My spouse, Nadine Changfoot, and my parents, Renée and Jim, are prime among them. Many years ago, at the beginning of my university studies in my native New Zealand, I sat with my Grandmother as she lay on her deathbed. At one point I told her of my intentions one day to write a book. I have never forgotten her smile and the complete conviction conveyed in her reply: "I know you will." This book, my first, is dedicated to the memory of Althea Forward.

Selected components of this text were published previously in article form, but all of these elements have undergone further, often significant revision and adaptation for their inclusion here. I thank the editors of the *Review of Politics, South Atlantic Quarterly,* and *Rethinking Marxism* for their permission to use this material. Back cover photo by Nadine Changfoot.

Abbreviations

Note: for *GS*, *MM*, *ND*, and *DA* the German edition is cited first, the English second. I have generally followed the German originals for these texts, using my own translations and adjusting accordingly. No notice of altered existing translations is given. Where English versions do not exist, the translations are mine. Any changes to other translations are noted in the text.

J. Habermas

BFN   *Between Facts and Norms: Contributions to a Discourse Theory of Law and Democracy*, Trans. William Rehg, Cambridge, Mass.: MIT, 1996.

KHI   *Knowledge and Human Interests.* Trans. Jeremy J. Shapiro. Boston: Beacon Press, 1971 [1968].

MCCA   *Moral Consciousness and Communicative Action.* Trans. Christian Lenhardt and Shierry Weber Nicholsen. Cambridge, Mass.: MIT, 1990 [1983].

PDM   *The Philosophical Discourse of Modernity: Twelve Lectures.* Trans. Frederic G. Lawrence. Cambridge, Mass.: MIT, 1987 [1985].

PT   *Postmetaphysical Thinking: Philosophical Essays.* Trans. William Mark Hohengarten. Cambridge, Mass.: MIT, 1992 [1988].

TCAI   *The Theory of Communicative Action: Reason and the Rationalization of Society.* Vol. 1. Trans. Thomas McCarthy. Boston: Beacon Press, 1984 [1981].

TCAII   *The Theory of Communicative Action: Lifeworld and System: A Critique of Functionalist Reason.* Vol. 2. Trans. Thomas McCarthy. Boston: Beacon Press, 1987 [1981].

T. W. Adorno

AT   *Aesthetic Theory*. Trans. Robert Hullot-Kentor. Minneapolis: University of Minnesota Press, 1997 [1970].

GS   *Gesammelte Schriften* (Rolf Tiederman, ed.). Frankfurt: Suhrkamp, 1970–.

HTS   *Hegel: Three Studies*. Trans. Shierry Weber Nicholsen. Cambridge, Mass: MIT, 1993 [1963].

MM   *Minima Moralia: Reflexionen aus dem beschädigten Leben*. Frankfurt: Suhrkamp Verlag, 1951.
         Minima Moralia: Reflections from a Damaged Life. Trans. E. F. N. Jephcott. London: New Left Books.

ND   *Negative Dialektik*, Frankfurt: Suhrkamp, s.t.w. 113, 1975 [1966]. (Also in *GS* 6).
         Negative Dialectics. Trans. E. B. Ashton. New York: Continuum, 1973.

T. W. Adorno and M. Horkheimer

DA   *Dialektik der Aufklärung: Philosophische Fragmente*. Frankfurt: Fischer, 1969 [1947].
         Dialectic of Enlightenment. Trans. John Cumming. New York: Continuum, 1972.

1

INTRODUCTION

This book is about the communication of the human condition and the condition of human communication. Its theme addresses central issues of concern for those interested in understanding the inheritance of Frankfurt critical theory and the contributions to contemporary democratic visions such understanding can offer. The focus is theoretical but the intent practical—which characterizes all worthwhile political theory. I hope to show the promise of a concept of communicative freedom coupled with an ethic of communicative interest in and respect for the other and for otherness that are inspired by a reconsideration of Theodor W. Adorno's critical theory. It is my belief that Adorno's highly complex but often misconstrued thought furnishes important insights for the development of critical social and political thought under contemporary conditions.

In making these contentions, however, I will directly challenge the work of one who has championed the possibilities of intersubjective communicative relations for freedom and for democratic society today and who claims a direct relation to the tradition of Frankfurt critical theory in which Adorno worked: Jürgen Habermas. Habermas aims to preserve the critical spirit of modernity and the original aims of Frankfurt critical theory during a time when critical reason has become subject to serious questioning. He values a social and political theory that would reassure modern selves of their identity and the possibility of their reason in the face of the disasters and disappointments with which enlightening and rationalizing political action has been associated in the twentieth century. Habermas believes that theoretically informed critique can remain reasonable while criticizing society, and indeed, that critical articulations are essential for freedom and democracy. He does not believe that we should give up on the idea of a rational society or on the possibilities of its realization through social change. But he thinks such an idea must be conceived according to his communicative theory and under the historical limit conditions of modern, differentiated, liberal–democratic society if the practical dangers associated with the utopian visions of planned socialist economies, neoliberal markets, or reactionary fundamentalisms are to be avoided.

For Habermas, critical theory itself took a 'dark' and ultimately fatal turn in the 1940s with the publication of Horkheimer and Adorno's *Dialectic of Enlightenment* (1972 [1947]), after which the development of its original program of a comprehensive social science with practical-political intent seemed impossible. From the 1960s, Habermas has led a broad-based effort among a new generation of critical theorists to reconstitute critical theory and recover this vision of a practical-political social science, an effort that culminated in his two-volume magnum opus, *Theory of Communicative Action* (1984; 1987). Central to this project was the clarification of the theoretical foundations for a universal human sociality by means of the concept of communicative rationality, which would meet the requirements of a *critical* social theory. While he has since stepped back from the original scope of this grand project, believing it to be overly ambitious at present, he has nevertheless remained true to the core concept of communicative rationality in his subsequent work. His social and political thought are still informed by a commitment to this notion, despite his shifts in focus and formulation. Recognition of the universal basis of communicative rationality, Habermas believes, offers the best hope for stability in the face of social complexity and human diversity, while at the same time it affirms the crucial political values of individual freedom, autonomy, and social solidarity.

I do not quarrel with Habermas about the importance of such calls for critique, communicative freedom, autonomy, solidarity, or achieving more effective democracy. Instead, I raise serious questions concerning his central ideas and the extent to which his theory actually meets the liberatory expectations of a critical social theory. In challenging Habermas's critical theory, I wish to propose an alternative reading of Adorno's critical theory that might better address these contemporary concerns. As a consequence, what I present here takes the overall form of a critique of Habermas via a recollection and interpretation of Adorno's work.

1.1. The Frankfurt School and Habermas:
A Snapshot View

Both Adorno and Habermas are major figures associated with so-called Frankfurt school "critical theory," a twentieth-century tradition of philosophy and social criticism that emerged in the context of Western Marxism. However, it should be noted that the appellation *critical theory* has proliferated in recent decades. It no longer primarily refers to the Frankfurt tradition but can apply to diverse theoretical perspectives and preoccupations in fields such as sociological theory, historiography, literary theory, and aesthetic criticism. For the sake of simplicity, in this book I shall use the term critical theory to refer to the Frankfurt tradition, though I acknowledge that many of the central concerns of critical theory are also taken up by others in the Western Marxist tradition, as well as in post-Marxist and poststructuralist theory.

Frankfurt school critical theory refers in the first instance to the writings of a loosely knit group of critical philosophers and social scientists associated with the privately endowed Institute for Social Research in Frankfurt, the first establishment in the West founded explicitly to give institutional expression and support to Marxist research (for that reason alone, a unique and remarkable institution). Under the directorship of Max Horkheimer, who took over in 1930, the Institute supported the work of a number of thinkers and researchers who were involved in developing a comprehensive Marxist theory of social analysis that addressed the changed conditions of twentieth-century capitalism. Horkheimer was an adept and visionary 'managerial scholar' who assembled a core group of intellectuals to develop a new program of theoretical and historical research that came to be described as critical theory. The Institute for Social Research came into existence officially in 1924 and was affiliated with and located at Frankfurt University during the 1920s and early 1930s. Forced into exile after the rise of Nazi Germany, the Institute was eventually moved to New York City, where it continued to operate with a reduced level of support and activities. The Institute was reopened in Frankfurt in 1951 with the return of several core members, where it sustains activities in conjunction with Frankfurt University.

But Frankfurt critical theory is more properly a tradition of thought rather than a school, per se. There was no collectively held doctrine or set of propositions followed by all members since critical theory was conceived in opposition to orthodoxy and aimed instead at a supradisciplinary approach (see section 2.1). Moreover, many of the foundational analyses and texts of the early figures that came to represent "Frankfurt" theory were written in exile from Germany—primarily in the United States and France. However, the measure of coherence that identifies this tradition for critical theorists is provided by the institutional setting (the Institute existed for the core members their entire careers), a founding 'manifesto' outlined in Horkheimer's inaugural address in 1931 to which he and other members repeatedly referred during their careers, and the Institute journal, *Zeitschrift für Sozialforschuung* (*Journal for Social Research*), in which members published their work. Admittedly, this coherence most clearly applies to the early period of the Institute for Social Research, but enough continuities have persisted by which a tradition of thought can be traced (even while the term "Frankfurt school" itself came into use only in the 1960s and was coined by outsiders). Among the figures commonly associated with Frankfurt critical theory besides Horkheimer, Adorno, and Habermas are Herbert Marcuse, Walter Benjamin, Friedrich Pollock, Otto Kirchheimer, Erich Fromm, Franz Neumann, and Leo Lowenthal, many of whom became quite well known in Anglo-American intellectual circles.[1] (I provide a more detailed account of the Institute and its development in Chapter 2.)

Indeed, what is called the Frankfurt school tradition of critical theory has proved to be one of the most enduring forms of critical reflection in the twentieth century. This endurance can be seen not only in the persistent if loose intellectual cohesion and complementarity of those originally associated with the Institute during their careers (although there were also serious disputes and falling outs, such as that involving Fromm). Continuity is also evident in the substantial influence of the teachings of core figures such as Adorno, Horkheimer, and Marcuse on young intellectuals in the decades following the second world war. Marcuse became a special authority for the student and counterculture movements of the 1960s, and critical theory acquired a rather mythical status in this period. Despite controversies with and condemnations from the student movement of the late 1960s and from New Left intellectuals, which afflicted Adorno perhaps most of all, the influence of Frankfurt school writings extended well into the 1970s. If there was a moment that signaled a crisis in radical social thought and practice, it may be the dashed hopes that followed the events of May 1968. As a crucial turning point for the popular movements for social change and their intellectual supporters, this moment fueled the development of alternate critical positions such as poststructuralist, post-Marxist, and feminist theory. A general decline in the influence of Marxism on critical thought has occurred in Europe and the West since the end of the 1960s, and Frankfurt critical theory was most closely associated with the Marxist tradition.

The 1990s, however, saw a certain resurgence in interest in Adorno in the humanities, especially by Anglo-American critical thought, which has, inspired by his work, reassessed the aesthetic as an ethical category. Adorno has thus become, for some, the "conscience of our political and aesthetic crisis."[2] Benjamin's work also maintains a substantial intellectual presence today—among other things he is venerated as a founding figure in the relatively new but expanding field of cultural studies.

But besides these legacies of philosophy and social analysis, perhaps the most important contribution to the endurance of Frankfurt critical theory is Habermas's grand effort to substantially revise and reconstitute this tradition for a whole new generation of students and scholars. In no small way is Habermas's success related to the crisis of the 'crisis of Marxism' in Western thought—the apparent decline in vitality of much Marxist discourse and analysis that emerged in the 1980s (see Agger, 1990).

While Adorno was a member of the inner circle of figures associated with the Frankfurt school from the 1930s to his death in 1969, Habermas is of a later generation. Habermas, whose relationship with Frankfurt critical theory began when he became Adorno's assistant during the latter 1950s, is widely regarded as the direct inheritor of the mantle of this tradition from Adorno. This inheritance, however, has been substantially transfigured under Habermas's intellectual leadership.[3] Notably, Habermas's transformation of critical theory involves an explicit rejection of Adorno's central negative dialectic and what I might call his aesthetic-critical theory, which were developed as responses to the latter's analysis of the fateful dialectic of enlightenment. Habermasian critical theory instead (sometimes) claims a heritage more directly from the original conception of critical theory articulated in Horkheimer's early writings. Yet Habermas has introduced a number of new and quite different aspects to the program of critical theory in an attempt to revitalize and continue its critical spirit in the face of various theoretical and practical difficulties attributed to its later 'Adornian' developments. Thus Habermas is a contemporary figure of continuity and discontinuity in the tradition of critical theory.

Habermas has championed the turn to linguistic philosophy in critical theory with the thesis that the theory of communicative action provides the key to a comprehensive understanding of social action. In conjunction with these philosophical and sociological elements, he has also developed a robust political theory. The analysis of the universal communicative presuppositions of speech affords insight into the shape of a rational and just politics at the same time as it indicates how a rationalized, self-reflective culture can also realize 'utopian' desires; that is, in traditional formulation, how the just citizen can also have a good life. Such bold and far-reaching claims rely on a theoretical move from a subject-centered, epistemological, and representational focus to an intersubjective, pragmatic, and linguistic one.

Habermas's rational orientation toward theory locates him within the modern tradition, but with a postmetaphysical twist: reason is no longer understood in the last analysis as a capacity or endowment of human subjects themselves (for this is a characteristic of subject philosophy). Instead, reason is to be understood as the organizing feature of linguistically mediated communication or communicative sociality itself. Human beings grow into language and their use of language transforms them: they are pragmatically 'communicating animals' whose needs, beyond basic physiological needs, and whose full life are realized only at the level of autonomous and free *communication* with others. It is ideally the life of fully rational linguistic communication that sets people free from the unreflective prejudice of tradition, the obscurity of myth, and the blind imitation of others. Reason and democracy are immanently related for Habermas. The rationality of modern language-use constrains and imposes limits, but it also establishes the genuine condition for the autonomy of the human self and the freedom for it to develop and grow. The specific idea of freedom here is tied to the act of human sociation through linguistically mediated truth-seeking. Any concept of truth that deserves its meaning entails the freedom to determine it. If truth is immanently related to practical language use, then the concept of freedom, too, can be discerned in the contours of linguistically mediated life. Clarifying the nature of reason can hence lead us to politically consequential conclusions.

Habermas's main critical claim is that the possibility of such a life has been systematically denied and distorted by the one-sided development of the potentials of modernity under the influence of capitalism and administrative power. Indeed, the logical and social limits of communicative action are limits beyond which only the subversion of language, society, and self occurs. The *telos* of communicative action—the free and equal achievement of mutual understanding and agreement—is undermined by all forms of systematically distorted communication, which becomes the new term for ideology. The critique of systematically distorted communication takes over certain aspects of the former Marxist critique of ideology and entails an idea of the conditions for non-distorted communication. Manipulative or distorted communication can be condemned not only because it is evidence of unfreedom, of domination or oppression, but also because it undermines the basis of stable and successful human interaction. Limited communication prevents genuine interpretive action and thereby denies the realization of the communicating actor's life, potentials, and meaningful relations with others. Habermas thus continues to be concerned with questions central to critical theory such as those of freedom, autonomy, solidarity, ideology critique, and the possibility of a genuinely rational democratic society. But with this turn to a linguistic, intersubjective-centered approach, he has necessarily abandoned as aporetic, dangerous, or at least paradigmatically outdated critical theory's fixations with the aesthetic and a 'new sensibility'—that is, with a substantially new ability to perceive and experience that would help constitute the liberated society. Such involvements were central to critical theorists' aims to foster a non-instrumental concern for and relationship to others, a new compassion or passionate care that could be universalizable. For Adorno, it should be noted, there were important limits to such new sensibilities. Christian love, as one example of an ancient "new sensibility," cannot be universalized in large, complex, modern societies; it is best suited to small, intimate communities where the intensity and identifications required for such ethical relations can be concentrated. Adorno, by contrast, sought a new sensibility and communicative ability that approaches the other not on the ethical levels of the familial or the intimate, which assume and oblige significant knowledge of and closeness to the other, but as a stranger, as different and alien. Adorno wanted to foster a "nearness by distance" (*MM*: 112/89–90) in which difference could be maintained, even celebrated, in a process of self-reflective contemplation, learning, and communication that would not require the kind of constitutive identification of traditional conceptions of community. A new sensibility was also important for better or more liberatory encounters with the non-linguistic sources of human existence, from human bodily drives and desires that were being increasingly manipulated by new media and industry technologies to the non-human otherness of the natural world that was being destroyed or assimilated by capitalist development. These preoccupations contributed so much to the critical theorists' utopian visions.

However, Habermas's model has by no means received universal assent among those sympathetic to the tradition of critical theory nor indeed has his theory been readily adopted as a political guide by any contemporary social movements dedicated to progressive democratic aims. Indeed, it is severely criticized and in general dismissed by contemporary poststructuralist and deconstructionist critics who themselves claim to articulate a far more compelling and defensible intellectual spirit that might be adopted in contemporary progressive and democratic struggles against domination and oppression. This kind of latter claim has become more commanding after the much heralded 'death' of Marxism, since critical theory in general is most consistently associated with Marxist theory and practice. Postmodernist critics are insistent of the need to abandon any kind of grand or totalizing theory in the face of the barbarous realizations and utter failures of the universalizing modern project in its various guises, including the brutal examples from the former Soviet empire. It bears mentioning in this context that figures of the Frankfurt school were highly critical of Soviet-style Marxism during a time when this was exceptional among left intellectuals in the West.[4] In light of the fall of actually existing European socialism, early Frankfurt figures such as Adorno—who was consistently critical of command as well as market economies—now deserve further attention and might even seem fresh to critical intellectuals today.

Adorno, I shall argue, was also centrally concerned with communication, with the way in which a communicative freedom could be fostered. Yet unlike Habermas, the former pursued this through the cultivation of an awareness of the 'objectivity of subjectivity' and reflection on the non-identical content of human sociality. Adorno presents a very different version of the communicative awareness and ethical understanding of reason than that theorized by Habermas—one that is, I will contend, quite incompatible and non-contiguous with Habermas's but still of great value today.

My general contention in this book is that, despite the many valuable insights and contributions to critical social theory offered by Habermas's theory, there are serious difficulties with and drawbacks to it that reach 'paradigmatic' proportions when gauged against the achievements of Adorno's critical theory. In the last analysis the communicative direction suggested by Adorno's negative dialectic indicates the more promising route for critical theory and democratic politics today. This is not to say that Adorno's theory does not contain substantive problems of its own—it does. Any critical theory today inspired by his theory will need to be aware of such problems while drawing on what is essential and valuable in the call of his work. For now, given that the Habermasian (mis)construal and criticism of Adorno's position are generally better known today than the actual content and claims of the latter's theory, clarification and elaboration are still necessary tasks. My specific argument, which I hope to sustain in various ways throughout the text, is that the focus on the aesthetic and the concerns with new sensibility and understanding born of an awareness of the objectivity of subjectivity (which animated much of Adorno's most important writing) are *crucial* for a critical theory and for democracy and cannot be abandoned without substantially weakening the possibilities of both. But it is precisely the critical Adornian insights into the objectivity of subjectivity that must be sacrificed if one is to accept the paradigmatic 'advance' Habermas offers.

Yet it is not that Habermas is all that disrespectful of his teacher. Adorno occupies a special position for Habermas not only in Frankfurt critical theory, but in the philosophical tradition itself. Adorno's remorseless critical insistence on the paradoxes of the "philosophico-historical concept of reason" inherited from Lukács and the Western Marxist tradition leads Habermas to describe him as "the most systematic and effective thinker" he has known (1986a: 97–98). Habermas's praise is for Adorno's unflinching stand in the face of the philosophical implications of the dialectic of enlightenment, without ever giving up on the critical idea of reason no matter how bleak the possibilities for freedom seemed historically. It is instead Adorno's inability to get beyond the limits of what is called subject-centered reason except by way of the allegedly inadequate appeal to aesthetic mimesis that Habermas finds his greatest and most unambiguous fault.

The crux of the Habermasian position is that Adorno fails to make the paradigmatic turn to the pragmatics of language and communication that must be made if critical theory is to break definitively with the philosophy of consciousness (*Bewußtseinsphilosophie*) or philosophy of the subject (*Subjektsphilosophie*). Central to my treatment of Habermas and Adorno will thus be the analysis of this so-called "paradigm shift," which I regard to be decisive in assessing their respective positions. More generally, given the influence of linguistic philosophy on social thought across the board, this switch may be one of the most important theoretical issues for critical social theory today. Hence the achievements—but really more important the *failures*—of this paradigm shift in critical theory provide general topics for the present work. But Habermas does not exactly claim to have given up on the utopian critique of Frankfurt school critical theory. For as Habermas has developed the core elements of his theory, which find their single most comprehensive expression in his major *Theory of Communicative Action*, he has also sought to use the characterization of a paradigm shift to establish the way in which the most worthwhile features of Frankfurt critical theory can be preserved in his theory. Not only is there here a claim to continuity with critical theory, but also a claim that the important limits of older critical theory can be traced to the 'paradigm' of consciousness philosophy—that its aporias and dead-ends can be resolved *only* in the shift to the theory of communicative action.

This meta-theoretical shift is inaugurated in the context of critical theory by Habermas and K. O. Apel and has proved to be highly influential among many social and political theorists over the last decades. Indeed, according to one Habermasian commentator, the paradigm shift in critical theory has brought with it "irreversible gains" (Benhabib, 1986: 345). This transformation in critical theory is inspired by the achievements of the more general shift to linguistic philosophy in twentieth-century philosophy and social theory pioneered by those such as Gottlob Frege, Ludwig Wittgenstein, Ferdinand Saussure, J. L. Austin and Noam Chomsky; of late, the work of Jacques Lacan has also been emphasized in association with a linguistic turn.[5] Habermas draws especially from the speech pragmatics of Austin and John Searle and from the transcendental-pragmatic arguments of Apel. The very phrase *paradigm shift* speaks to the significance of this dimension in Habermas's theory, and I think it not an exaggeration to say that this meta-theoretical and methodological shift provides the basis for much of his substantive theory within and after *Knowledge and Human Interests* (1971a), although evidence of the turn to language and communicative theory is present as early as Habermas's inaugural lecture at Frankfurt University in 1965 (*KHI*: 301–17). Even before this his commitment to free public communication in the context of the structural transformation of the (bourgeois) public sphere is central to his *Habilitationschrift* (1989c). But it was only with the emphatic paradigmatic shift in *Theory of Communicative Action* that Habermas ceased to struggle with the reconstruction of historical materialism (see Habermas, 1979a) and explicitly *replaced* it with his new theory. It is also in *Theory of Communicative Action* that he formulates his most devastating critique of Frankfurt critical theory.

The paradigm shift is thus ostensibly the *Aufhebung* of older critical theory. The German *Aufhebung* is an apt term for this shift (although it is rarely used in this context) for, among other things, it underlines in Habermas's relationship to Frankfurt critical theory the sense of negation and preservation. This said, however, the present effort should not be understood as dogmatic: an original critical theory is not to be defended against its watering down, corruption, or destruction in the new critical theory. Neither can Habermas's theory simply be dismissed from the perspective of postmodernity as modernist, rationalist, or formalist and hence itself outdated (the accusation of modernism and the commitment to a rational society may also implicate Adorno from this position). One of the contentions of the present work is that Habermasian critical theory is altogether a *different kind* of critical theory to that committed to negation—which might group Adornian, poststructuralist, or deconstructionist critiques together (this is an assessment Habermas himself would not entirely disagree with, of course). Yet Habermasian theory has more in common with what critical theory rejects as traditional theory than Habermas would like to admit. This is why the paradigm shift can be emphasized so usefully: understanding Habermas depends on understanding his translation of the language of critical theory. What follows in these pages is a critical examination of the logic and arguments that lead Habermas, and those who by and large agree with him, to abandon the older 'paradigm' of critical theory for the new line of critique.[6]

1.2. Conflicting Paradigmatic Issues

Naturally, the criticism of the philosophy of consciousness and subjectivity was a dominant concern for Adorno, as summed up in his critical concept of the dialectic of enlightenment itself. But, according to Habermas, Adorno is nevertheless trapped within the paradigmatic limits of the subject's concern with knowing and acting even while he remains such an unyielding critic of its philosophical and social self-reflections. In the absence of the turn to language and communicative action, Habermas sees no defensible alternative to the subject of modern philosophy and he will not tolerate its utter effacement as might be discerned in structuralism or poststructuralism. For him, the ultimate emptiness of the philosophy of consciousness must be overcome by the theory of communicative action which accounts for subjectivity in a far more satisfactory way. This is to be achieved by moving the self-reflection of reason into this new field rather than, as in Niklas Luhmann's systems theory, for example, attempting to overcome the subject simply by switching from a metaphysics of subject and object to a 'metabiology' of relations between systems and environments that succeeds only to the extent that it loses any purchase on *critique* (*PDM*: 368–85). Adorno is also important in this respect for Habermas (and for myself) precisely because he sought to take the self-reflection of reason to a higher level and thereby to negate the philosophy of consciousness *without* sacrificing a profound and unrelenting critique of domination.

That Adorno did not finally succeed in this endeavor, according to Habermas, is arguably less important than the spirit of the former's critique. Habermas's critique of Adorno is certainly intended to be final, to foreclose on the project of the negative dialectic once and for all. But, in contrast to his earlier criticisms of Adorno that advocated a break with the orientation toward reconciliation or utopia, Habermas now recognizes a fundamental utopian element in Adorno's critique that he, along with others such as Albrecht Wellmer (1985; 1991) and Seyla Benhabib (1986), believe is (indeed, must be) preserved in the theory of communicative action for it to qualify properly as a critical theory. In Wellmer's words, Adorno's utopian projection of a "'non-violent' synthesis" is not to be found in some new relationship to the Other of discursive reason, but rather is precisely the regulative idea that discursive reason has of itself, rooted in the conditions of language (cf. Habermas, 1986a: 156–57; Wellmer, 1991: 14). Once the move to the theory of communicative action is made, an ethic of discourse can be uncovered in the dialogic relation between participants in rational speech that meets Adorno's requirement for the recognition of difference—*but within rather than beyond the world of logos*. A normative foundation for critique is then to be discovered within a communicative rationality that draws upon the suppressed rational potentials of modernity and hence offers theory a secure basis from which to criticize current conditions.

It is indeed precisely a freedom equivalent to the freedom projected by Adorno that Habermas claims to have determined with the theory of communicative action—and *without* the need for a radical rupture with capitalist modernity. Whoever "meditates" on Adorno's enigmatic statement that the reconciled state would "find its happiness where the alien remains distant and different in its lasting nearness, beyond the heterogeneous and beyond that which is one's own" (*ND*: 192/191) will become aware, Habermas contends, "that the condition described, although never real, is still most intimate and familiar to us. It has the structure of a life together in communication that is free from coercion. We necessarily anticipate such a reality . . . each time we speak what is true. The idea of truth, already implicit in the first sentence spoken, can be shaped only on the model of the idealized agreements aimed for in communication free from domination" (Habermas, 1983d: 108–9). What Adorno was looking for, Habermas asserts, were the structures of "reciprocity of mutual understanding based on free recognition," in which "the ideas of reconciliation and freedom are deciphered as codes for a form of intersubjectivity" (*TCAI*: 390–91). Although this form of intersubjectivity is, for Habermas, idealized in presuppositions made most transparent in the rather specialized form of discursive speech, it can be discerned even at the level of everyday speech and action.

For Habermas, this avenue of inquiry is far preferable than the resolution to leave the potentials of modernity completely behind, which he sees as philosophically irresponsible and politically dangerous or regressive. According to Habermas, it is especially the radical critiques of reason and language by such post-Nietzschean critics as Michel Foucault and Jacques Derrida that entail a loss of the subject and of reason, the abandonment of enlightenment in an attempt to escape from its dialectic of reason and domination. The radical critique of reason and language ultimately escapes the (totalizing) domination of reason and language only at the price of its own coherence. The critique of instrumental reason must, for Habermas, remain rational if it is to have a voice at all, but this effort continually seems, at root, to refer to something *beyond* reason, *beyond* language, for the sake of which the truth of its critique stands.[7] Habermas believes there is something fundamentally wrong with such programs of critique.

Although Habermas is rather less critical of Horkheimer and Adorno in *The Philosophical Discourse of Modernity* (1987) than he is of the other, mostly post-Nietzschean figures discussed in this text, it is nevertheless significant that Horkheimer and Adorno are included in the radical line along with these contemporary critics. His inclusion of them ironically lends Adorno a contemporaneity that Habermas no doubt does not really intend, but which has not been lost on commentators (see the introduction and essays in Pensky, 1997). I draw this parallel between Habermas and Adorno to suggest branching critical routes from similar sources and concerns. Each figure is to be seen in his own way as negotiating alternative, yet incompatible paths away from the philosophy of consciousness and the subject. As such, I want to affirm the relevance of Adorno's critical theory distinct from Habermas's. But I also suggest that Adorno's position is nevertheless divergent from current poststructuralist critical theory that seeks to address quite similar concerns. These distinctions, I think, make Adorno's theory a stronger contender for progressive allegiances in light of Habermasian and dialectical critiques of postmodernism. The work at hand seeks to clarify these alternatives in order to show what has been lost, sacrificed in the shift to Habermasian theory, yet what must nevertheless be preserved for a reconstructed critical theory at the turn of the millennium.

Nonetheless, many current commentators sympathetic to the reconstruction and revitalization of Frankfurt critical theory accept in large part Habermas's critique of Horkheimer and Adorno and his assessment of the latter's contribution to critical theory. Habermas does appear to offer a way out of the self-consciously aporetic critical theory that Adorno develops in his major texts, and perhaps this also enhances the former's appeal. Many critical writers who align themselves with the Habermasian project and in opposition to poststructuralist critical theory find Habermas's formulation of the issues for critical theory compelling and hence largely ignore Adorno. For those who embrace full-fledged poststructuralist theory, a selective appropriation of Adorno is possible, but significant revision or abandonment of older critical theory also seems necessary. My sympathies and position seem to lie somewhere in between the two.

We may now discern two central and related issues concerning the paradigmatic transitions that are to be addressed in the present study. The first concerns the very real problems with the philosophy of consciousness and subject philosophy and the entwinement of critical theory with these problems. This issue requires an account of the main reasons why Habermasian theorists regard as necessary the general paradigm shift in critical theory. This entails a specific elaboration of Habermas's critique of Adorno, which is given primarily in Chapter 4 along with a more general discussion of the paradigm shift. Adorno's own unsystematic critiques of the philosophy of consciousness appear especially in sections 2.2, 4.4, and Chapter 5. For Adorno, as for Habermas, the kind of thought represented by the philosophy of consciousness contains fundamental faults. For the purposes of the present study, there is no question that an alternative is required.

The second main issue is whether, as Habermas contends, Adorno is finally to be located *within* this thinking, even as the latter is fundamentally critical of it (although not quite in the kind of 'paradigmatic' way Habermas advocates). In Chapters 2, 4, and 5 I present my reasons for thinking that Adorno's critical theory offers a route away from the philosophy of consciousness that is more promising than Habermas's. In the course of my contrasts of Adorno's and Habermas's critical theories, I contest the success of Habermas's solution to the aporias of Frankfurt theory and, more broadly, to the aporias of subject and consciousness philosophy themselves. Due to the entwinement of the paradigm shift with the substance of Habermas's theory, this is also hence a contestation of the Habermasian inheritance of critical theory, a contestation undertaken for the sake of the democratic potential lost in the abandonment of the negative dialectic. While Habermas's systematic misunderstanding of Adorno enables him to present the paradigm shift and the development of his theory in a rational and compelling way,[8] he neglects the crucial arguments and claims of Adorno that threaten his position most centrally. These arguments and claims in no small part address consciousness philosophy, subjectivity, intersubjectivity, and ideology critique. Habermas's criticisms of Adorno as well as his theory of communicative action beg many questions concerning these topics—questions Adorno attempts to answer most centrally.

The substance of the study opens in Chapter 2 with an exploration of some main motifs of early Frankfurt critical theory. This serves as an introduction to some of the central issues pursued in the book. The theme of this chapter is the crisis of ideology critique, which all contemporary critical theory has been obliged to address in some way. This includes a discussion of the decisive dialectic of enlightenment to which both Habermas's theory and Adorno's later work respond. In Chapters 3 and 4, I turn to an examination of the specific achievements of the paradigm shift as they appear through the lens of Habermas's notion of communicative rationality. Chapter 3 examines Habermas's theory as a *critical* theory of society, that is, as a theory of social pathology or repression, with a particular focus on the analysis of the Marxist concept of real abstraction in section 3.3. In this chapter I assess Habermas's view of the systematically suppressed rational potentials of modernity from the perspective of the critique of reification. In Chapter 4 I converge on Habermas's claim to have discovered the universal basis of sociality in the pragmatic relations of speech. Having established the intellectual context of Habermas's engagement with critical theory in the previous chapter and the basis for his own paradigmatic shift in the early sections of this one, a reconstruction and assessment of his critique of Adorno follows in second half of Chapter 4. The central Habermasian criticism of performative contradiction (which is leveled at poststructuralism as well as Adorno's theory) is given special attention with respect to the radical critique of reason and the negative dialectic. Here I offer a defense of Adorno on the basis of *dialectical* consistency rather than Habermas's preferred *performative* consistency, and draw out the inadequacies of Habermas's notion. Finally, in Chapter 5, I offer a further critique of Habermasian theory as non-utopian coupled with an interpretation of Adorno that attempts to move his thought in promising directions for contemporary concerns. In the final sections I investigate the possible alternatives toward which Adorno's thought points that can be drawn from a reading of his aesthetic-critical theory. I defend the Adornian notion of the mimetic 'shudder' as a pivotal point through which to access an alternative communicative ethic and freedom appropriate for a renewed critical politics.

2

CRITICAL THEORY AND THE ECLIPSE OF 'IDEOLOGY': THE EARLY FRANKFURT VISION AND ITS TRANSFORMATION

'Ideology' is a key concept in Marxist critical theory, though its proper meaning and use have been subject to intense and lengthy debate.[1] Its problematization as an analytical category and critical concept under conditions of 'late' capitalism or postmodernity has required that it be rethought significantly, if not completely abandoned. Indeed, many alternatives have been developed to take its place in contemporary critical theories. Since the late 1950s, moreover, conservative thought has included an end of ideologies thesis corresponding to the view that fundamental social change does not offer an advance over capitalist democracy.[2]

But there is also a distinct sense that contemporary politics can no longer be understood adequately in terms of coherent and identifiable positive political ideologies. This condition exists not only as a result of mass or catch-all political parties in the twentieth century and the transformation of political contestation in an era of televisual and sophisticated mass-mediated politics. Indeed, political parties themselves are in a period of critical transformation if not in outright decline as a result of such changes and other factors such as the less autonomous and smaller role of the political state itself in the globalizing political economy. Neither is the decline of ideology quite a condition of the failed political projects of 'previously' existing socialism in Eastern Europe or the century's deradicalization of left political parties in the West to the point at which, in the 1990s, so-called "Third Way" social democratic parties can hold power in almost all European countries while continuing to implement capital-friendly neoliberal restructuring. New modes of political dominance also emerged in the 1980s such as Thatcherism and Reaganism that deployed ideological strategies in new and complex ways and have colonized and transformed the political space in which older ideological battles were once fought. Indeed, severely complicating contemporary ideological mapping are the shifts or transformations in spatial and temporal experience under the conditions of multinational or late capitalism, which has problematized the historical consciousness itself. The seriousness of this new postmodern condition or "dilemma" of representation corresponds to a disjunction in our very perceptual abilities, which were themselves formed under a different cognitive environment (high modernism) for much of the century and which have not yet evolved to match the experience of the new "postmodernist hyperspace" (Jameson, 1991; see also Harvey, 1989).

Moreover, resistance has also proliferated in the twentieth century with multiple critical positions and objects of contestation that have fragmented political opposition to dominant social power. It is difficult to conceive of a systematic logic to the production of ideas, which the concept of ideology as the logic of the idea suggests, if there is no determinant system or level of society onto which ideas can be mapped. Not only capital and class, but the operation of patriarchy, environmental destruction and pollution, consumerism, heterosexuality, Eurocentrism, and racism are among those manifestations of social power producing vital resistance movements. However, the critical theories that have accompanied these new movements of resistance do not often claim to be addressing the systematic *totality* of social relations as Marxist theory claimed to do for the (revolutionary) working class. Neither do they necessarily seek the *universal* liberation from domination and ideology toward which Marxism aimed, though there are still some positions that do make this claim, if in modified form.

At the global political level, the conflict between the two grand, contesting ideological visions of a universal political order—the free world versus communist society—has given way to the regressive flourishing of increased regional instability, intensified regional social and military violence, religious and political fundamentalisms, racism, ethnic hatred and exclusion, and genocide. But again, these new conflicts tend to be divided along particularistic lines such as those established by ethnicity or nationalist identities rather than between contesting political causes with universal visions, which the concept of ideology used to name as encompassing theoretical or visionary constructs. Overlaying the global system is nevertheless the same basic political relations of domination and inequality between the 'developed' centers and the 'underdeveloped' periphery that became established with the European imperialisms in the sixteenth century. But current neocolonial domination, which operates through free trade, foreign investment and development, international aid, and the dissemination of Western consumer culture instead of direct rule, and which is enforced by the disciplinary efforts of international organizations such as the World Bank, the W.T.O., and the I.M.F., is far harder to identify and to effectively resist today than were the spatially centered colonial administrations for the former resistance movements of national liberation.

Politics, however, concerns far more than battles between ideological positions or cultures, be they universalist or particularist. Conversely, the question of ideology is politically important far beyond the articulation and dissemination of a specific logic of ideas. The need to get beyond a relativist view of ideologies (or their equivalents) and a simple pluralist view of politics are twin tasks centrally important to critical theory. Our aim in this chapter is to consider how Frankfurt critical theory began to recast the critique of ideology early in what might be called a growing crisis in ideology critique in the first half of the twentieth century that has only been fully realized at century's end. The Marxist roots of ideology critique were substantially transformed though not completely abandoned during the trajectory of Frankfurt critical theory's account of the historical transformation of capitalist society. Yet this is an indication more of critical theory's adherence to a non-dogmatic dialectical materialism than of any loss of faith. Indeed, critical theory seeks to respond in general to the historical need for new critical knowledge of society and politics under ever changing social conditions. Its social ontology thus cannot be static, which means it does not quite hold to a social ontology at all.

The critique of ideology that concerns us here includes but entails more than a *theory* of ideology. That is, it is also oriented toward overcoming the *power* ideology exerts on human beings. Ideology critique is thus often regarded as essential for a critical social theory that seeks social change. In Marxist theory, the critical concept of ideology acquires crucial political content by naming the ideational part of the relations of social domination: the 'false' ideas and systematic blockages that mask the real underlying class relations of domination by presenting them as something other than they are or hiding them completely from social subjects. Ideology operates in the service of those with material interests in perpetuating these relations of domination. To criticize ideo-logical views is thus to attempt to reveal what otherwise might seem to be rational or reasonable 'ideas' as operations of domination and there-fore not at all as rational or as reasonable as they seem. What appears as universal, legitimate, natural, empirically factual, or simply unalterable aspects of life or human nature are really historical and changeable, merely hidden particulars that masquerade as universals in a historical milieu. Inherent in this notion of ideology is the desire to overcome it, to dis-pense with falsity and disguise in the interests of a 'true' condition free of such distortion.

What might constitute such a projected true state of affairs is revealed by the practical-political dimension of critical theory. This is not supposed to offer just another 'positive' ideology but a state free from the pejorative and deceptive senses of ideology themselves (see Geuss, 1981). The true state of affairs in this sense is equivalent to political freedom—the utopian projection that inspires critical theory to work for liberation. But it is just such a utopian projection, along with its desirability as a political force, that has been seriously called into question with the problematization of the critical concept of ideology. One of the major themes introduced in this chapter and indeed pur-sued in this book is how the critique of that which was named as ideology can be understood (within the tradition of critical theory) and defended without abandoning the political motivation provided by a certain utopian articulation.

I will begin this chapter with a rehearsal of some main themes in the original program of Frankfurt critical theory and its intellectual his-tory in order to provide context for the major arguments of this book. This will by no means be a comprehensive treatment of critical theory but a highly selective account relevant to present aims. My guiding motif is the crisis of ideology critique, which might also be taken as a manifes-tation of the more general crisis of Marxism and critical thought in the twentieth century. Coupling the present chapter with the next, the im-portant differences between Adorno's and Habermas's respective ap-proaches to the concept and critique of ideology will be discussed in order to assess the value of their critical theories. It will also be useful to examine some contemporary poststructuralist responses to the question of ideology along the way (introduced in section 2.1.2). Tracing the path of Frankfurt critical theory away from its early program in section 2.2, I give an account of Horkheimer and Adorno's analysis of enlightenment as a fateful dialectic bound up with the highest urges of intellectual thought and culture. The overall discussion in this chapter will also serve as a genealogy of certain concerns that emerge in the Habermasian critique of Adorno's critical theory to be discussed in Chapter 4. But the reconstructive argument I pursue later in this chapter aims to begin the alternative interpretation of Adorno's critical theory (explicitly against the Habermasian view) that I will develop over the course of the entire text and that I hope will offer promising insights for the self-understanding of contemporary critical theory.

2.1. THE PROGRAM OF CRITICAL THEORY AND THE PROBLEM OF IDEOLOGY CRITIQUE

2.1.1. The Institute for Social Research and the Program of Critical Theory

During the 1920s, the Institute for Social Research conducted historical research that employed a fairly orthodox historical materialism. Under Carl Grünberg, the Institute's theoretical program centered on Marxian political economy and emphasized the history of socialism and the labor movement. Many Institute figures at this time emerged from or had strong links with the labor movement, the German Communist Party (KPD) and the Social Democratic Party (SPD). The Institute also maintained relations with the Marx-Engels Institute in Moscow, occasionally participating in joint projects. Grünberg's achievement was unique in the German (and not only the German) academic world at this time. For now a full professor who was openly committed to Marxism taught political economy at a major university where Marxism and the history of the labor movement were recognized as legitimate academic pursuits, where they could be studied for the award of higher degrees, and where Institute members became part of the permanent teaching faculty (Wiggershaus, 1994: 34).

When Grünberg suffered a serious illness and had to step down, Max Horkheimer was appointed to the position of Director. Horkheimer was the son of a bourgeois, Jewish factory owner and had rebelled against his father's intention for him to take over the family business. Instead, Horkheimer chose an academic career and was drawn to socialism. Although sharing the disappointment and disillusionment felt by other leftist intellectuals, activists, and later Institute members at the failed European revolutions following the First World War, especially the German revolution of 1918, he remained a committed socialist who was convinced that capitalism and class domination must be abolished if human suffering was to be alleviated. The first Institute publications under his leadership continued the focus on Marxist political economy—indeed, political economy would remain central to the Institute's activities right up through the 1940s. But Horkheimer was far from an orthodox thinker or an uncritical defender of Soviet Marxism. Neither did he (or any of the core Institute members he assembled) affiliate directly with the socialist parties in Germany. The interest of his early essays from the 1920s—paralleling and influenced by others such as Karl Korsch and Georg Lukács—was to explain the failure of socialist revolution despite the presence of 'objective' revolutionary conditions. By the time he took over the Institute, Horkheimer had formulated a vision of a new research program intended to assist in advancing a critical knowledge and a critical politics that would contribute to the revitalized struggle for an emancipated society.

However, while questions of theory and practice remained important, and while many themes and projects central to Grünberg's Institute were maintained under Horkheimer during the 1930s, the new vision of critical theory tended to take theory as its politics rather than forge intellectual links with the political movements of the time. Indeed, dissatisfaction with the existing political possibilities (including those presented by the Soviet Union) motivated the articulation of a new political vision in the face of the decline in class consciousness, which became more urgent with the working-class embrace of fascism. There was a pressing need to comprehend the new social formation with more sophistication and depth than was permitted with the prevailing reductionist, scientistic Marxist model that privileged an economic 'base' at the expense of the social, political, and cultural spheres, which were neglected as mere epiphenomenal superstructure. Revision and further development of Marxist theory under these changed circumstances were clearly in order.

The Institute preoccupations with the analysis of the new picture of capitalist society that had been emerging in the 1920s and 1930s can thus be usefully understood at the intellectual level as a response to the crisis in the theory and practice of Marxism and the analytical and political limits of existing ideology critique. Indeed, regarding the latter, Horkheimer's first major essay at the Institute consisted of a critique of his Frankfurt University colleague Karl Mannheim's *Ideology and Utopia* (1936 [1929]). Mannheim was an important opponent because he was widely seen as offering an alternative to the critical theory being developed at the Institute. Horkheimer's 1930 critique of Mannheim thus provides a useful context for understanding the former's articulation of the original program of critical theory.

Mannheim's influential sociology of knowledge, which he explicitly conceived as a revision and application of Marxist theory, sought to develop a new concept of ideology beyond its use as a party instrument that merely impugned an opponent's ideas as disguised manifestations of class interest. Instead, Mannheim refused to exclude Marxism itself from such an analysis by extending the concept of ideology to apply not just to the deceptions of 'ruling-class ideas' but to all theories—including those reflecting the interests of the working class.

The sociology of knowledge seeks to reveal the 'situational determination' of all cognition and thought such that the structure of any particular representation can be understood in relation to the specific historical structure and social conditions out of which it emerges. It supplements ideology as deception with a notion of ideology as a socio-historically bound worldview (*Weltanschauung*). Mannheim accordingly distinguished between the "particular" concept of ideology, which refers to distortions that "range all the way from conscious lies to half-conscious and unwitting disguises; from calculated attempts to dupe others to self-deception," and the "total" notion, which refers to "the ideology of an age or of a concrete historico-social group, e.g. of a class . . . of the total structure of the mind of this epoch or of this group" (Mannheim, 1936: 55–56). But once the "total" concept of ideology is generalized in this manner and all theories at all times are understood as ideological in a non-moral, reflective sense rather than as 'false' in some way, it falls to the sociology of knowledge itself to reveal the meaning of each epoch and their development. For otherwise the sociology of knowledge would amount merely to a cataloguing of differences. Horkheimer criticizes this result as a repetition of just the kind of idealist metaphysics Marxian theory is out to demolish.

Drawing parallels to the metaphysics of Dilthey's philosophy of history, Horkheimer cites as evidence Mannheim's expression of "reality" as "the ascent of human beings"—that is, his evolutionary conception of human value, his related reference to the "essence" of humanity and to an "ineffable element" that in this case can only mean the divine. The sociology of knowledge, despite its protestations to the contrary, points to a meaning in history that is above history, a context beyond context that it conveniently leaves unexamined. For Horkheimer, "there is no adequate justification for claiming that, in a thoroughly conditioned and mutable reality, the 'development of humanity' alone should occupy this exceptional position. Nor is it convincing to argue that, of all kinds of knowledge, the anthropological is not ideological" (1993b: 136). Mannheim's approach amounts to a mode of assessment of the history of thought that relies on something other than social science and there-fore unnecessarily mystifies history and social existence.

Horkheimer does not deny that Marxism escapes historical de-termination—indeed, critical theory is most attentive to the question of its own conditions of existence and emergence. For Horkheimer, how-ever, the truth or falsity of a position or theory cannot be decided simply by reference to its socio-historical determination. The question of ideol-ogy is instead inherently *political*. That is, ideological positions are al-ways articulated in a context of social conflict and struggle, which cannot be abstracted from any assessment of their truth or falsity. Thus besides Mannheim's recourse to metaphysical rather than scientific explanation, Horkheimer objects to the absence of the political dimension in his con-cept of 'total' ideology. The Marxist analysis of society as divided into classes in conflict is opposed to any notion of society that somehow escapes the contradictions of class antagonisms and, consequently, it is opposed to any meaningful notion of a 'total' worldview. This theoretical position cannot be reduced to the ideology of a specific social group without de-politicizing its view of the ideological distortions, deceptions, and deployments arising from social interests in conflict. Consequently in the sociology of knowledge, for Horkheimer, "attention is diverted from the social function of the 'ideology' to exclusively intellectual con-siderations" that "leads to the idealist reinterpretation of existing contra-dictions as mere oppositions of ideas, 'styles of thought,' and 'systems of *Weltanschauung*'" (1993b: 148–49).

After Horkheimer assumed the Directorship of the Institute, the concern with the critique of ideology became central to Institute work. This was motivated by the concern to develop a Marxist-inspired, postmetaphysical and materialist conception of history that would unite various disciplines in the interests of a comprehensive vision.

Horkheimer's inaugural address as Director in January 1931 outlined the new research program that he and other Institute members would refer back to on many occasions throughout their careers. Later critical theorists have also taken special notice of this early program, in particular following Habermas's explicit invocation of it in order to contextualize his revision of the tradition in *Theory of Communicative Action*.[3] Essentially, Horkheimer calls for the cultivation of a new rela-tionship between social philosophy and the empirical sciences that is inspired by the Marxian vision of a critical social science. Social philoso-phy, for Horkheimer, concerns the great principal questions such as "the relationship of the individual to society, the meaning of culture, the for-mation of communities, or the overall status of social life" (Horkheimer,

1989: 31), while the empirical sciences investigate concrete social phenomena as they exist in reality. The new formulation should conceive of each in terms of "an ongoing dialectical permeation and evolution" for neither should or can be immune from criticism or correction by the other. Drawing on the latest in scientific techniques of social investigation, a 'supradisciplinary' organization of research was proposed that would bring together "philosophers, sociologists, political economists, historians, and psychologists" in order to "pursue their philosophical questions directed at the big picture . . . to transform and to make more precise these questions as the work progresses, to find new methods, and yet never lose sight of the whole" (1989: 31–32). This integration of philosophy and science would demystify metaphysical social philosophy—even Marxism was criticized as having declined into a dogmatic, reductionist, and objectivist materialist metaphysics—and it would overcome the fragmentation of the sciences via this supradisciplinary materialism.

Kellner (1989) emphasizes this supradisciplinary approach as what is most distinctive about critical theory's early program. It is to be distinguished from an interdisciplinary approach, which fosters communication across disciplines but allows them to remain detached and independent. In Kellner's words, "Critical Theory is guided by the conviction that all inquiry, all thought, all political action and all informed human behavior must take place within the framework of a comprehensive and global Critical Theory of society which contains a synthesis of philosophy, the sciences and politics" (1989: 44).

Hence each member of Horkheimer's circle at the Institute initially took specific research responsibilities that would contribute to this overall vision: Lowenthal was to work in the sociology of literature, Pollock political economy, Fromm the psychological dimension, and Adorno the sociology of music. Marcuse later joined as a fellow philosopher.

In a series of essays in the 1930s, Horkheimer and other Institute members elaborated this vision. These writings were intended as programmatic for what emerged definitively as Frankfurt critical theory and thus were also taken as points of departure by many among the core group associated with the Institute. Horkheimer's general approach was to distinguish the new critical theory from the prevailing European philosophical movements and positions, which were collectively referred to as "traditional theory." As the distinctive term for the Institute approach, "critical theory" was adopted at first as a prudent code word for its Marxist theory while its members were in exile in the United States—an environment quite hostile to the theory associated with socialism and the

Soviet Union. But thereafter the term became thoroughly associated with the Horkheimer circle and the specific tradition they inaugurated.

Horkheimer discerned two broadly defined sides to traditional theory or 'bourgeois' philosophy and ideology,[4] each opposed to the other but nevertheless related uncritically to the existing society as attempts to harmonize human relations within its essentially contradictory social conditions. On one side was the new metaphysics of the early twentieth century, among which Horkheimer included Romantic spiritualism, *Lebensphilosophie*, and material and existential phenomenology. These intellectual movements, he argued, are akin to the theological spirit (in which they are rooted) that offers to the bourgeois individual a metaphysical reassurance of genuine identity with the supernatural or suprapersonal, a true reality that confirms that his or her real suffering is but appearance in the grand scheme of things. (These philosophies might hence also be seen as equivalents to what Marx criticized in his early writings as the false, idealistic critiques of bourgeois society and politics in the first half of the nineteenth century, and they extend in various lineages to include New Age spiritualism at the end of the twentieth century.)

On the other side, looming larger, was positivism in its various manifestations. By using the goals and methods of the natural sciences, chiefly physics, as models for the philosophical determination of valid knowledge, positivism is radically opposed to all metaphysics. But, as Horkheimer observes, the positivist aversion to questions concerning what a thing *is* extends its critique of metaphysics to all knowledge claims that do not or cannot admit of scientific verification. Since such knowledge can only concern the *appearances* of things of which observation allows the discovery of laws, all thought can be divided into that which counts as knowledge and that which does not. Scientific knowledge is viewed as authoritative and reliable, whereas all non-scientific knowledge is not really knowledge at all but rather 'fancy' or 'nonsense'. "Besides science there is art" (Horkheimer, 1972a: 139). Once the distinction is no longer recognized between what an entity *appears to be* and what it *is*, valid knowledge of the human condition can be attained only through the behavioral sciences like psychology, physiology, or biology. Valid social or political knowledge is not thereby abandoned, according to the positivist position, but rather it must meet the strict requirements of scientific form and method in order to be counted.[5]

But more insidious than this scientization of politics is the participation of science and the scientistic worldview in what I will later discuss as the dialectic of enlightenment. Instead of acting as a force of rational progress in human knowledge and freedom as the Enlightenment philosophers had hoped, the commitment to scientific truth free from mystical taboos or ideological taint declines into technological fetish and a myopic epistemology. Science instead introduces new constraints to knowledge and acts as an ideological weapon for a new class of rulers. Science's progressive philosophical opposition to the questions that occupied 'ideological' metaphysics ends up functioning in the interests of the newly established order by reducing politics merely to contesting value judgments and the manifestation of historical struggles to the abstract givens of empirical study (1972a: 178). Indeed, for Horkheimer the concerns of metaphysics should not be regarded as simply meaningless, no matter how misguided and false the particular ideas were.

Yet positivism, by radically eliminating the *knowing subject* as a determinate moment in cognition, erases all difference between existing individuals and all difference between the historical moments of theory. The positivist principle that all theoretical disagreement and conflict are to be decided by some form of scientific verification is extended in time and space, which harmonizes all individuals under the unity of the 'one'. It thereby posits an "eternal fact" of an "even more general character than a law of nature" (1972a: 148). Hence, following Horkheimer, one can ultimately discern a 'secret' or unstated metaphysics in positivism, itself one of the most explicit and trenchant bourgeois expressions of anti-metaphysical thought, because it defines absolutely what counts as truth through an eternally valid and untouchable principle. In large part positivism and metaphysics are "simply two different phases of one philosophy which downgrades natural knowledge and hypostatizes abstract conceptual structures" (1972b: 40). Therefore they lack the specifically *critical* perspective of a genuine, open-ended pursuit of truth because they each insulate certain historical values and "abstract conceptual structures" from doubt and criticism. A critical perspective that refuses this kind of hubris and philosophical irresponsibility is available only to a theory that is able to properly grasp the dialectical relation of intellectual and material reality. For critical theory, neither positivism nor 'bad' metaphysics can thus truly advance the self-understanding of reason (*Vernunft*).

Theorizing the relation between intellectual and material reality turns us toward the dynamics of comprehension itself. On Horkheimer's understanding of dialectical materialism (or critical theory), a concrete understanding of the knowing subject is crucial for any adequate social theory; conversely, a historical account of society is likewise essential for any adequate notion of the knowing subject. Only by adequately grasping these two aspects can theory hope to penetrate the hypostasis of the individual's own perceptual abilities that occurs in current society. The scientific Marxism of the time likewise had no theory of the subject, which not only compounded its inability to adequately explain the failure of socialist revolution but also meant it was unable to say why a new, 'inevitable' socialist society was even desirable. The subsequent attention critical theory gave to Freud and psychoanalysis was new in the context of Marxist theory, and it was intended to address the need to account for the subjective aspects of social existence far better than philosophy and sociology had managed to date.[6] "The facts which our senses present to ourselves are pre-formed in two ways," Horkheimer writes: "through the historical character of the perceived object and through the historical character of the perceiving organ ... and yet the individual perceives himself as receptive and passive in the act of perception" (1972c: 200). It is this that entails an adequate conception of the social totality in which the individual's nature and perceptual capacities are developed and formed, for otherwise such a radical historicizing of human traits would not make sense—that is, it would not be possible to *make sense* of historical development and change at all.

For the early Horkheimer, the critical theory of society finds the meaning of the whole not in the 'facts' that exist, that can be scientifically determined, and not in the dreams produced by metaphysical desires, but in the idea of the concrete transformation of contemporary society "into the right kind of society" (1972c: 218). What gives it its *critical* character in contrast to traditional theory's ideological harmonizing of the individual to the status quo is its purchase on a future freedom promised by the (radical) structural transformation of the present society. A critical theory of "society as it is," Horkheimer argues, is "a theory dominated at every turn by a concern for reasonable conditions of life" (1972c: 198–99). Evocative of Marx's theory of alienation and critique of capitalist society, critical theory

> is motivated today by the effort really to transcend the tension and to abolish the opposition between the individual's purposefulness, spontaneity and rationality, and those work-process relationships on which society is built. Critical thought has a concept of man in conflict with himself until this opposition is removed. If activity governed by reason is proper to man, then existent social practice, which forms the individual's life right down to its least details, is inhuman, and this inhumanity affects everything that goes on in society (1972c: 210).

This concern with the realization of a genuinely rational society expresses the centrality of transformative politics for the intellectual endeavor of a critical 'theory'. Such a commitment follows from the conviction that a new set of social relations is necessary for a new way of thinking, acting, perceiving, and experiencing that might realize freedom. Indeed, in a response to Horkheimer's essay "Traditional and Critical Theory," Herbert Marcuse contended that philosophy represented an *interest* of human beings in freedom and happiness, an interest that nevertheless could not be realized merely in and through philosophy but required socially transformative political praxis. Insofar as philosophy reaches its limit with "the concept of reason as freedom" in Idealism, "the philosophical construction of reason is replaced by the creation of a rational society" (Marcuse, 1968b: 137, 142). The rationality that is to guide the future society cannot be merely the functional rationality of planned production or distribution embodied in conventional bureaucratic direction. Such planning tends to ally utility with scientized politics in a massive administered world constructed to satisfy not the genuine needs of people but those of the system itself, which are projected as the actual needs of its social subjects. Marcuse argued that beyond this there is a crucial link between the regulation of production and the *rational interest* of "the freedom and happiness of the masses" (1968b: 144). This "organization of the administration of the social wealth in the interest of a liberated mankind" cannot simply be formal or procedural for freedom and happiness are substantive, existential experiences of a concrete way of life.

Yet unlike the political efforts of the philosophical tradition that culminated in Hegel, critical theorists cannot and ought not mark out the definitive or proper structure of the new society, its institutions or legitimate political power, nor the precise substantive shape given to the free and happy life. All this must "occur as the free creation of liberated individuals" (1968b: 157, 135). Critical theory hence does not put forward blueprints for a new society, even though ideology critique expresses an interest in social transformation. Rather, in Marx's words, the task of a critical theory is to clarify the interests of those engaged in the struggles of the times with the aim of a liberated society in mind: to "show the world what it is fighting for" (Marx, 1974a: 15). It thus orients itself toward history and historical social movements without a dogma, attempting instead to remain true to the progressive development of historically emergent social relations identified within the 'womb' of the existing system.[7] Liberation, for Marcuse, was to be the result of successful resistance to the domination of capitalism, which could take an increasing variety of forms but which in the end still depended on some final event, a "Great Refusal," that negated capitalism. Only after that could human freedom be real and actual, if it was indeterminate at the present time.

Thus Marcuse argued that philosophy and theory alone were finally inadequate for a utopian consciousness that might inform and aid groups struggling for progressive change. Expressing a major theme of critical theory, he contended that the theoretical consciousness needed to have a concrete relation to what he called "phantasy." Contrary to positivism, phantasy is understood not as mere fancy—external desire—but actually as a kind of legitimate cognition that points toward "the already possible unfolding and fulfillment of needs and wants" (1968b: 155). Marcuse consistently stressed true as opposed to false human needs—the "'biological' dimension in which the vital, imperative needs and satisfactions of man assert themselves" (1969: 16–17). He persisted with a search for the soul of revolt in marginalized groups as well as in peoples in peripheral countries as an alternate or supplement to the integrated and transformed proletariat. These positions are sometimes taken to indicate a problematic left Hegelianism that implies a 'bad' metaphysics of nature or philosophy of history. Yet Marcuse nevertheless consistently emphasized the historical orientation of critical theory on such points. Critique must finally find its 'confirmation' (but not 'foundation') in historical struggles of resistance and critical activity, which themselves in turn give rise to new theoretical critique along with new, progressive needs. "That the true interest of individuals is the interest of freedom, that true individual freedom can coexist with real general freedom and, indeed, is possible only in conjunction with it, that happiness ultimately consists in freedom—these are not propositions of philosophical anthropology about the nature of man but descriptions of a historical situation which humanity has achieved for itself in the struggle with nature" (Marcuse, 1968a: 192). It is this historicizing of "the fulfillment of needs and wants," which, when articulated as what is "already possible," politicizes critical theory and gives it its transformative, liberatory orientation.

Indeed, the conservative force of the integrated working classes in the West, the collusion of socialist parties in the limited Western representative democracies, along with the failures of Soviet socialism, were evidence to Marcuse that the development and flourishing of a "new sensibility" was crucial internally to the practice of any successful revolutionary movement. This, however, required very different forms of organization than the traditional modes of nineteenth- and twentieth-century radical politics.

If the socialist relationships of production are to be a new way of life, a new Form of life, then their existential quality must show forth, anticipated and demonstrated, in the fight for their realization. . . . Understanding, tenderness toward each other, the instinctual consciousness of that which is evil, false, the heritage of oppression, would then testify to the authenticity of the rebellion. In short, the economic, political, and cultural features of a classless society must have become the basic needs of those who fight for it (Marcuse, 1969: 88–89).

Some have consequently seen just this kind of alternative mode of organization coupled with a new sensibility emerging in the new social movements, especially the peace and ecology movements. For Eder (1982), the new social movements aim to advance beyond modern society toward a post-industrial order in part by articulating new values and a new mode of life, which is consistent with what Marcuse and other critical theorists called for (Kellner, 1989: 220–21).

Despite such continuations of spirit, however, it is possible to discern limits to and problems with the original program of critical theory that allegedly affect its durability and contemporary development. Horkheimer's effort to distinguish critical theory from traditional theory and to move beyond metaphysics is dogged by the apparent anomalous reliance on certain categories and concepts critical theory is supposed to have abandoned as elements of traditional theory. Many of these notions seem extremely problematic from perspectives at the end of the twentieth century. Horkheimer's confidence in the progressive outcome of history as a result of heightening contradictions in capitalism and the "new barbarism" that accompanies it cannot be theoretically grounded, which he realized, but nevertheless his confidence in this early period implies a philosophy of history that receives very few advocates today. His belief that "there will emerge in the future age the relation between rational intention and its realization" (1972c: 217) seems to suggest the possibility of a (completely) transparent society beyond the stage currently reached by capitalism. This possibility perhaps can be traced to the Hegelian idealist desire to overcome the forcible separation of subject and object, which Horkheimer seems to endorse by claiming that "their identity lies in the future, not in the present" (1972c: 211). Indeed, Horkheimer invokes the philosophy of the subject at moments when he touches upon the reason of the future: "[humankind] will for the first time be a conscious subject and actively determine its own way of life" (1972c: 233). Moreover, he seems to fall into a related metaphysics at other times when he asserts that "the thrust toward the rational society . . . is really innate in every man" (1972c: 251). Marcuse's later utopian call for the creation of a new Subject or 'new man' through an aesthetic transformation seems to have a strong affinity with such conceptions.

Habermas has pointed to the determinate systemic limits and paradoxes of the philosophy of consciousness (or the subject) as the real reasons the original program of critical theory foundered. This, he argues, becomes most clear in the 1940s with *Dialectic of Enlightenment*. Horkheimer and Adorno reject the Hegelian-Marxist (ironic) return to an objective idealism in Lukács' theory of reification and class consciousness without finally breaking with the desire to project a radical unity to theory and practice envisioned for the new society. But the problem precedes and is even deeper than this. With the rejection of any return to objective reason—that is, any hope of *identifying* the basis of social solidarity that the metaphysical tradition found through a harmonized configuration of the natural and social orders—there seems to be no basis on which to judge the value or desirability of what is to be expressed through and in the future state of freedom. The Marxist recovery of alienated subjective powers and capacities through the achievement of a comprehensive autonomy and freedom, which would satisfy needs directly through the actualization of those powers and capacities, cannot be represented substantively.

But neither, Habermas contends against Frankfurt theory, can such meaning be indicated unproblematically by reference to the repressive-expressive contents of phantasy, the sensuous power of imagination, or the sphere aesthetic mimesis. The problem is that there simply cannot be an unambiguous reading of Marx's overcoming of alienated human powers and capacities or the satisfaction of needs in themselves precisely *because* the identification of such human capacities and needs—what Marcuse later repeated as "the already possible unfolding and fulfillment of needs and wants" in the creation of an *"aesthetic ethos"*—always depends on *interpretation*. And the proper activity of interpretation cannot simply be assumed. That is, any condition free from reification and capitalist domination will still require the determination of *which* powers and capacities are to flourish and *which* needs are to be thereby met. The *facticity* of capacities and needs, for Habermas, which always grounds itself historically in the social structures into which human beings grow, still demands a separate determination in order to be recognized, to acquire *validity*. There is nothing automatic about this recognition of capacities and needs, even though the level of material production and structure of the relations of production place real limits on the scope and content of this recognition. This interpretive dimension entails processes oriented toward mutual understanding and agreement that are different from the historical capacities of material production and their matching needs. For Habermas, these levels of facticity and validity cannot—or should not—be collapsed into one another in an unreflective way. As we will see, Habermas attempts to rescue the practical interpretation of needs from the repression/expression model by transforming it into the linguistically mediated activity of free communication with others. This practical-political recovery of the self-reflective formation of the species can be recognized, he argues, only by the paradigm shift to the theory of communicative action.

Frankfurt school studies in political economy had already revealed that the development of the forces of production no longer seemed to pose a critical threat to the relations of production, and that indeed progress in technological productive capacity no longer necessarily produced conditions for social and cultural progress at all but actually contributed to increased reification and domination. The apparent disjunction between the forces and relations of production had to be explained with recourse to a new theory of the capitalist state and law (see Scheuerman, 1994), as well as a new approach to ideology and culture in general.

If, according to Horkheimer, "(t)here are no general criteria for judging the critical theory as a whole, for it is always based on the recurrence of events and thus on a self-reproducing totality" (1972c: 242), then how might critical theory gain a *theoretical* purchase on the "self-reproducing totality" itself? How might it do this without smuggling in an external value orientation and contradicting its own radical historicizing and critical premises? If just this sort of attempt is misguided, then one might ask what alternative self-understanding could critical theory have that would also avoid weakening itself into an ideology, in the manner of the sociology of knowledge. Horkheimer's programmatic early work contains tensions that seem to be resolved only by recourse to strategies more appropriate to traditional than critical theory, which he really wishes to avoid.

This is the point at which Horkheimer and Adorno undertake a thoroughgoing and radical critique of reason and reification under the heading of the dialectic of enlightenment that seeks to reveal an alternate rationality in conjunction with an ethics of cognition. From Habermas's viewpoint, it is a deeply paradoxical affair that cannot hope to succeed, for Horkheimer and Adorno submit subjective reason "to an unrelenting critique from the ironically distanced perspective of an objective reason that had fallen irreparably into ruin" (*TCAI*: 377). The totality, as we have inherited it in thought and in social relations, is fundamentally untrue, as

Adorno would emphasize. Yet it must still be grasped at least as such, which does establish a tension at the core of critical theory. From a poststructuralist perspective, these tensions in the early Frankfurt critical theory are vestiges of the idealist, humanist metaphysical tradition that are unwarranted by critical theory's own "methodology of suspicion" (Hoy, 1994: 114). On this reading, critical theory's aspirations toward a "totalizing" theory must be abandoned if it is to avoid falling back into a philosophy of history. It must relinquish the very desire for a *theory* that informs critique and, if it is to remain true to its spirit, instead write critical *histories* such as those exemplified in Michel Foucault's work.

The notion of totality, of grasping the concept of the whole of human relations, has been a central feature in the tradition of Western Marxism—indeed, it would seem to be elemental (see Jay, 1984). It is a concept that is explicitly rejected by poststructuralism and post-Marxism because it is seen as a hangover from the imperialist, metaphysical philosophies and linked with the errors of revolutionary utopian desires for a new age characterized by the unity of subject and object, the harmony of spirit and reality, individual and collective. Insofar as any kind of *positive* totality is invoked, such a concept is also rejected by a consistent negative dialectic. But as a number of writers have pointed out, the concept of totality itself should not be automatically equated or associated with some kind of totalizing urge toward total control or complete knowledge of everything that exists, much less with totalitarian thought or the mythical subject-object unity. Marxism already properly poses a challenge to all philosophical systems that might make use of 'totality' in a 'totalizing' way. The dialectic, Jameson has argued, is not a philosophy in that sense but something else: "Its ideal (which famously involves the realization and the abolition of philosophy all at once) is not the invention of a better philosophy that . . . seeks to do without premises altogether, but rather the transformation of the natural and social world into a meaningful totality such that 'totality' in the form of a philosophical system will no longer be required" (1991: 334). Later, I will contend that it is precisely the negative dialectic and the crucial *productive* tension arising from the 'untrue Whole' that presents a consistent and promising response to the contemporary need to acknowledge the limits of theory while not finally requiring us to abandon a purchase on what its leading advocate, Adorno, called the "non-existent social totality" (*nichtexistente Gesamtgesellschaft*). The idea of a non-existent totality is a way of indicating a critical, utopian orientation without suggesting that one already has or could have all the answers.

Another dimension to the problems that emerged in connection with the original program of critical theory concerned Horkheimer and Adorno's deepening critique of science. Overcoming the separation of philosophy and science desired by Horkheimer seemed less and less possible in the face of the hardening methodological exclusivity of the sciences, the increasing integration of science into industry and politics, and the appeal of positivism as a philosophy and an ideology. The failure of psychoanalysis to become accepted as a science had further alienated critical theory from the sciences, since many Institute members besides Fromm—especially Adorno and Marcuse—incorporated psychoanalytic insights into their theory and saw psychoanalysis as a parallel to Marx's vision of critical social science. By the time of the Institute's return to Germany and Horkheimer's installment as Rector of Frankfurt University in 1951 (Horkheimer would not produce any significantly new work from this point on), the hope of integrating the sciences into a supradisciplinary program had been severely inhibited under the analysis of the eclipse of reason, the dialectic of enlightenment, and the critique of positivism. Yet Adorno continued to engage in empirical work through the 1940s and 1950s—for example, in his involvement with the Princeton Radio Research Project and *The Authoritarian Personality* (Adorno, et. al., 1950). He even seemed to present an Adornoesque version of Horkheimer's original program in a 1951 lecture delivered in Germany shortly before he was forced to return for two years to the United States for immigration and financial reasons (Wiggershaus, 1994: 454–46). Despite this, the early hopes of the critical theory of society were, at best, put on hold. Adorno developed his aesthetic-critical theory at a meta-theoretical level with the hope that this could inform and further something of the original aims of critical theory in new ways, which I will indicate in section 2.2 and argue in more depth in Chapter 5. Adorno's later efforts will be thoroughly misunderstood if his concern with the aesthetic is regarded as a despairing aestheticization of reason, a misguided Nietzschean transmutation of Marx, or some such view.

That Adorno did not withdraw politically—despite suffering various accusations of resignation, excessive abstractness, quietism, etc., during the halcyon days of New Left activism—is also evident from his continued and active critical participation in the public sphere during the 1950s and 1960s. He maintained a high profile as a public intellectual in postwar Germany, giving radio talks and lectures and writing on prevailing political, cultural, and social issues (see, for example, the work assembled in Adorno, 1998). But the apparent lack of an addressee for the kind of liberatory spirit that critical theory sought to awaken had led

Adorno to characterize critical theory during his exile as a "message in a bottle" waiting out the foreseeable future (Wiggershaus, 1994: 279), a view he found difficult to relinquish during the rest of his life.

2.1.2. Post-Marxism and the Recasting of Politics

Frankfurt theory and Habermas are not alone, of course, in responding to the need to rethink the freedom of democracy in the absence of a philosophy of the subject. Ernesto Laclau and Chantal Mouffe (1985), for example, engage in a seminal effort to move the discourse of the socialist project beyond the essentialist political and epistemological bottlenecks created by the ostensible need for a unifying or universalizing theory of society (as a social totality) that would encompass ideology, social conflict, resistance, difference (race, class, gender, sexuality, culture, etc.), and domination. They also seek to revitalize critical thought under the conditions of a postmodernity in which, as Lyotard (1984) has definitively put it, there is widespread "incredulity" toward all such metanarratives of ideology and truth, resistance and revolution, identity and difference, and so on. Laclau and Mouffe aim to reorient the political self-understanding of the (radical) Left away from a theory that essentializes antagonism and the agents and sites of political action from an external point of view (the theory of history and class struggle). In the latter, privileged points from which historical change is to be set in motion (for example, the Revolution, the General Strike, the Party) are consequently designated as the focus of political organizing. Instead, Laclau and Mouffe conceive of a radical democracy that recognizes the fundamental openness of *the social* and of social division and antagonisms that constitute the identities of individuals and groups.

> If the various subject positions and the diverse antagonisms and points of rupture constitute a *diversity* and not a *diversification*, it is clear that they cannot be led back to a point from which they could all be embraced and explained by a single discourse. . . . The discourse of radical democracy is no longer the discourse of the universal; the epistemological niche from which 'universal' classes and subjects spoke has been eradicated, and it has been replaced by a polyphony of voices, each of which constructs its own irreducible discursive identity. . . . Juridical institutions, the educational system, labor relations, the discourses of the resistance of marginal populations construct original and irreducible forms of social protest, and thereby contribute all the discursive complex-

ity and richness on which the program of a radical democracy should be founded (Laclau and Mouffe, 1985: 191–92).

As a result of their step away from 'totalizing' theory—a rejection of 'high' or 'meta-' theory (all of which are essentially equivalent to Lyotard's metanarratives)—post-Marxist and poststructuralist critical thinkers hope to avoid theoretical dangers as well as the danger of *theory* itself: the intellectual arrogance, ethnocentrism, or imperialism associated with claims to comprehend the *whole* of identity and difference. They also claim for themselves an improved critical eye that is more attuned to the changed historical experience of late capitalism and more attentive to the particular needs of its diversity of individuals and groups. Although Laclau and Mouffe misrepresent the critical theory of revolution here—it is rather *counterrevolution* or conservative reaction that seeks to lead particulars *"back* to a point from which they could all be embraced and explained" (191; emphasis added)—the value of their call is the importance it places on rethinking alliance politics among oppressed and marginalized groups. The key political categories in Laclau and Mouffe's recasting of the radical democratic project as an alliance politics are those of the 'equivalence' and 'articulation' of struggles against domination and oppression, which are to be contrasted with the universalization and thereby assimilation of such struggle under a single dynamic of resistance. In order to preserve and remain sensitive to difference but nevertheless provide a coherence to radical democratic politics, 'chains of equivalence' must be articulated among the diverse groups and identities struggling against specific dominations and oppressions. Here, one might argue, is a valuable notion of an antagonistic totality as alliance politics centered on the hegemonic project of radical democracy that does not require a single representative or theory for its existence.

From the perspective of critical theory, however, a wholesale and undialectical rejection of categories that, while featured among those traditionally central to metaphysics, are not *in themselves* necessarily or wholly metaphysical, introduces different dangers. Accepting diversity, even celebrating it, *without* the communicative effort to meet with, to comprehend, to cooperate with, and possibly—or perhaps even probably—to contest with otherness, risks a different apathy or passiveness that infects the relations of self and other. Such a tendency to passivity lies at the opposite pole of the violent imperialism of assimilation that is supposed to be done away with. It does not consist of an utter break with its dialectic.[8] The ethical call of a critical theory like Adorno's, as we will see, is so thoroughly concerned not only with opening up to the other, letting the other be, but also with allowing and encouraging the other and otherness to open up, to speak and communicate, and to contemplate its representations, to engage with them. Without this kind of ethical call, ostensibly critical, postmodern thought may risk consequently falling back into some form of positivism (which is sometimes alleged against Foucault and his followers), or it may produce a new, as yet unrecognized myth or metaphysics in the absence of adequate replacements for modern critical concepts such as the subject, nature, interest, the social totality, reason, or history (as scientism or Mannheim's sociology of knowledge do). All of this may prematurely foreclose on the real political gains projected by contemporary theorizing that are to be derived from a postmetaphysical, yet ethically conscious and negative dialectical critical theory.

Perhaps just what is at issue in this respect is whether 'master-codes' or 'master narratives' such as the subject, the totality, or history are required for philosophically defensible critique at all.[9] Once one recognizes that language and communication are historical, have inextricably historical components out of which no timeless abstraction can legitimately be conjured, then one must, in some sense, assume a direction for history. Otherwise, as I contended earlier, history becomes simply the reified logging of specific facts and statistics with no possibility of making any *sense* of this data. Sense-making is just what the historical understanding achieves. A further issue is how to deal with the assumption of a history for critique without removing one's own position, the position of critique, from examination, doubt, and possible revision or rejection. This is an obligation to give an account of one's own premises just as one gives an account of and criticizes others'. For critical theory, such self-reflection intends to be *internal* to the theory, to the mode of inquiry, which acknowledges its own historicity at the same time as it criticizes the lack of such acknowledgment in 'ideological' thinking—or, as Adorno was fond of saying, in the "one-track mind" (*eingleisige Gedankengang*).

What is clear is that ideology critique has been transformed in poststructuralism and certain forms of post-Marxism, severed from a cognitive connection to systematic social-theoretic analyses or universalizing 'storied' accounts of domination, which raises crucial questions concerning the very terms of left/progressive, democratic critical theory itself. Less clear are the final implications of the abandonment of some kind of cognitive relation to a concept of the social whole that animated critical theory's original program. Careful consideration of the question of critique and its relation to democracy, history, and the future of democracy, I would argue, thus continues to be necessary.

It is worth noting at this point that Habermas does not recognize a 'sea-change' in or radical break with modernity that some theorists attribute to the condition of postmodernity.[10] For Habermas, the structure of the contemporary situation has not essentially changed, only its appearance or surface has altered. Yet he thinks that the great progressive modern effort to bring about a new state of affairs has dissolved, largely as a result of the crisis in and "exhaustion" of the specific utopian project that found historical expression in the cause of the welfare-state and which crystallized around the potential of a society based on social labor (Habermas, 1986c: 3–4). The current phase of modern society is characterized instead by Habermas as a period of "new obscurity" in which, among other things, the older utopian-modernism has given way to critiques of modernity arising out of neoconservatism, old-conservatism, and a relatively new "anti-modernism." Habermas views this anti-modernism that has sometimes joined conservative critiques as an attempt to step outside the horizon of the modern world (that is, as a *post*modernism). But, he argues, it is impossible to achieve (or institutionalize) such a radical discontinuity and distance from the modern without the risk of introducing far worse conditions.

Habermas, by contrast, remains committed to the liberal-democratic spirit of the Enlightenment, which he sees as worthy of preservation if only for the fact that its potential has not yet been fully realized. He believes that modern society has brought to consciousness and to social and political institutions certain universal structures that represent, if not the final and complete fruition of rational human development and historical learning, then the conditions of their potential and possibility as such. Indeed, for Habermas, the institutions and rational universal structures explicit or lying potentially in modernity are *binding* on us. As a consequence, these evolutionary gains cannot be denied or left 'behind' without risking dangerous regression. For Habermas, postmodernism is a version of philosophical modernism that tends to become a 'young conservatism' because it obscures—through its uncritical resort to the aesthetic or (following Martin Heidegger) the ecstatic— rather than enlightens (1983b: 14). One of Habermas's main contentions against postmodernist or poststructuralist writers is thus that the collapse of validity into power is not only philosophically illegitimate and at root a performative contradiction, but is politically highly ambiguous. Jay voices a similar concern with Foucault's later attention to the political potentials of sexuality and pleasure: "If there were no truth, but only 'truth effects' expressing certain power relations, then how could one be confident that his call for a 'general economy of pleasure not based on sexual norms' (Foucault, 1980: 191) would not lead to a new form of oppressive power, of the kind, say, attacked by Marcuse as 'repressive desublimation'?" (Jay, 1984: 528).

I agree in general with those such as Habermas, Harvey (1989), and Jameson (1991) who identify a new condition of late capitalism in which the surface appearance and experience of life has substantially changed without altering the basic structure of the capitalist system. That capitalist society tends to produce new configurations to its superstructure is by no means a new observation at a general level. Indeed, it was Marx himself who offered an account of modern capitalist society in which things appear to remain the same while being essentially different and under constant flux and change. (Marx's contemporary, Baudelaire, can also be mentioned in this context for his parallel observations on the ephemerality of modern experience.[11])

Yet philosophy, Bernstein writes, "was late in absorbing the lessons of modernism; which is perhaps why it receives denominations—'poststructuralism' 'postmodernism'—drawn from different histories, different temporalities; and equally why it has proved so difficult to perceive that the claims of philosophical modernism . . . are best understood as the progeny and continuers of the project of critical artistic modernism, the project of revealing a *rationality*, which must itself be construed as coextensive with what is meaningful, which is neither subsumptive (deductive) nor procedural in character" (1995: 171–72). Later I shall argue that Habermas does not adequately acknowledge or address the critical claims of the philosophical modernism articulated by Adorno and his efforts to reveal just such an alternative rationality. To a certain extent, Habermas parallels postmodern concerns by raising problems with the modern impasse of the 'traditional' idea of theory and ideology critique, but from a different philosophical perspective to those of full-fledged poststructuralist critics and with modified aims to those of Adorno. Instead of pursuing the logic of ideology critique to its limits like Adorno, Habermas seeks to transform its concept, and with it the idea of critique, into something else via the paradigm shift. Quite early on, in fact, Habermas criticizes the Frankfurt school concept of ideology, which he sees still tied to the notion of unmasking critique despite its thorough problematization of ideology.[12]

It is time now to examine the crucial turn in critical theory that the crisis of ideology critique engendered. Before the radical critiques of reason introduced by poststructuralism and deconstruction, a similar radical move was made in critical theory by Horkheimer and Adorno in their *Dialectic of Enlightenment* (1947).[13]

2.2. THE DIALECTIC OF ENLIGHTENMENT

2.2.1. Necessary Illusions

Ideology critique would appear to become ineffective if ideology itself no longer *functions* simply to mask and deceive. If the notions of, for example, cultural or political legitimacy, universality, or 'unchangeableness' themselves do not appear to grip or motivate people in a definitive and fundamental way, then demystifying them would hold no guarantees of a critical, enlightening effect. According to Marx's version of critical theory, critique oriented toward the practical change of what 'is' is successful at least partly because of the motivational effects of such critical enlightenment. Yet by no means does it wholly rely on enlightening effects; indeed, it is also a theory of why enlightenment is not enough for such motivation (see also section 3.3).

But if, for example, the form consciousness takes today is overwhelmingly that of *cynicism*, as Sloterdijk (1987) holds with special reference to Germany and which others also discern in the British and American contexts (Bewes, 1997; Chaloupka, 1999), then the naïve acceptance of ideological representations has been replaced by an 'enlightened false consciousness' that knows very well what is dressed up as universal is really in someone else's interests. This nakedness no longer has a practical unmasking effect but creates a quiet cynicism lived as a private disposition. It is rather a matter of self-preservation that drives a demoralized enlightened consciousness "to put up with preestablished relations that it finds dubious, to accommodate itself to them, and finally even to carry out their business" (Sloterdijk, 1987: 6). Such a notion of a cynical reason is a further interpretation of what we might understand as the enduring crisis of modernity, which is not only cultural, but social and political.[14] Indeed, Sloterdijk claims inspiration from the pioneering analysis of the fateful dialectic of enlightenment that Horkheimer and Adorno provide, in which the social crisis of the Enlightenment tradition, the crisis of the notion of ideology, and the desperate hope for an alternative to nationalism, liberalism, and (official) Marxism are all expressed. For Sloterdijk, this condition can be countered by a recovery of the quite different and vital ancient notion of *kynismus*, which affirms aesthetic resistances to the social phenomena that reproduce the postmodern cynical, enlightened false consciousness.

However, it may be premature to affirm our current situation as largely 'post-ideological'—either as a cynical age of resigned reason, as the expression of a radical plurality of utterly contingent historical knowledge practices, or, in the conservative mode, in terms of the final end of ideologies (and 'history') heralded by the triumph of Western capitalist democracy.[15] It is clear that the phenomena the concept of ideology and related concepts attempt to name have undergone substantial transformation in the twentieth century and that new ways of thinking them are required. It is also evident from our discussion that the tradition of Frankfurt critical theory, while quite clearly associated with *Ideologiekritik*, is also intent on problematizing the political and critical notions of ideology. From its critique of science, technology, and enlightenment philosophy, one becomes aware of further political dangers arising from the focus on ideology as a critique of false consciousness.

For the phenomena *ideology* is designed to name do not operate simply to mask 'real relations' but are somehow entwined in all conceptual thinking and in the conceptual grasp of the real. If this is so, then the effort to overcome ideological distortion through the use of theory alone—a better, more enlightened and true theory—is fundamentally misguided. Moreover, the belief that a liberatory political project can be guided by theoretical critique without offering some kind of account of the metaconditions through which critique itself becomes possible is internally limited. Such a position risks imposing a different ideology with a new set of blinkered dominations, exclusions, and oppressions in the place of one discredited by the new, authoritative theoretical critique. This latter has been a lesson presented over and over in the history of critical theories from Marx's day to the present, though clearly taking on significant new dimensions in the second half of the twentieth century. The feminist critique of Marxism, the postcolonial critique of 'white' feminism, and the deep ecology critique of anthropocentrism are ongoing examples of this. Our response should be to rethink the whole but in some new, non-essentialist, non-exclusionary, non-dominating fashion that might be able to accommodate at least this aspect of all these critical positions. Cynical reason, of course, is deeply pessimistic that theoretical or practical liberation is any longer possible and, as a result, has lost faith in social philosophy itself.[16]

Such an effort to rethink the entire approach to ideology critique is indeed just what Horkheimer and Adorno inaugurate in *Dialectic of Enlightenment*. Adorno, especially, pursued the development of critical theory in response to the implications of the dialectic of enlightenment in his subsequent work (although the origin of his negative dialectic can be found earlier, emerging especially from his engagement with the work of Walter Benjamin; see Buck-Morss, 1977). No less scandalous than earlier texts that bear witness to the nihilism and foundation-less constitution of modern society, *Dialectic of Enlightenment* is a text that many subsequent critical theorists have taken as their point of departure. Habermas's program for the renewal of the normative foundations of critical theory can in many respects be interpreted as a prolonged engagement with the (misread) implications of its central theses. It is just this turn in critical theory, beginning with the work related to *Dialectic of Enlightenment* and all the deeply disturbing implications that flow from it, that Habermas wishes to reject and replace. But he, like them, wishes to provide an account of the metaconditions that make critique possible and at the same time present a critical theory of ideology and social pathology.

The main difficulty or problematic for those caught in the wake of Horkheimer and Adorno's watershed *Dialectic of Enlightenment* was thus how to conceive of critical reason once conceptual thought itself is implicated in the domination of society. What can the response be to a situation in which the development of *theory* (let alone the movement of any historically constituted collective subject) can no longer represent the genuine development of reason? What does one do when the historical progress of enlightenment and civilization bears more resemblance to a progress in efficient and deadly means of domination and destruction than a progress in a universal human history (which, at the beginning of the new millennium, seems empirically true more than ever)? When demystification simply leads to remystification, when shedding the light of cognition casts even longer shadows of domination, one may doubt the very sense of the traditional distinction between *Verstand* and *Vernunft*.

For Horkheimer and Adorno writing in the 1940s, the difficulty of recovering an adequate intellectual, moral, social, and political life that would correspond to the ability to think without delusions and unnecessary domination was indeed immense. The consistent response of critical theory to such problems has been to delve ever deeper into the conditions of reason itself, into the possibilities of non-dominating cognition, conceptual thought, and perception, all of which bear upon the formation of subjectivity and intersubjectivity in ethically and politically important ways. It is also to relentlessly criticize the mass deception of consumer culture and the political economy of technological civilization for its denial of the potential for a truer life. Negation would seem to be key if there can be no further enlightening *theory* that could be contrasted to the baleful entwinement of the universal reason of enlightenment, the unreason of domination, and the delusions of ever more myths. A better way of thinking that somehow was not abstracted from the encounter with the objects of thought could offer the most promising starting point for coming to terms with this terrifying condition of foundationless existence. It might thereby allow social beings to face the abyss without the fear that throws up delusions like walls. As Horkheimer and Adorno write in their study of this condition: "While the horror admits of no truth against which it could be judged, it moves within reach of the truth negatively, in its immeasurable illogicality [*im Unmaß seines Widersinns*]; those unable to discriminate [*die Urteilslosen*] are kept separated from this truth only by the complete loss of thought. Self-controlled enlightenment coming to power [*Gewalt*] is itself able to break through the limits of enlightenment" (*DA*: 217/208).

The struggle with the question of what it is that limits the thought that limits thought has consequently led followers of Adorno in two opposite directions. Those who retain a strong negative critique but give up the belief that an authentic rational society is possible lean toward poststructuralism or deconstruction; others (led by Habermas) retain the idea of a rational society but abandon the negative dialectic (Zuidervaart, 1991: 206). Critical negation relies on a dialectic, and the dialectic, for poststructuralism, is a theoretical artifact of the philosophy of history that cannot therefore be preserved. Yet without the dialectic—a dynamic of development—strong negative critique points nowhere particularly new, and indeed the idea of change itself seems to lose its profound content. Without the dialectic, negation may instead accept the materials of the present, those at hand, and instead seek to articulate sites of resistance to power that do not appeal to a systemic theory of domination beyond that inherent in the symbolic systems of discourse themselves. In this case, discourses are instead understood as themselves material, or at least as having material effects, which then reveals them as strategies for the maintenance and enhancement of the social power of those who articulate them. Strong negative critique operates as an unrelenting negativity that is conscious of the impossibility of finally resolving or mitigating the contradictions and aporia of reason and domination. But non-dialectical negative critique does not open itself to the possibility of a new state of affairs that might be beyond the dialectic of enlightenment itself, a state of affairs critical theory refers to as a qualitatively "new historical epoch," the "liberated society" (and all such equivalents). Instead, the fall of man is irrevocable, irredeemable on this earth.

Yet for many critics today, the idea that no true referent exists somehow beyond the eternal play of signifiers seems to dissolve the most profound hopes of philosophy, namely, the (utopian) promise inherent in the concepts of reason and truth themselves. If philosophy itself has come to an end instead of perhaps undergoing a transformation that might see it live on in some way,[17] then one may wonder if there can only be endless critique and negation, endless dynamics of power and resistance, endless suffering and guilt born of the unavoidable and inevitable violence done in all 'civilized' action. Would this not be an intolerable, debilitating condition for those interested in progressive change? Without some form of normative foundation, Habermas and his followers contend, critical theory risks becoming immobilized, inoperative, mute, resigned (which is just where Habermas thinks Adorno ends up with the negative dialectic, as we will see in more detail in Chapter 4).

The eternal play of signifiers and the concept of truth, however, should not be thought of as mutually exclusive. If such eternal play or constant negation is revealed as the proper activity of self-reflective thought, then the potential for democracy goes beyond public participation in deliberative decision-making. Democracy cannot avoid the positivities that all politics involves (even some postmodernists now call for a strategic essentialism to improve political efficacy), but the key question is how participants respond to this in an ongoing way. The politics of negation prevents the slide into dogmatism or instituting an unfounded and unfoundable closing off of challenge, conflict, struggle, contemplation, or reservation at some point that is deemed reasonable. But it intends that something more should come of this, that democracy concerns reconcilement between self and other in the political field and that this will lead to a more profound liberation from unnecessary suffering at other levels of individual and social life. In short, constant negation and problematization might be precisely the kind of vital communicative activity that defines and invigorates the decentered, diverse, disagreeing, and contesting 'universality' of a democracy coming to itself, while it paradoxically calls on participants to recognize the insufficiency that is revealed in the activity of negation itself. The more the world is shown to be other than or in excess of what it is, the more it becomes possible to challenge and resist the systems of domination that establish that world and reassure us that it is in fact as it is.

Thus there is an unavoidable and highly significant tension in the negative dialectic that should always bring pause to any concrete utopianism. For it counsels that as soon as we think we are 'beyond' the dialectic of enlightenment, we most certainly are not; as soon as we think the liberated society might be upon us, we become blind to the sacrifice that establishes it in thought and in reality.

Critical theory, as I present it, is a theory that requires a grasp of the negative dialectic, which is to be distinguished from either conventional science, metaphysics, or simple negation. The devilish negation of everything that Goethe's Mephistopheles represents is different from the ruthless critique of everything existing for which Marx called. As such, negative dialectic is a form of thought permanently in tension with its own drive. Critical theory's self-consciousness of this tension, which, in its greatest practitioners such as Adorno, is performed with admirable artistry and verve by way of its very presentation or *present-ing* of the process of thought itself, should not therefore be dismissed as merely contradictory, incoherent, or, more darkly, as nihilistic. For such awareness is crucial to the ethic elicited by consistent critical thought itself. The sense or spirit of the negative dialectic cannot be articulated precisely as a question of *theory*, in the form of a system of conceptual thought or method and nor should one expect that it could be. Indeed, language itself has a 'double character' that makes it a model of dialectic, and it is this sense that must be reconstituted in some way without implying that this double character can or should be overcome. "As a system of signs, language is required to resign itself to calculation in order to know nature and thus gives up the claim to be like nature. As representation, it is required to resign itself to the image in order to be nature whole and gives up the claim to know nature" (*DA*: 24/17–18). These two sides of language are equally false if taken as adequate models on their own, yet they present an irresolvable tension if taken together.

The negative dialectic is always bound up with the obscurity, indeterminacy, and radical contingency of being, of the present opening onto the future and the recollection of the past, of the historical emergence, perception, and articulation of new needs and unfulfilled desires. It maintains an orientation to *truth*, however, by center-staging the experience that is integral to adequate cognition, by its reflective performativity of thought-action. This, I shall argue later, requires critical theory to think the aesthetic dimension of thought-action in a profound way. What is clear is that the dialectic cannot be presented as the kind of Grand Theory or with the pretensions to Truth that have been so effectively criticized by poststructuralism and deconstruction and by Frankfurt critical theory itself.

Let us now turn to *Dialectic of Enlightenment* itself. After some preliminaries regarding the text, I examine selected main ideas and relevant criticisms from Habermasian and poststructuralist perspectives in order to draw out its ethics of communication. Instead of a detailed and comprehensive analysis of the text, I offer an interpretation primarily designed to show that a transformation began to occur that opened a new, if difficult, path for critical theory to negotiate. I aim to counter the dominant perception that this phase inaugurated the decline of critical theory (which will perhaps also help dispel some of the more egregious misunderstandings).

2.2.2. Myth and Enlightenment: Quandaries of Dialectical Thought

Dialectic of Enlightenment has proved to be a text of enduring interest in critical social and political theory, one that has attracted a great deal of study and attained important influence well outside the tradition of Frankfurt critical theory. While the authors' own cautious historicization of the text in the Preface to the 1969 edition is tempered by the suggestion that it still then held significance, scholars today remain concerned to assess its continuing relevance from a variety of perspectives.[18] The question of its continued relevance, however, is complicated substantially by the difficulty presented in understanding its important arguments, which has in turn led to an abundance of seriously distorted and misleading interpretations—including Habermas's.

In addition to its unremitting critique of Enlightenment philosophy and scientism, postmodern thinkers have been attracted by *Dialectic of Enlightenment*'s analysis of the self as a social text—that is, the self as an entwinement of reason and power—as well as its attempt to recognize and incorporate the irreducible extra-rational content of reason and thought. Indeed, many commentators have pointed to the kinship between postmodern and poststructuralist concerns and those expressed in *Dialectic of Enlightenment* and in Adorno's thought in general.[19] Late in his life, Foucault (1988; 1991) indicated approvingly the affinities between his work and that of the Frankfurt school, even suggesting that his work would have benefited from an earlier reading of critical theory (though this declaration can be read ambiguously). On the other hand, postmodern critiques of this document reject its Marxist and utopian codings and its recourse to a revised critical dialectic that is allegedly made in the name of an authenticity or "comprehensive reason" that simply does not exist (Böhme and Böhme, 1983: 18). One should, however, remain cautious in drawing too close a likeness between early critical theory and postmodern or deconstructive positions, as will be suggested later, for the role of the dialectic and its (negative) utopian vision are decisive in the former.

Conversely, the critical notoriety of *Dialectic of Enlightenment* has continued to vex thinkers such as Habermas who are concerned with preserving what is progressively worthy in the inheritance of critical theory and more broadly in modern social philosophy. Thus at minimum one may locate *Dialectic of Enlightenment* as an ambiguous yet highly influential text in twentieth-century theory that can figure—albeit uncomfortably—on either side of the quarrel between modern and postmodern theory (at least as this manifests in the contemporary Frankfurt versus French post-Nietzschean debate). My task in the remaining part of the chapter, however, is not to comment directly on current disputes between postmodern and Habermasian critical theory. It is instead to suggest, via an exploration of *Dialectic of Enlightenment* with special reference to select Habermasian and postmodernist criticisms of this text, that the critical theory subsequently developed by Adorno constitutes a distinct and alternative line to that taken by Habermas (or poststructuralism, for that matter, but I cannot argue that here). This will set up the main thrust of my overall argument that seeks to delineate an Adornoesque path that reaches right through Habermas's reconstitution of critical theory. A quite different communicative ethic can then be drawn from Adorno's work than that which Habermas develops.

Horkheimer and Adorno introduce a radical critique of reason to critical theory in *Dialectic of Enlightenment*, which at one level attempts to come to terms with the crisis of the critique of ideology but at others a bewildering and apparently outlandish set of theses are offered on a range of topics from literary criticism and philosophy to mass culture and anti-Semitism. The text's obscure and fragmentary presentation permits the precise meaning of its complex and intertwined arguments to be seriously disputed, while having the virtue of remaining enigmatic and deeply suggestive. Interpretation of the text is also clouded by the replacement—largely for fear of the American authorities in Germany—of Marxist-inspired critical terms that were present in the shorter 1944 mimeograph with alternatives in the published 1947 version. A very careful and reflective approach is required to *Dialectic of Enlightenment*, as with all of Adorno's texts, an approach he sought to encourage through his very mode of writing. Inaugurated during the authors' exile in the United States in a period of fascism, world war, increasingly 'colonized' and administered modern culture, and under conditions hostile to critical or Marxist thought, this text is also undoubtedly colored by its time.

Habermas (*TCAI*: 366ff) and Dubiel (1985) emphasize these distressing historical conditions faced by Horkheimer and Adorno as radical thinkers in the 1930s and 1940s in their contextualization of the turning point in critical theory. According to Habermas and Dubiel, three historical experiences were decisive for the development of critical theory: the bloody oppression of Stalinism, the co-optation during a capitalist crisis of labor movements into the fascist transformation of politics, and the new levels of integration of mass society in the United States achieved through the production of mass culture. All these experiences converged in the disappointment of failed revolutionary expectations. From a more sympathetic perspective, as Geyer (1997: 669) puts it in the German context in particular, the conditions of its coming into being mark *Dialectic of Enlightenment* as "a founding text for a German history of the twentieth century."

Yet it would be a mistake to collapse the conditions of its genesis with its claims to validity. The social-theoretic orientation of *Dialectic of Enlightenment* is nevertheless often described, especially with its context of composition in mind, as a dark and pessimistic 'critique of instrumental reason' that extends and develops Max Weber's rationalization thesis, Marx's theory of commodity fetishism, and Freud's theory of repression into a totalizing view from which there is no escape (for example, as is done by Whitebook, 1995). This is a misleading and narrow interpretation, for it denies the hopeful aspects of its outlook and the theoretical resources it musters to propose an alternative to the dire dialectic it analyzes. I hope to draw attention to the existence and complexity of this specific alternative toward the end of my discussion.

The text's critique of contemporary society and the baleful history of civilization should be familiar to most with a passing acquaintance with critical theory. Once the rationalization of culture adapts to the basic mode of capitalist production and once individuals adapt their needs to suit mass-produced cultural products, the way is clear for the exercise of social and political power through an autonomous system of production and consumption that has assumed the status of a 'second' nature. In this system of production and consumption aided by the great twentieth-century advances in science and technology (especially mass communications technology), signification and meaning have become almost entirely fluid such that needs articulation and interpretation relate less and less to what might constitute the real interests of human beings and more and more to the reproduction and expansion of this system itself. Neither explicit and overt political domination nor mystical worldviews and ceremonies are any longer required in order to maintain class domination because the individual internalizes system requirements, thereby reproducing a subject suited to conformity and to the consumption of the system's commodified products rather than to the 'freedom' that bourgeois ideology promised. But the authoritarian character of this new subject is consequently a danger to the development of bourgeois democracy, and new sets of constraints must be introduced to compensate. Culture itself, which was never fully separable from its material conditions of existence, becomes so thoroughly integrated into the totalizing system of production, reproduction, and consumption that it ceases to function as ideology at all and seems no longer even to be recognized as representing or constituting any critical distance.

Hence the basic dialectical thesis of the culture industry chapter of *Dialectic of Enlightenment* states that 'culture' has become industry and 'industry' has become culture. Although perhaps the most infamous chapter of the book, its central argument concerns the false promise offered by the culture industry, the *deception* in the satisfaction realized by the consumption of its products rather than any proper theory of what culture is or should be.[20] Along with the other 'Excursuses' and chapters on the concept of enlightenment, *The Odyssey*, Sade, and anti-Semitism, the text aims to show how Western culture and civilization are fundamentally entwined with subjectification and the domination of all that is other to identifying reason, of all that is natural and beyond rationalization but which nevertheless provided and continues to provide the conditions for culture itself. Even critical philosophy itself is unable to be separated or abstracted from this process without negation. Indeed, the anti-metaphysical thrust of this critique entails that today thought itself, no matter how rigorous, cannot uncover a pure rational object below false appearance. Moreover, never was such an object available in any and all past societies. Thus enlightening ideology critique, if it is to continue at all, cannot remain bound to unmasking the particular in the universal for the sake of the true universal but must somehow acknowledge the relations of domination and hence the corruption immanent to all symbolic thought as well as to all currently known practical cultural life.[21]

The focus for Adorno is subjectivity since subjectivity is the category brought to full universality only under modern capitalist society.[22] As such, it is not of course a category *exclusive* to capitalism. The primal history (*Urgeschichte*) of subjectivity Horkheimer and Adorno trace in *Dialectic of Enlightenment* is supposed to uncover the presence of an elemental bourgeois subjectivity in the earliest myths of Western culture. The principles of 'bourgeois' subjectivity and exchange predate capitalism as a world-historical system because they are elements of the kind of praxis that is part and parcel of the beginning of human society itself. Class society begins when the principle of the self can be maintained only in relation to others by way of domination of those others who must in turn sacrifice their own self-formation. But domination, as the principle of subjectivity, extends back to the very hominization of human beings in which the principle of self-preservation wrenches itself from its embeddedness in nature, and thus in some sense precedes even class society.

Identity thinking is the term Adorno uses to describe the subsuming, classificatory consciousness that fetishizes the sign itself, the primary element of cognitive presence, as the thing it represents. Identity thinking in one sense, then, represents the dominant principle of enlightenment itself—the form of reason that brought humanization to the species by opening up the world to instrumental control. 'Things' are abstracted by their hermetic names and become independent of the wider locus and context; concepts identify objects as particular examples of a universal and come into being for a human cognition beyond and unconstrained by the immediacy of sensual and imitative life. Identity thinking is essential to the very self-preservation of the species because it allows an instrumental organization of reality for the sake of human ends. Thus identity thinking is necessary for all thinking that is concerned with the differentiated existence of the things themselves as well as the selves that conceive them. It cannot simply be done away with, and Adorno does not propose this. While one may "still be capable of seeing through the identity principle," Adorno writes, "nothing can be thought without identification—each determination is identification" (*ND*: 152/149).

Identity thinking is not quite the *opposite* of Adorno's preferred dialectical thought. It is instead a poor, inadequate, incomplete type of thought that is better understood as a moment or aspect of thought rather than equivalent to the whole of thought itself. But it is a baleful moment toward which the subject always tends to the detriment of dialectic. Identity thinking is easy enlightenment, knowledge content in its reification or fetish of the sign. But it is the instrumental power of identity that is to be resisted by critical thought because instrumentality is historically aligned with *social* power. The identity principle thus names more than just a type of thought because its form is entwined with and predicated on social domination. Against Durkheim, the social character of categories of thought does not express social solidarity but testifies to the "inscrutable unity of society and domination" (*DA*: 28/21). Corresponding to the development of collective and individual, universal and particular, are parallel and primary relations of social domination that clothe themselves in the appearance of ever more rigorous knowledge of 'reality'. "The distance between subject and object, the presupposition of abstraction, is grounded in the distance to the thing itself [*Sache*] which the master has gained through the mastered. . . . With the end of the nomadic age, the social order is established on the basis of fixed property. Estate and labor step apart. . . . The universality of thought—mastery in the conceptual sphere—like the discursive logic it develops, is raised up on the foundation of real domination" (*DA*: 19–20/13–14). The critique of the "dialectic of enlightenment," then, in convicting each new episteme or paradigm of truth with reverting to myth, thereby also convicts it of ideological support for the rule of a succession of classes—priestly, aristocratic, cleric, capitalist.

Adorno thus advocates an awareness of the historical, social, and intellectual processes by which the object is distorted, transformed, limited, reduced, violated—in short, dominated—by the concept. The term *object* here signifies variously all subject matter that is intended to be captured in a concept or idea, and thus includes not only natural objects but other subjects as well as ideas and concepts themselves. Thought, Adorno argues, is driven to the dialectic "by its own inevitable insufficiency, by the guilt of what it thinks" (*ND*: 17/5). But the material processes of cognition are seen to be extraordinarily extensive and also to imitate political relations that are reproduced in different forms at *all* levels of social existence. Thus not only do we dominate nature for the sake of self-preservation, but we humans dominate ourselves and our 'inner' nature, sacrificing a political liberatory knowledge of ourselves to an instrumental interest in maintaining control:

> In the moment in which men and women cut themselves off from the awareness of themselves as nature, all of the aims for which they keep themselves alive—social progress, the improvement of all material and intellectual powers, even consciousness itself—are nullified, and the enthronement of means as ends, which in late capitalism takes on the character of open insanity, is already perceptible in the primal history of subjectivity. The domination of men and women over themselves that establishes their selfhood is inevitably the annihilation of the subject in whose service it is committed because the dominated and repressed substance that is dissolved through self-preservation is nothing other than the life force by which the achievements of self-preservation are solely defined: it is in fact just that which is supposed to be preserved (*DA*: 61–62/54–55).

This critique is not, thus, just a critique of the inadequacy of concept and thing, of the violence inherent in all identifying abstraction. Far more than this, it involves a critique of the whole 'reality' or world that is brought into being in conjunction with the specific forms of identity thinking and their sacrificial logic of substitutability. The philosophical and anthropological genealogy of this logic of substitutability are traced in *Dialectic of Enlightenment*, which arrives at the spectacular present hegemony that secures modern exchange society. Though reality is undeniably real, it is also real only to the extent to which our cognitive capacities accord with historical relations of social domination. Hence, again today, what is at stake for critical theory is not just a critique of science or positivist and idealist epistemology. For example, the issue is not whether to turn science and technology from evil, wrong, destructive, or exploitative uses toward good, progressive, and rightful applications, in the same sense that, following Marx, the critique of surplus value extraction does not thereby simply prefer just and equitable exchange. This is because exactly such value hierarchies of right versus wrong, good versus bad, illegitimate versus legitimate, repeat the structure of the dialectic of enlightenment and do not lead to an effective break with its logic. To resist this fateful dialectic instead requires a new science, a new cognition for which a corresponding *moral* critique would be largely superfluous because unnecessary social domination and suffering caused by class society would have been eliminated along with the enthrallment to identity.

Part of the problem with the contemporary orientation of scientific knowledge toward control, as well as all identity thinking, is that the central cognitive validity of aesthetic mimesis is abandoned. For Adorno, there is an "indelible mimetic moment in all cognition and all human practice" (*ND*: 153/150). Identity thinking is not the opposite of mimetic thought *per se* either, but an unreflective and unacknowledged form of mimesis itself. I will have much more to say about the concept of mimesis, since it is a central category in Adorno's articulation of what might constitute communicative freedom. For now, we might understand aesthetic mimesis as the gesture of philosophy toward that which is sacrificed for the power of conceptual thought. It represents a consciousness of the non-identity at the heart of all identity and calls for thinking to reorient itself accordingly. As such, it also thus implies the possibility of a different existence or reality and corresponding set of social relations. The 'fetish' of the identifying consciousness, by contrast, is the repression of a non-dominating mimesis by a "mimesis of death" that renders the cunning subjective reason nature-like for the purposes of domination. Rational action—which, for example, the practices of myth and magic are also—can affect a disenchanted reality that is to be manipulated as it is tamed only by becoming like it, by becoming instrumental reason (*DA*: 64/57). A reified world must be matched by a deadening reason that numbs and bewitches the subject who uses it. But whereas magic, like science, still pursued aims, it did so through a mimetic relation that self-consciously participated with its object and did not merely manipulate it. Science in fact exchanges mimetic representation for universal interchangeability, liquidating its objects as did fate, a feat in which everything in nature becomes repeatable (reflecting the abstract repeatability of industry) and thereby mastered as knowledge (paralleling the social domination of class) (*DA*: 16–17/10–11, 19/13).

Horkheimer and Adorno offer a psychoanalytic-anthropological critique of the ideology of human civilization that does not quite seek to write or present an alternative philosophy of history, but rather aims to give an account of the presuppositions of our current instrumental subjectivity that are repeated in the earliest of myths. The process that first produced myth was enlightenment, and this process has developed and evolved uninterrupted (although in a by no means 'happy' way) to the thoroughly 'enlightened,' scientific civilization of the present. This process does not have a beginning, however, for enlightenment has emerged with a natural character or growth (*Naturwüchsigkeit*) that cannot be eradicated. There was thus no golden age before domination that we could yearn for or attempt to recover. On the other hand, enlightenment is therefore not wholly natural either and in principle can be further altered, possibly in a progressive way. Hence this is an *historical* thesis and not, as Habermas implies, an *ontological* one.[23] While domination of nature establishes a certain continuity in human history, this domination produces qualitatively different historical forms (mimesis, magic, myth, science) and thus presents the possibility of its own transformation. What is required for such further transformation, Horkheimer and Adorno argue, is a *re*-cognition of this process and a reduction in domination in order to break the hold of mythical regression instantiated by the dialectic of enlightenment. "Enlightenment is more than enlightenment," Horkheimer and Adorno write: "Through the announcement in which spirit confesses its domination and retreats into nature, it dissolves the claim to domination that enslaved it directly to nature . . . Every advance of civilization has renewed together with domination that prospect of its pacification" (*DA*: 46/39–40). Horkheimer and Adorno repeatedly allude to this potentially 'good thing' about enlightenment and reason, which is part of what they mean by reconciliation, even while they describe reason's worst excesses.

The fateful course of enlightenment thus designates the progressive freeing of human subjectivity from its subjugation to blind or unreflected processes and beliefs paradoxically through a series of new dominations and myths. Enlightenment concerns knowledge, but also social organization, capacities, and power. Each new epoch believes itself to have rationally overcome the backwardness and limitations of the previous one. But the process of emancipation has always enacted with its achievements and progress the repetition of the primal form of domination that undermines its enlightening efforts at every turn. The modern perspective introduces a unique time-consciousness not only of its own period but of previous epochs as well that are then relativized against the pressure to realize the new that drives the modern spirit. Despite this, the recognition of the *dialectic* of enlightenment throws into doubt the very notion of any purely rational progress in human civilization, including the modern self-understanding as 'progressive'. Thus, in the modern era, the mythic powers of the gods of the natural world that influenced human social life are replaced not with a sober and secular knowledge of true social relations and their foundations but with profane myths of faceless and inhuman economic or social forces that govern human society. That there is a facticity to these social forces does not negate but rather composes part of their mythic appearance. Moreover, new, demonized social enemies replace the deities and demons who used to cause calamity out of sight—but with a vengeance, of course, for modern enlightenment has forsaken the advantages of a mimetic relationship with nature that animism at least could explicitly invoke to outwit or appease the invisible malevolents. A compulsive repetition of unrecognized error is manifested such that, like a pendulum, this dialectic ensures that "enlightenment reverts to mythology, from which it never knew how to escape" (*DA*: 33/27).

It can be easy to view this (incorrectly) as a Weberian anti-modernism and thoroughgoing anti-progressivism that testifies to the structural impossibility of the desired reconciliation of this process (as does Whitebook, 1995: 3, 6–7). Indeed, the Habermasian critique focuses on both practical and theoretical aspects of Horkheimer and Adorno's argument. If theory production itself (reason oriented to enlightenment) is called into question, then critique, paradoxically, is also brought under suspicion and must be rendered "independent even in relation to its own foundations" (Habermas, 1987: 116). The practical consequence of this is that it destines the radical critic to political quietism since every positive thought becomes suspect (McCarthy, 1978: 108). The radical critic is left, as is alleged in Adorno's case, to gesture toward the alienated yet autonomous sphere of art in order to find a critical sensibility beyond totalized commodification and society itself. The price is muteness and impotence, for the aesthetic can have no legitimate practical-political bearing on society.[24]

For Habermas, the principal consequence of the radical critique of enlightenment as domination is that the concept of reason becomes blurred, which threatens to destroy the rational inheritance of Western culture itself. Horkheimer and Adorno's theory is said to fall into a performative self-contradiction because reason is criticized with its own 'tools'. Habermas here remobilizes the well-worn logical critique of skepticism or relativism (that the skeptic must presume at least one absolute:

the validity of his own position, and hence contradicts himself) against poststructuralists and deconstructionists as well as against Horkheimer and Adorno. But Adorno already recognized the formal and hence unpenetrating level of this kind of objection to relativism after which "the fiber of relativist thought remained more or less untouched" (ND: 46/35). Relativism/skepticism cannot be effectively criticized from a strictly logical or (quasi-) transcendental position because each—relativism/skepticism and the logical/transcendental—represents the opposite side of the same unreflective and undialectical coin. One radically doubts that universally valid knowledge can be produced at all while the other desperately desires such knowledge and foundation for fear of the terrifying condition that its absence would entail. Neither recognizes how fully their position is produced by contradictory social conditions, nor why a consciousness of non-identity and social contradiction would render such philosophical and political concerns far less pressing.

Neither does Habermas's objection of performative contradiction come close to addressing the philosophical position of the negative dialectic, as I shall argue in more detail later.[25] Indeed, its abstract level seems to beg the question of the nature of reason that is precisely at issue since it uses the presuppositions of *logos* to establish the sense by which all statements must operate, including those which challenge this sense of *logos* and its presuppositions. Moreover, by claiming that a rational critique of reason must be disallowed while simultaneously claiming that consistent rational critique is nevertheless possible can itself be seen to be contradictory. The objects of social criticism are already rational objects, and it is just their rationality that is under scrutiny. This was a basic insight of Hegel's social philosophy that had already revealed the emptiness ensuing from Kantian attempts to insulate or radically separate the rational subject from the history that composed it.

It is hence exactly the conditions of thought that are to be self-reflectively addressed by critical thinking in order to reveal how reason's very existence cannot be self-sufficient but instead depends on precise relations to that which is non-reason. Further, it is to reveal how reason can *turn into* the unreason or rational irrationality that is to be criticized. In short, there is no object that is not already infused with the history that perceives it. Adorno contrasts his own dialectical thought to the equally false extremes of foundationalism and skepticism/relativism not as a happy middle or synthesis but as a qualitatively different form that refuses their parameters. He appeals to this new form of thought in order to break the spell of identity thinking that holds society and philosophy in thrall. For Adorno, critique *is* performative contradiction, and this is part of its point. Adorno's effort is to show that such new self-consciousness need not be thought as incoherent in a theory that operates according to determinate negation and does not require or desire the identity of the Absolute.

It is interesting that the Habermasian charge of performative contradiction against Horkheimer and Adorno is paralleled in a different way by Hoy's (1994) more differentiated and qualified poststructuralist critique of the latter, but with no more success.[26] Hoy alleges that, since the authors of *Dialectic of Enlightenment* state that their critique "is intended to prepare the way for a positive notion of enlightenment which will release it from entanglement in blind domination" (*DA*: 6/xvi), their own critical philosophy remains "parasitic" on the enlightenment theory of knowledge it so vehemently criticizes. That they never specify the positive notion of enlightenment in the end casts doubt on any faith in reason or even critical reason (1994: 115–16). Despite Horkheimer and Adorno's admirable critical *activity* in this text, Hoy contends that their commitment to dialectical thinking means they are unable to break with the enlightenment concern of achieving a "superior grasp of reality" that renders their project hypocritical because dialectical thought cannot claim superior *knowledge* or a superior *moral* position (1994: 126). For Hoy, who doubts the very possibility of any critical theory adequate to its name, "superior knowledge" of reality is implied in the truth-falsity distinction to which all theory testifies. Horkheimer and Adorno's own argument indicates that, once the Absolute is abandoned, no further 'true' theory can come of critical negation; yet the dialectical assumption persists that one is nevertheless possible. For this argument against Horkheimer and Adorno, Hoy must, like Habermas, deny that (negative) dialectical thought really constitutes a theory, or at least a non-contradictory one. Abandoning an attachment to the dialectic allows Hoy (not quite like Habermas) to read the critical *theory* of *Dialectic of Enlightenment* as a fragmentary writing in the mode of the post-Nietzschean critical *history* that he wishes to defend.[27]

Adorno surely maintains the truth-falsity distinction, but his understanding of the value and meaning of theory (versus error or ideology) cannot be measured in terms of its correspondence or approximation to reality and certainly not according to any speculative identification of consciousness. Truth is, rather, an inherently *practical* and *historical* idea. It should not be understood as some transcendent, abstract, or eternal property that endows properly qualified statements, but as the achievement of a self-reflected interest in freedom. Truth, like falsity, is historical, part of the human world, and its fragile, temporal substance is consequently quite fleeting. "Open thinking," which pursues truth, relies not on any official documentation supplied by philosophy but on "the consistency of its exposition [*Durchführung*], the density of the texture," in order to hit its mark (*ND*: 45/35). In a contradictory world, philosophical truth can only be expressed negatively—that is, as the representation of the insufficiency of its own striving. For nothing can remain utterly stable and absolutely present, calm and composed, completely self-identical and lacking contradiction. Thus the materialist dialectic that Adorno presents is a mode of thinking that, without positing a method or a theory that is to be 'applied' to its subject matter, nevertheless pursues truth through the consistent *performance* of its negative critique, its determinate negations. The knowledge generated is a critical knowledge (which does resemble the critical history of Foucault), but whose claim to truth arises from its perception of the contradictory and therefore non-existent (*nichtextistente*) or absent social totality in which all thinking occurs, including its own (which is non-Foucaultian). To limit truth to the determination of the 'facts' is to be reconciled to the social domination (reification) that presents them as such and hence it is to be blinded to their existential truth.

The key difference to Habermas's theory is that there is no aspect of the totality that is insulated from contradiction, for the operation of reason itself depends on the non-identical, the extra-rational or un-reason. The universal is at once both absent and present. One of Adorno's key themes, to which I will return during the course of this book, is that the non-identity of reason with itself does not imply an incoherent critical position nor undermine every effort to combat domination. It does not imply giving up on any access to truth, but it does require us to reconceive what we mean by truth and how truth can operate in society. The key difference to Hoy's poststructuralist position is thus that the very contradictory nature of the social totality has a truth-content: it points toward reconciliation, toward a thinking and acting in the world and with each other that has somehow come to terms with the insufficiency of identity and no longer fears the nonidentical as a threat to the stable relations of self and other. Just this vision of the reconciled condition is to supply the truth of the philosophy.

In fact (contrary to Hoy), Horkheimer and Adorno *do* suggest an alternative notion of enlightenment that is utopian, yet not *merely* or pointlessly so,[28] and that does, in this unique but difficult way, maintain a relationship to truth over falsity. Horkheimer and Adorno's alternative notion of enlightenment, which I will examine in relation to a communicative ethic shortly, emerges from their critique of contradictory society.

This social-theoretic dimension, which includes a thoroughgoing critique of capitalism and class domination, is essentially ignored by Hoy, who fails to recognize the reproduction of class society in identity thinking. This link between identity thinking and class domination constitutes, in effect, Horkheimer and Adorno's theory of class consciousness without the Lukácsian subject-object of history. Their 'superior grasp' is not of reality directly, which is what enlightenment thought has always claimed to provide, but of the way in which *thinking* is also at the same time a *doing* and an *experience* that emerges from (present contradictory) social conditions and possibilities. If one accepts that reason depends on its other—indeed, that reason emerges in a constant and conflictual relation to what is outside itself—then one cannot appeal to the self-sufficiency or transcendent structural operation of language. Even though we are thoroughly linguistically mediated beings, language remains dialectical and therefore language as such cannot be the only "nature" we can *know*.[29] Neither can one appeal conversely to a primordial Being, an authenticity, a prior unity of spirit and matter, or comprehensive reason that has been lost in the course of history and that must be recovered for any hope for freedom, truth and justice. Adorno does not opt for either of these latter alternatives.

This is also why *Dialectic of Enlightenment* does not present an ontology at all, for it testifies to the continual fluidity and movement of historical being and consciousness and of history and nature itself. "The traditional antithesis between nature and history," Adorno writes, "is both true and false; true insofar as it expresses what has befallen the moment of nature; false insofar as it apologetically reiterates the concealment of history's natural emergence [*Naturwüchsigkeit*] by way of conceptual reconstruction" (*ND*: 351/358).[30] Nevertheless, if neither an epistemology nor an ontology is invoked, and if the social totality is 'non-existent' (un-presentable) yet somehow still figurable in indirect fashion, then how can Adorno properly claim to refer to truth and falsity or achieve a philosophically defensible knowledge at all? The gesture toward reconciliation may simply end up being empty, or at best futile, which is just how many critics of Adorno have seen it. Horkheimer and Adorno's counter-formulation of the enlightening subject and its constitution, which is the 'positive' topic of *Dialectic of Enlightenment*, outlines in this transitional stage what this knowledge might be. It suggests a communicative concept that bridges intersubjective and interobjective relations at the meta-theoretical level through an aesthetic theory. I offer a preliminary examination in this final section and in the following chapter.

2.2.3. Beyond the Sacrificial Logic: Toward a Justice of Cognition

The philosophical anthropology that informs Horkheimer and Adorno's study is crucial to its full comprehension (as is its critique of capitalism and domination). As should be clear, it is an anthropology that does not rely on an essential nature yet points to the possibility of a new state of freedom through a re-cognition of the process of self-formation. The Odysseus chapter in *Dialectic of Enlightenment* analyzes Homer's epic *The Odyssey* as a narrative constitution of a new individual appropriate to the propertied relations and social order of the emerging Greek political economy. Its theme uncovers the process of reason as a progress of sacrificial exchange that provides a continuity to the advanced exchange society of late capitalism. "The pivotal point at which myth becomes enlightenment and enlightenment becomes myth," Hullot-Kentor (1989: 21) explains, "is sacrifice, and the transition from myth to enlightenment is progress in the power of substitutability." The formation of the self-identical self in this epic depends on the introversion of sacrifice; its unity is preserved only by a cunning of reason that continually renounces itself in order to preserve itself. This describes history as the introversion of sacrifice, history as renunciation (*DA*: 63/55) for the sake of home life and its fixed property.

The concept of fear thus designates an important continuity in Horkheimer and Adorno's anthropology and operates as a key in the account of the capitulation of enlightening thought to domination. The consciousness of 'knowing that' first establishes the difference between nature and human being, but it is constituted through the relation of unknown to known and mastered, and therefore continues and transforms innate primal fear as specifically *human* fear of the unknown and uncontrolled. Identifying thought—which allows explanation—emerges from the primal urge to overcome fear and, as such, enlightenment is a radical extension of mythic fear (*DA*: 21–22/15–16). Overcoming the dialectic of myth and enlightenment is thus bound up with overcoming human fear and the (historical) way in which the reassurance that arises with knowing takes the form of mastering and dominating. Any notion of free communication worthy of its name cannot tolerate the presence of fear.

The singularly most successful strategy of subjective reason in overcoming the fear of the uncomprehended, hostile, and threatening forces of nature is likewise a primal anthropological feature: imitation or *mimesis*. Just as the witch doctor puts on masks and represents the demons in order to steal their power, so modern science determines the facts in order to control the nature thus revealed. The difference between science and magic is that the latter could still be conscious of the act of imitation and knew its representations were efforts to become part of the things to which they referred. For science, by contrast, concept and sign are understood to imitate exactly the abstract processes of nature as they are given, but must then give themselves over to nature completely, lose themselves in it, in order to master it completely. Science capitulates to the existing social relations of domination in a way magic did not by virtue of the former's fetishism of subjects and objects alike. Magic, on the other hand, rather than simply an early form of myth, becomes an inchoate form of dialectical thinking since it still recognized the sem- blance of subjectivity and its objects.

Horkheimer and Adorno thus open up an *aesthetic* theory of acting in the world that emphasizes the *distance* between reality—the objectified and separated nature toward which instrumental action is now possible— and its representation, which exists only as history, as a 'second nature,' as historical re-presentation at a mimetic level. The self-reflective *performative* effort of perception and understanding mediated by reason depends on maintaining—not erasing—the presence of this distance between representation and reality, which themselves remain in dialecti- cal tension in the communicative actions of historical beings. Bringing this state of affairs to consciousness, which is perhaps the preeminent aim of Adorno's work (especially in *Aesthetic Theory*, as we shall see in Chapter 5), is to make possible the production of meaning without un- necessary suffering and sacrifice. This is the possibility to which modern art testifies. Even Shapiro's (1989: 22) appreciative reading of Horkheimer and Adorno seems to neglect the latter's commitment to historicity and the recognition of the aesthetic power operating in perception and intel- ligibility when he opts for Foucaultian genealogy because "critical theory in general, and Adorno to some extent (although his position is ambigu- ous here) base their readings of the reification of the self on a model of an authentic model of intelligibility." Instead of ontology, which Adorno rejects, there is an aesthetic theory of appearing in the world, of repre- senting truth, that does not depend on a notion of essential authenticity but does appeal to an autonomy and freedom of such bringing forth and making present.

Using the salient example of anti-Semitism to demonstrate the debased potential of Western civilization, Horkheimer and Adorno argue that the historical development of enlightenment and cultural progress produces further myth and wretched regression not primarily as a result of any evil contrivance "but rather by enlightenment itself, petrified with fear of the truth" (*DA*: 4/xiv). There is a 'necessary illusion' involved in conceptual thought, which, in the socialized and 'civilized' individual, determines perception itself, but which constantly veils its operation from everyday consciousness. "Perception," Horkheimer and Adorno write, "is mediated directness, thought in the seductive power of sensual nature." Yet "(o)nly the self-conscious labor of thought can again elude this hallucinatory power" (*DA*: 203/194). It is precisely the possibility and actuality of this second and subsequent labor of reflective contemplation that they see fleeing from the world. The philosophical tradition collaborates with science, industry, charismatic leaders, mass media stars, commodification, consumerism, etc.—the entire political-economic-cultural complex culminating in their historical stage of (monopoly) capitalism—such that the individual is in effect removed from any active participation in the world. Instead, as the individual is subjected to the increasingly pre-formed and pre-thought, his or her capacities for independent thinking atrophy.

Yet Horkheimer and Adorno do not simply contrast a contemporary *passivity* and subjectification in the individual to an earlier or potential *activity* of the subject that was or could be (more) fully intentional and self-conscious. This would resemble a progressive liberal critique and invoke an alternative, happy story of the Enlightenment (which in many respects corresponds instead to Habermas's version of critical theory). Rather, the flattening of culture and the removal and replacement of individual autonomy and spontaneity produces a partial, incomplete, 'easy' enlightenment that suppresses a very different and quite distinct mode of thinking compared to the one-sided 'shedding light' characteristic of the Enlightenment project itself. This would be the potential for a negative dialectical, but nevertheless liberatory, approach to subjectivity and objectivity. The alternative Horkheimer and Adorno favor is not a robust, autonomous actor counterposed to the passive automaton of post-industrial consumer culture, but an 'active-passive' figure of cognition who is capable of moving through the phases of thought in order to re-cognize (*Anerkennung*) the objects of consciousness in a practical-political moment. The truth of objects is not to be found somehow 'inside' them, 'below' their conceptual appearance, but in their essential conceptual or linguistic appearance *as* semblance—in the double manifestation of the truth in their illusion. Only in this way can objects be approached without domination.

The problem is that today the individual "no longer summons up the active passivity in which the categorical elements can be adequately formed from the conventionally pre-formed 'given,' and from these elements the 'given' formed anew so that justice is done to the perceived object" (*DA*: 211/202). The systematic suppression of the consciousness of non-identity allows the primal fear of the unknown to manifest itself in the inadequate knowing of our contemporary period, which, given the destructive capabilities contained in the great technological advances of the twentieth century, has serious, potentially disastrous results for politics, morality, and culture. An awareness of the *action* of cognition is necessary for 'justice' to be done to the object, which in turn reveals a 'justice' of cognition that might lead to a social and political justice for subjects predicated on non-dominating communication. What could be the basis of this unusual ascription of *justice* to the process of *cognition*?

"In a certain sense," Horkheimer and Adorno write, "all perceiving is projecting."[31] Anti-Semitism takes root as a repression born of the fear that the subject's own self is implicated in the other, the object; it is projection deprived of re-cognition. "The person chosen as enemy was already perceived as enemy. The disruption lies in the subject's lack of discernment between its own and alienated share in the projected material [*zwischen dem eigenen und fremden Anteil am projizierten Material*]." Thus the "pathological aspect of anti-Semitism is not projective behavior as such, but the absence of reflection in it." (*DA*: 196, 199/187, 189). The anti-Semite fails to see that it is partly his own image he hates and fears in his enemy.

We throw our own light upon the world with our perception of it, but the self that perceives is synthesized in this process just as much as the world that is lit up by perception. The 'outside' world is created by the subject only from the traces it leaves behind on the 'inside,' on the senses, from which the self learns to detach itself and understand again as external. "In order to reflect the thing as it is," Horkheimer and Adorno contend, "the subject must give back to it more that he receives from it." And this "more" that is given back is the signification that in turn constitutes the identity of the perceiving self, whose inner depth "consists in nothing other than the tenderness and richness of the external world of perceptions" (*DA*: 198/189). Identity thinking, by contrast, is thought that does not recognize the distance between its representations and the object, thought that lights up the object for itself but fails the receptivity and reciprocity its signification obliges. It fails to be generous to the object, to "give back more than it receives," and consequently ends up robbing itself of the richness offered by sensuous communicativity.

It is precisely at this point that the question of *communication* can be confirmed as an ethical endeavor requiring great care and attention from participants. The dimensions of communication encompass not only those of the subject's relationship to other subjects and to objects, *but also those of the object's relationship to subjects.* For if the subject is itself not transcendental but rather is constituted in the "tenderness and richness" of the reciprocal relations and dynamics of its (subjective) *objectivity*, then a vital moment of communicative freedom occurs in the awareness of how objects 'express' themselves to us. This is not simply a call to re-enchant or re-animate nature, and neither does its resistance to reification secretly connect truth with a "universal reconciliation" that "includes the interaction of human beings with nature, with animals, plants, and minerals" (*TCAI*: 381; see also Grenz, 1974: 57–58). Rather, it constitutes a de-centering of the subject without complete erasure or deracination, in order to allow the subject to come to terms with the nature of its reason. This aims to mitigate the *contradiction* between humans and "nature" rather than to erase the division. Odysseus's masterful sacrifice is a sacrifice for the sake of ending all sacrifice: A self that masters itself "not in order to coerce itself and others, but for reconciliation" (*DA*: 63/56), where reconciliation means that the antagonisms are stilled between subject (individual) and object (the non-identical—all the historical perturbations that lie within the object). This does not mean that their difference is eliminated or that some kind of pure bliss should descend (the Lotus-eaters represent an entirely regressive model). Neither does it mean that conflict or competition between people disappear, for what it would *recover* is the politics repressed by the progressive rationalization of sacrifice: the capacities for free, private, and public aesthetic self-formation and self-representation. It would be a self-conscious recovery of non-reason in order to complete a reason that is irrational and irrationally fearful without it. Progressive enlightenment is thus nevertheless to be found in and through the reason and the self it establishes, even though this reason and self have done their utmost to contradict and repress this possibility. This describes the Adornoesque effort to use enlightenment against itself, to draw upon the communicative ethic that gives a "priority" to the object or to the object's "preponderance" (*Vorrang des Objekts*) in order to recognize the objectivity of subjectivity. Contrary to Whitebook (1995: 14), Adorno's alleged inescapable choice between the two "poisons" of violent ego unification and utter lack of unification does not apply.

Attentiveness to the complexity of this 'intersubject/interobjectivity' is thus crucial for a self-formation and reflective awareness that no longer damages the life it creates. This idea is at the heart of Adorno's critical theory but it is often lost underneath objections to an alleged paradigmatic limit within the subject-object dualism or the dismissal of the dialectic's persistence in his thought. We will continue to return to this issue of attentiveness throughout the present text.

2.3. CONCLUDING REMARKS

The differences between the 1930s program of critical theory and the transformation inaugurated in *Dialectic of Enlightenment* turn on the difficulty of conceiving a comprehensive and global critical theory once even the noblest aims of social philosophy have become suspect as part of the reproduction of myth. The historicization of knowledge that materialism achieves is intended to break the power of myth, but it can do so only by remaining true to the non-identity of its own identifications and thereby cannot present itself as a comprehensive *theory*. The knowledge that is to contribute to bringing about liberation is inherently a partial, incomplete knowledge, especially when it is thought at the level of the totality. Instead, the subject of social philosophy, as a social text, can only be understood adequately with recourse to an aesthetic conception of self-representation that constantly bears in mind the mediated distance between reality and its intelligibility in conceptual form. The spirit of the supradisciplinary program of a comprehensive materialism that has a grasp on the whole continues in the ongoing attempt to connect critical accounts of historical experience with a theoretical grasp of the intertwined processes of perceiving, thinking, and acting. But it gives up its aim to offer a comprehensive and global theory that would coordinate the diverse disciplines as though from an Archimedian point or fully rational future.

3

Habermas and the Critique of Reification

3.1. The Habermasian Critique of Reification in Late Capitalism

With the term *ideology* Habermas refers to the way in which lifeworlds are structured so that domination cannot appear as class-determined or even as domination as such. Premodern forms of ideology constrain the lifeworld to a "structural violence" (1987b: 187) that immunizes from rational criticism certain core understandings characteristic of the sacred. Class domination cannot come to light as contingent under these structural conditions of communication. In antiquity, for example, when *reason* first becomes politically important in explicit ways (acquiring a higher value than the depth of belief in myth or the fear of naked power), generalizable interests are suppressed while a hierarchy of particular interests defines the good of the whole through rationalizations of power tied to metaphysical and religious worldviews.

This structural limitation erodes under the conditions of modern society. For Habermas, the specifically modern form of understanding develops as the lifeworld becomes rationalized and differentiated into the spheres of science, morality, and art and as relatively autonomous administrative and economic spheres of instrumental and strategic reason are split off into subsystems.[1] As this occurs, the possibility of the former, structurally limited ideological interpretations maintaining a foothold in everyday life becomes more and more tenuous because reaching understanding relies more and more on rationally redeemable *claims to validity*. Modern understanding, for Habermas, entails at root that knowledge and belief are opened up to *rational criticism* and publicity. Hence modernity does not only result in a *loss* of meaning due to the ethical emptiness of a totalizing instrumental reason (as might be said of Max Weber), but rather meaning and understanding develop new forms based on *communicatively* achieved understanding and agreement. Indeed, contra Weber as well as Horkheimer and Adorno, modern disenchantment does not simply substitute an expanding, formal, "de-worlding" instrumental reason for ruined ethical structures. Instead, a qualitatively new modern communicative ethos is created that replaces the older structures but which is also accompanied by contradictory processes: "The communicative potential of reason first had to be released in the pattern of modern lifeworlds before the unfettered imperatives of the economic and administrative subsystems . . . could thereby promote the cognitive-instrumental dimension to domination over the suppressed moments of practical reason" (*PDM*: 315).

Instrumental reason does greatly expand and takes over new spheres of life, which we will soon examine, but it cannot be totalizing (except, perhaps, in the most pessimistic moments of a Weber or a Foucault). For Habermas, this overall process in fact increases the potential for a genuinely rational society because shared lifeworld contexts lose the unquestioned givenness of traditional authority and become more and more subject to the interpretive efforts of participants. New meanings are established that depend on discursively achieved consensus formation among large numbers of people. In short, for Habermas this creates a growing *interpretive need* in modernity. This is a need that depends on valid reasons being given for beliefs (or the assumption that such reasons could, in principle, be given), where this 'validity' can be intersubjectively recognized through discursive means. In principle, the modern understanding cannot permit the 'immunization' of any belief from such rational criticism and discussion. Thus for Habermas, the rational presuppositions of language brought to consciousness in modern society present the possibility of achieving a free and democratic life for all—that is, free from the disguised or hidden exercise of class power.

The ideological problem for a critical theory to comprehend, then, is why explicit relations of domination continue to remain obscured in the modern (capitalist) period, a period in which, as Marx memorably put it, "All fixed, fast-frozen relations, with their train of ancient and venerable prejudices and opinions, are swept away, all new ones become antiquated before they can ossify." Under these radical conditions in which "All that is solid melts into air, all that is holy is profaned," Marx thought that a critical theory and an enlightened consciousness would develop by which human beings would "at last be compelled to face with sober senses the real conditions of life" and their real human relations (1978: 476). How is it, then, despite capitalism's destruction of the *ancien régime* and its constant revolutionizing of social relations and production, that human beings nevertheless failed to be "compelled to face with sober senses the real conditions of life"? This is the task Marx sets for himself in comprehending the new form of mystification characteristic of capitalist society. Beyond his earlier critique of the 'German' ideology, Marx's analysis of commodity fetishism in *Capital* using the theory of value aims to show how class domination continues in capitalist society despite there being no explicit institutional or ideological embodiment of such relations.

Habermas addresses this question of continued hidden relations of domination in capitalist society with his version of the Marxist theory of reification: the thesis of the *internal colonization of the lifeworld* by systemic intrusion. This thesis explains for Habermas why the potentials for free and undistorted self-formation inherent in modernity are systematically denied and suppressed under conditions of capitalist development. But before examining Habermas's position in detail, let us reconstruct the important aspects of the social theory that identifies this phenomenon.

According to Habermas, Marx was limited by a conception of human society that was structured fundamentally by laboring activity. Drawn from Hegel's social philosophy, this conception could not adequately bring into view the communicative dimension of *symbolic interaction*.[2] Symbolic or communicative interaction is essentially separate and distinct from laboring activity, and for Habermas the communicative rationality governing linguistically mediated interaction in fact takes theoretical and evolutionary priority.[3] Labor became a central political category for Hegel because it was only through labor—through its synthesis of the subjective and objective—that the individual came to be recognized by others; private property was only a moment in the subject's struggle for recognition (Avineri, 1972: 88–89), which ultimately leads to an *ethical* goal. Thus labor was always *social* labor for Hegel and Marx, since one labors not only for oneself but necessarily for others. For Habermas, Hegel's account of recognition is more complex, especially in the latter's early theological writings and his Jena lectures. Habermas distinguishes Hegel's insights into the importance of intersubjective recognition from the eclipse of intersubjectivity in Marx (see Habermas, 1974). According to the Habermasian critique of Marx, a "meta-theoretical significance" is attached to the category of "objectification" that explains the becoming of the species in history via the material medium of labor. This is said to entail a learning process focused on the rules of knowledge and know-how that cannot include intersubjective relations satisfactorily because it conflates intersubjective learning with technical learning. This priority of objectification suppresses and cannot explain the acquisition of the rules of knowledge pertaining to the activities of language, culture, and social interaction. Such knowledge instead depends on the determination of meaning and context (that is, interpretation), which entails a knowledge of ourselves not a knowledge of nature (Benhabib, 1986: 61–62).

This interpretive knowledge and its correlated learning capacities and processes constitute vast domains and reservoirs of communicative resources in society, which are contained in the spheres Habermas associates with the lifeworld. Actors draw on these resources and develop them in their action coordinated by communicative rationality (sharply distinguished from strategic or instrumental rational action). Sociologically speaking, lifeworld mechanisms thus govern the social reproduction of interpretive schemes, legitimate authority, and instilling life aspirations; the constitution of obligations and the social integration of diverse identities, behavior, and social memberships; and finally, socialization via successful interpretations, motivations for action, and personality formation (*TCAII*: 140–45). As we will see in Chapter 4, these diverse and complex social functions operate under sets of assumptions that prioritize the action of raising and redeeming validity claims.

In contrast to this medium of communicative learning and understanding, the systems media of money and power coordinate action through calculations or the pursuit of instrumental goals (purposive-rational action). These systemic spheres constitute crucial modes of action that reproduce the material basis of society through instrumental labor, technological control, administrative organization, and strategic goal-oriented action (clearly central and essential aspects of market societies). The lifeworld requires substantive reproduction at the level of its material substratum, and this can only be secured by purposive-rational actions in relation to nature along with instrumental and strategic relations among actors. The 'system' thus designates an objectification of the lifeworld necessitated by the need for survival, and as such it is a universal characteristic of human society on Habermas's view. But, precisely because Habermas understands these processes as 'survival imperatives' along the lines of biological system imperatives, which have become autonomous in complex societies detached from binding traditions, the coordination of instrumental and strategic activity can no longer be represented as a *consciously* cooperative effort—as collective intentional embodiment. Society, in other words, is not a collective *subject* whose elements can be known in advance. "Survival imperatives require a functional integration of the lifeworld, which reaches right through the symbolic structures of the lifeworld." (*TCAII*: 232). Large-scale, integrated economic activity simply cannot be coordinated in the special, communicatively *rational* way that all the forms of mutual understanding and agreement coordinate action by requiring subjects to raise and redeem validity claims.

A key condition of modernity is then revealed. As a result of the higher demands placed on the processes of reaching mutual understanding in modern society, there is a heightened potential for disagreement and conflict: reaching understanding becomes 'riskier' *because* it is rationally motivated (*TCAI*: 70). But at the same time, this heightened threat of 'instability' in the communicative medium is offset by the development of systemic steering media that remove the need for communicative understanding and agreement. Steering media that are differentiated out from lifeworld locations *compensate* for the increased risks of disagreement and conflict and the demands of communicative action, Habermas argues, by *replacing* language as a mode of coordinating action in certain contexts. They replace language as 'delinguistified' media—the media of money and power attain symbolic forms that do not require a hermeneutic attitude in order to establish their meaning. By replacing language with a generalizable code according to which actors can make calculations with respect to future, empirically measurable conditions, actors are thereby relieved of *responsibility* for their communications. That is, these increasingly complex webs of communication do not require subjects who must back up their claims with rationally defensible reasons or assume or assess them in the communications of others (*TCAII*: 263). The switchover to these delinguistified media describes precisely the concurrent emergence of spheres of modern administrative power and economic interaction. The political sphere thus becomes governed by *power* relations directed through the formation of bureaucracies and the state, and the economic sphere by the exchange of commodities through the medium of *money*. One of the most significant evolutionary values attached to the development of these delinguistified media is that they allow (specific) actors to gain new and greatly improved degrees of freedom of action oriented to success (*TCAII*: 264).

In the modern period, Habermas argues, the comparatively rapid development of the forces of production (the division of labor, labor power, and the technical organization of relations with nature) is permitted by this relative autonomy or uncoupling of systemic spheres from lifeworld contexts. But, according to Habermas, such productive development is, significantly, also only permitted by a corresponding development in the lifeworld institutions that 'anchor' the differentiated subsystems *back into* the lifeworld. The primacy of the lifeworld is such that spheres of purposive-rational action cannot simply exist and operate on their own as a matter of course. Although these spheres are delinguistified, the media through which they function involve generalizable symbolic (and therefore social) meanings that must be stabilized.

But the media themselves are not simply *equivalent* to their action contexts, as Marx pointed out. That is, 'value' is not an inherent property of that very special commodity money, just like the value of any exchangeable commodity cannot be found in the properties of the commodity itself. Similarly, 'power' does not simply reside in the mere existence or assertion of hierarchy or in the de facto administrative and coercive agency of the state. For this reason, the system spheres themselves cannot in principle stabilize the necessary respect for value and power. Such fundamental stabilization must be found elsewhere. According to Habermas, the character and value of money in modern capitalist society are established instead by the formal institutions of bourgeois civil law such as those of property and contract, and secured by reserves such as gold. By itself, the monetary medium does not "arouse adequate 'confidence in the system' merely by virtue of its functioning" (*TCAII*: 266). Hence the confidence required to secure the system of the circulation of money is supplied by the medium of consensus formation in language, which is only available in lifeworld institutions such as law and the intersubjective recognition of standards. Likewise, the modern state requires *legitimation* for its exercise of power, which is an even more demanding and distinct form of consensus. Essentially, both power and money are thus media that require consensually oriented anchors in lifeworld institutions.

What complicates matters is that these autonomous spheres of action do not function unproblematically. First, as systems of purposive-rational action replace spheres of the lifeworld that were coordinated communicatively, certain sacrifices, pain, and costs are necessarily also experienced.[4] This is despite the 'relief mechanisms' of the independent subsystems. New freedoms for purposive-rational action are gained only at the price of costs incurred by the *devaluation* of the lifeworld for coordinating action. Symbolic elements of the lifeworld lose their power to contribute to the reproduction of culture, society, and person since they tend to be reduced to aspects of an 'environment' for purposive-rational actions. This development is what Habermas calls the "technicizing of the lifeworld" (Habermas, 1987b: 183), which should be distinguished from the admittedly ambivalent technologies of communication that publicize and that compose a public sphere in which the responsibility of the reader/hearer is greatly developed and enhanced. The former is also another way of conceiving the spread of instrumental reason into more and more areas of life.

Furthermore, when systems spheres experience blockages or crises in their coordinating functions, which may be due to internal limits or contradictions or external, environmental factors, then recourse for addressing or solving such crises may be made to the powerful resources of coordination located in the lifeworld. One of Habermas's most central critical theses is that certain *essential* spheres of communicatively structured symbolic reproduction cannot be replaced successfully by such systems media without pathological side effects. This rests on the quasi-ontological distinction between spheres of purposive-rational and communicative action corresponding to system and lifeworld that come into conflict and competition. Consequently, when *communicative* action is made subject to the dictates of *systems* media, "the *mediatization* of the lifeworld assumes the form of a *colonization*" (*TCAII*: 196). What occurs is not necessarily a destruction but a transformation or assimilation of lifeworld processes into the employ of systems needs. Mediatization is thus distinguished from colonization by the latter's subjection of irreplaceable lifeworld elements to systemic requirements. Mediatization enables the creation and expansion of purposive spheres of action whereas colonization inhibits and distorts essential communicative spheres that are also developing or already exist. Habermas offers as an empirically verifiable example of lifeworld colonization an account of 'juridification'[5]—the tendency for law to extend deeper and deeper into social life in modern welfare-state capitalist societies, which increasingly limits the ethical scope of individual action and consequently obstructs the possibilities of autonomous self-formation. Reification, understood in this way, produces pathological side effects in the lifeworld spheres in which it takes hold, yet the origins of these experiences are not readily accessible to participants just as the true origins of modern European colonialism were not readily apparent to colonized peoples in the periphery.

Thus Habermas contends that through internal colonization, systemic domination of the lifeworld can remain hidden from direct view—even in a differentiated and rationalized modern society. In Habermas's view, a critical consciousness of reification remains for the most part out of reach in mass society by virtue of the cultural impoverishment and fragmented consciousness that is produced by it (*TCAII*: 355). Cultural impoverishment refers to processes that diminish and disempower the interpretive capacities of everyday consciousness, a prominent example being the dominance of expertism in all forms of cultural knowledge. Expert cultures attached to the three broad spheres of formal inquiry become less and less able to contribute to the enrichment of everyday life (less able than they once were, arguably); esoteric discourses develop while mass education declines, unable to incorporate expert knowledges into accessible forms of comprehension except as authoritative but ultimately mysterious fact. The differentiated and specialized spheres of the rational lifeworld become increasingly split off from the everyday; consciousness becomes 'fragmented' and unable to apply the modern standards of validity in a unified manner: "In place of the positive task of meeting a certain need for interpretation by ideological means, we have the negative requirement of preventing holistic interpretations from coming into existence . . . *everyday consciousness* is robbed of its power to synthesize; it becomes *fragmented* . . . In place of 'false consciousness' we today have 'fragmented consciousness' that blocks enlightenment by the mechanism of reification" (*TCAII*: 355). Repeating Weber's and Lukács' critiques of reification, Habermas argues that the potentials of everyday communication are thus atrophied and systematically limited.

It is important for Habermas that systemic colonization of the lifeworld is nevertheless not inherent to or automatic in a modern, rationalized lifeworld and indeed that mediatization thus has rationally established limits. Otherwise a fateful dialectic would again threaten the reason he wishes to preserve from reification. Since reification does not represent the congealed form of alienated human labor turned back upon itself and working through the capitalist class relation, it can in principle be overcome without necessarily finding an alternative mode to instrumental relations with nature or to instrumental/strategic relations between actors within the relatively autonomous and circumscribed systemic spheres. But reification cannot even be overcome unless a strict distinction is drawn between mediatization and colonization, which correspond to rationalization and reification respectively. Using Habermas's bi-level social theory, the *class-unspecific* effects of reification on the lifeworld can be theorized without the need for a theory of (class) consciousness. In part it is the usefulness of this distinction between mediatization and colonization that I would like to challenge.[6]

Indeed reification, according to Habermas, only describes the expression and experience of class domination insofar as a largely unbridled capitalism still dominates the character of system imperatives. The operation of the system according to generalized media and differentiated subsystems is hence a theoretically (and socially) neutral affair for Habermas since such operation has a rational core appropriate to a liberal (and secular), differentiated modernity. What is unnecessary and contingent is the capitalist appropriation of the essential resources of the lifeworld through its domination at the level of the system. Human emancipation and the achievement of a rational society, for Habermas, thus demand the liberation of the lifeworld and a certain wresting of democratic control of the system away from capitalist domination.

3.2. CAPITALISM AND SOCIAL CRISIS

Following from this Habermasian understanding, there are implicit in Marx's view of social crisis two views of 'systemic' and 'lived' crisis that refer respectively to the spheres of system and lifeworld.[7] The first takes the point of view of the observer-thinker and analyzes the systemic crises of the capitalist mode of production as a whole, crises such as stagflation and the tendency of the falling rate of profit. The second takes the point of view of the participant in a crisis, which is found in the historical chapters of *Capital*, and documents experiences such as alienation, suffering from mental and physical illness and from deprivation of the necessities of life, resentment, aggression, and struggle against capitalist development and domination. While these two perspectives of systemic and lived crisis are said to run through Marx's analysis, the theoretical problem of linking them is left unresolved, namely, the precise relationship "between action contexts out of which lived crises emerge and objective-functional interconnections among action consequences that lead to systemic malfunctioning" (Benhabib, 1986: 128). Indeed for many, the question of this link is the central problem of a critical social theory.

According to Habermas, Marx attempts with the theory of value to solve the question of translating theoretical or observational statements about the "economic subsystem" into theoretical or observational statements about the "workers' lifeworld" (*TCAII*: 336–37). Unfortunately, the theory of value—the aim of which is to comprehend what Marx calls 'real abstraction'—relies for Habermas on a dialectical logic that ultimately refers to an a priori ethical conception of creative laboring activity in order then to explain deformations in intersubjective contents. In Habermas's view, Marx distinguished alienation from the objectification of labor only by assimilating the "species life actuated in work" to aesthetic productivity so that he could "conceive social labor as the collective self-realization of producers" (*PDM*: 64). This ethical a priori is assumed rather than demonstrated because Marx does not doubt that the model of purposive-rationality based on the subject-object relation is fundamental for social action.

The formal abstractions such as abstract labor, capital, the state, and the commodity are condemned by Marx to pass away once the mystical autonomy of the process of capitalist accumulation is revealed as a 'fetishistic' distortion or falsity rooted in alienated labor. It bears mentioning here that Marx's use of the term *fetish* in *Capital I*, Chapter 1, to describe capitalist society's ideological mystification should also be understood in its historical context, and that he meant it to have an alienation effect on his audience. This term was commonly used by European missionaries and colonizers to describe the 'false,' pagan iconology of non-Western peoples who were to be converted to the true way of Christianity. The imperialism of (at least institutional) Christianity thus accords with the imperialism of capitalist expansion. Marx was well aware of the irony, and he used it to good effect here. However, such language and orientation have, across the breadth of Marx's work, led to one of the great ambiguities in Marxiological study: Is Marx's own science, which aims to reveal "the real conditions of life" and assist revolutionary change, a science of society in the Enlightenment tradition that can provide critical-political knowledge of the actual historical process in rationalistic terms? Or is it a whole new thing altogether, more like a secular, yet holistic science of the world in a tradition closer to that of the great religious-metaphysical explanations of nature, human being, and eschatological visions of the future of the cosmos?

Most important in this question is to recognize that its political and historical dimensions cannot and ought not be abstracted, which is in my mind revealed by Marx's use of fetish to describe capitalist reification. As such, Marx's reference squarely recognizes the broader and deeper dialectic of enlightenment operating in both the (institutional) Christian church as a cultural phenomenon and nineteenth-century capitalism as a rationalizing political-economic process. But again, the practical-political question of just how these mystical forms will fall away even once they are revealed and named remains historical and not quite under theory's jurisdiction.

According to Habermas, "Marx is convinced a priori that in capital he has before him *nothing more* than the mystified form of a class relation" (*TCAII*: 339). For Habermas, Marx's view automatically denies the evolutionary value of the differentiation of state and economy, which are nevertheless systemic developments free of class-specific identity and hence worth preserving in undistorted form even though they are historically associated with the rise of capitalist society. Because Habermas sees Marx holding to an unexamined notion of a ruptured ethical totality—from which the latter is said to derive his lifeworld concepts such as objective class interest—he interprets the Marxist idea of the future socialist society as involving a de-differentiation issuing from the enlightened and unifying power of reason. This is a conception that can be dismissed from a systems theory perspective as just more idealist illusion (*PDM*: 67).

Where Marx sees the 'irrational' operation of the capitalist system as a contradictory totality conceived as a social ontology, Habermas does not rely directly on an ontology but refers to the concept of rationality from which the two distinct and potentially conflictual modes of social interaction are derived. Yet a 'quasi-ontological' distinction is drawn by Habermas between the spheres of lifeworld and system themselves. As we have seen, he aims to explain reification not as real abstraction conceived in terms of the totality of exchange society but as the effect of specific overextensions of systemic objectification (which can take the form of either 'monetarization' or 'bureaucratization') into essentially non-objectifiable public and private contexts of life.

The social system is 'irrational,' or rather 'a-rational,' only in the sense that it is *functionally* integrated—it "reaches right through the structures of the lifeworld"—and hence cannot accord with a concept of intentional order. As a social *system*, however, it has its own functions and imperatives at a level beyond the reach of the rational intent of its human 'parts.' Therefore there is a rationality to the system as a whole *beyond* the intentionality of its social subjects.

One of the obvious implications of Habermas's view is that the system of production cannot be coordinated successfully by a bureaucracy without significant distortions in its operation. Hence Marx's call for the apportionment of labor-time in accordance with a definite social plan, which would also be coordinated with the historical needs of the community (Marx, 1954: 83), appears from Habermas's systemic point of view to hark back to a premodern ideal of system-coordination subjugated to lifeworld dictates (while at the same time looking forward to a society based on social rather than alienated labor). The assumption of systems theory in this context—that the hypercomplex conditions of modern life cannot simply be overcome short of an act of will on the magnitude of extreme totalitarianism—is an assumption that fits neatly with Habermas's general view of the achievements of modernity that need to be preserved. (In this respect, Habermas's liberal sociology meets his non-essentialist, pluralist, democratic political theory.) For Habermas, the uncoupling of system spheres—an achievement of bourgeois freedom—is an advance understood to be immanent to freedom itself and must be preserved in some form in a 'post-capitalist' society.[8]

With reference to the bureaucratic coordination of social production, it is also possible to speak empirically of pathologies in the
operation of the system that are due to constraints imposed by an
uncoupled lifeworld.[9] One might regard part of the failure of the cen-
tralized direction of production in the former Soviet Union as documenting the results of such bureaucratic constraints on functional
integration. On the Habermasian view, the market ought not be so
suppressed as a coordination mechanism for the sake of the health of
functional integration. Complex societies, according to Habermas, "are
unable to reproduce themselves if they do not leave the logic of an
economy that regulates itself through the market intact" (1991b: 40).[10]
On the other hand, the modern bureaucratic state in Western capitalist
societies, in contrast to its actually or previously existing communist
alternative, faces many national limits to its *raison d'être* of administrative control and organization of capitalist markets. This dimension has,
however, paled in comparison to the newer level of globalizing arrangements such as free trade agreements and monetary unions that
have reduced the power of national governments substantially in relation to that of international administrative bodies and multinational
capital. Both forms of state face these constraints in varying proportions, in addition to developments in international political economy
such as the internationalization of capital and production. However,
the welfare/warfare-state of the present period of late capitalism (the
'welfare' side of which is currently in substantial decline) finds itself
burdened with different crises resulting from the way its steering functions relate to capitalist society. For Habermas and his followers, the
crises of the state in late capitalism do not indicate fundamental contradictions or problems with the state and its function *themselves*, but rather
indicate the way capitalist contradictions and crisis are displaced *onto*
the state via the state's steering capacity.[11] The system encroaches on
this institution of the lifeworld in very observable ways.

Hence, for Habermas, the formation and structure of the modern
social system and the corresponding institutions of the lifeworld are
mediated by the historical development of capitalism. Yet they are not
wholly *determined* by capitalism. From a historical perspective, the development of society toward a genuine modern and enlightened form can
be said to have been skewed and atrophied by specifically *capitalist* development. The present capitalist-distorted social totality is 'irrational'
because of what it denies to its members—a rational and more stable life
largely free of specific 'reification effects' that otherwise could, in principle, be provided.

Yet it is difficult to see how Habermas could maintain a critical idea of 'irrational' capitalism in this sense, especially given his view that the functional integration of systems of purposive-rational action are an unavoidable fact and necessary condition of human society and indeed of a healthy democracy itself. Conceding the functional need of a free market and differentiated social complexity (in the systems theory sense) is no small concession to the status quo of capitalist society itself. The major task here would be to demonstrate a clear and unequivocal distinction between totalizing, pathological *capitalism* and the preferred ideal-type of a modern, differentiated, post-liberal society that somehow nevertheless *contains* capitalist production and markets. Habermas's 'radical reformism' demands a rationalized capitalism alongside a lifeworld emancipated from the domination of the system. This entails accepting capitalist social organization while ensuring that capitalist imperatives do not dominate the institutions of the lifeworld and the state on which the former nevertheless depend.

Habermas attempts to develop such a conception in his analysis of the relations between civil society, the state, and the economy, which are viewed as autonomous spheres interacting differently with each other in cooperative, competing, or contradictory ways. The sphere of civil society, in contrast to the highly organized and structured systems of state and economy, is a unique and crucially important source of guidance for a democratic political administration that addresses steering problems arising in both systems. Civil society, Habermas writes, "is composed of those more or less spontaneously emergent associations, organizations, and movements that, attuned to how societal problems resonate in private life spheres, distill and transmit such reactions in amplified form to the public sphere" (*BFN*: 367). Civil society functions as the social basis of diversified and more or less autonomous public spheres in which relevant issues, questions, and problems of society are raised and receive public consideration. Clearly, this is dependent on acceptance of the principles of free and open communication that undergird the notion of democracy and hence cannot be applied to totalitarian states. The informality and unstructured nature of the groups participating in such a public sphere are virtues. For the "wild" complex of the public sphere, which forms an important "context of discovery," elicits spontaneous articulation and communication "more sensitively" and "more widely and expressively" than other institutionalized forums. Unlike formally constituted and procedurally regulated public spheres (for example, parliament or the public bureaucracy), the informal public sphere has the crucial advantage of "*unrestricted* communication" (*BFN*: 307–8).

In a democracy, the publics of civil society and the procedures of democratic opinion- and will-formation institutionalized within a constitutional framework allow the influence and communicative power generated in autonomous public spheres to be transformed via law into administrative power, which thereby secures the socially integrative force of communicative solidarity at the level of the political system. Under the conditions of the democratic constitutional state, the communicative presuppositions and processes of deliberative politics operate as the most important "sluices" for the "discursive rationalization" of popular sovereignty (BFN: 299–300). Likewise, the "structures of recognition" inherent in everyday communicative action are "transferred" through law to the level of "abstract and anonymous relationships among strangers" that secures social integration reflexively when other action systems fail (BFN: 385).

This is of course an idealized model, for Habermas recognizes that the administration, economy, and powerful social interests dominate the main institutions of the public sphere such as the mass media and parliament. The non-institutionalized associations, organizations, and movements of civil society are largely peripheral and lack effectualness when compared to these actors and systems. Although the informal public sphere's superior sensitivity and responsiveness to critical developments, latent problems, and unarticulated need interpretations indicate a central importance not only for a genuine democracy but also for effective political steering, its "signals" and "impulses" are often too weak to initiate new learning or affect decision-making in the political system (BFN: 373). Only under certain critical conditions which engender "periods of mobilization" does Habermas believe that the balance of power can shift from the political system toward civil society. Only then can the groups of civil society "acquire influence in the public sphere . . . through its own public opinions, and compel the political system to switch over to the official circulation of power." Outside of these situations, the public sphere and civil society remain rather sedentary, subject to social power, distortive manipulations that hide the circulation of "unofficial" power and the depoliticizing process of mass media information selection and presentation (the "kernel of truth in the theory of the culture industry") (BFN: 373, 377, 379). As a consequence, Habermas advocates a tighter regulation of the mass media by which they can better serve the interests of deliberative politics and assume the mandate of an "enlightened public whose willingness to learn and capacity for criticism they at once presuppose, demand, and reinforce" (BFN: 378).

For Habermas, the preservation of the constitutional state, which guarantees a liberal public sphere, allows an ongoing process of democratic opinion- and will-formation as long as the reifying encroachments and mystifying interferences from the systems of economy and power can be held in check. Thus the formal guarantees of law and the steering capacities of the state are limited and can achieve only so much, for they are in themselves unsuitable for establishing or fostering emancipated forms of life (*BFN*: 372). These depend instead on the freedom and spontaneity associated with the actual practices of autonomous citizens and groups and can only develop in the course of democratization processes. On the other hand, the democratic movements emerging from civil society must themselves "give up holistic aspirations to a self-organizing society" and limit themselves to "indirect" influence on the autonomous political subsystem, since no single "macrosubject" can claim to represent and direct the interests of a differentiated and complex modern society (*ibid.*).

Thus there is a happy medium to be achieved in the interrelations between the autonomous spheres of economy, state, civil society and the public sphere where each operates without disrupting or overburdening the operation of the others too much and where each ideally reinforces and contributes to the development of the other. This would be the condition of a stable democracy, although clearly not simply a one-dimensional, static state, since there will always be the "tension between facticity and validity" that drives democracy onward. Under current conditions, the groups of civil society become most insistent and shrill during afflicted and conflictual conditions, since they represent society's "consciousness of crisis" (*BFN*: 357). During these times they can most clearly affect normative and institutional change. Most of the time, however, their voices are marginalized, co-opted, or suppressed, while civil society and the public sphere are deformed by social power.

Habermas believes that his "self-limitation of civil society," which restricts democratic movements to indirect influence of the political administration, is not an incapacitation since there is no natural state monopoly on the technological knowledge used in decision-making. But on the other hand, political steering also can (should) only indirectly manage functional systems and highly organized spheres of action (like capitalist markets) (*BFN*: 372). Thus Habermas wishes to protect the complex systems of administration, social power, and economy from overly aggressive challenge or transformation by democratic movements. He would allow the continued operation of the current capitalist system pretty much as it is now as long as a liberal public sphere is preserved (and reinforced) from which opposition to the excesses of social and economic power can be mobilized.

But here it becomes clear that in order for capitalism to be distinguished from ideal-typical modern society, 'capitalism' must be downgraded from the Marxist idea of a contradictory class society, in which the principle of exchange and the phenomena of reification operate most completely, to a kind of abstract economic activity, albeit an economic activity that systematically gets in the way of emancipated human life. In other words, the capitalist economy becomes a system in the systems theory sense, which operates functionally even while it tends to encroach on and distort essential forms of sociation. As an organized system of activity, it must remain autonomous from the normative, communicatively structured lifeworld, despite its necessary institutional anchoring, for without such free operation Habermas believes that the material *and* democratic fruits of modern differentiated society would be in danger. Indeed, it is only in this way that the economy organized through capitalist production and markets can be distinguished as a "piece of norm-free sociality" (*PDM*: 349) that comes into competition with the 'non-economic' (or rather, non-reifiable) rational needs of the lifeworld. Capitalist modes of activity are to be protected for the material, 'self-preservative' benefits they bring to liberal-democratic society; autonomous administrative and technological power unsubjected to direct democratic regulation are to be protected for similar reasons. Without these systems Habermas believes that the very democratic way of life brought to the fore in the modern period is threatened.

Reification, I would insist, following those such as Horkheimer and Adorno, goes deeper and is more primal than capitalist class society or bureaucratic, administrative objectification, although it is under capitalism and modernity that reification finds its most extensive and highly developed forms. If reification is a phenomenon of simple commodity production prior to capitalist society, then the pathologies identified by Habermas cannot be removed simply by placing limits upon specifically *capitalist* class activity. Neither can democracy properly be achieved in a sense outside discriminate domination and exclusion.

Since Marx, to speak of the capitalist 'economy' abstracted from its social relations of domination has been suspect as the kind of false or faulty abstraction of which classic political economy is guilty. Despite the tendency in Marxism itself to fall into an economism that usually hypostatizes Marx's distinction between the levels of base and superstructure, the crucial dialectical standpoint from which such concepts are developed, and which negates all economism or determinism, is that of the *social totality*. Capitalism, from the Marxist perspective, must always be understood in the last analysis at this level, as *capitalist society*, conceived in terms of the concept of the *mode of production* that is its dominant. A common mistake in reading Marx is to equate his use of the concept of production with that of the economy.

Now Habermas is well aware of this; where he directs his attack is against what he sees as the assumptions behind Marx's concept of the social totality, which the former reads as limited to an expressivist notion based on the philosophy of the subject. However, this is a very limited and in my view incorrect reading of Marx's concept of the totality under capitalism. As Postone (1996: 71–83) has argued, Marx instead employs his concept of the totality to transform the classic opposition between subject and object (and hence between 'labor' and 'nature') by analyzing and grounding this problematic socially in the historical forms of capitalist society. What Marx views through the concept of the social totality is lost in this respect as Habermas translates it into a radically differentiated notion in which a methodological gestalt shift allows the switch between lifeworld and system perspectives without ostensibly losing sight of 'society' itself. This is intended to resolve the problem of the overextension of the basic concept of purposive-rationality that constrains Marx (as well as Weber and Frankfurt critical theory) to instrumentality, and it is intended to comprehend reification in its specificity.

But Marx's concept of labor cannot be reduced to a form of purposive-rational action; indeed, it is just such a reduction of labor in modern political economy and the parallel capitalist reduction of the worker to instrumental action that Marx is out to *criticize*. Habermas avoids the question of Marx's concept of labor by his prior step of theoretically limiting labor to a sphere of purposive-rationality solely concerned with the material reproduction of society along the lines of survival imperatives and distinct from the reproduction of inner or 'socialized' nature. Remarking on this limitation, Dallmayr (1984a) argues that Habermas's designation of human relations with nature as strictly instrumental actually erases the possibility of safeguarding the integrity of *social* bonds by removing "nature" as a possible barrier to their instrumentalization. Moreover, the distinction between goal-rationality and instrumental rationality is essential for Marx, for it is through this distinction that he can abstract the capitalist system as a reifying system independent of actors' intentions and needs.[12]

In Habermas's social theory, there is no sense in which the differentiated form of a functionally integrated social system related to a socially integrated lifeworld ought to be transcended *itself* in order to bring about freedom. Indeed, such a prospect would contradict the whole point of conceiving society unavoidably as a bi-level totality with necessary functionally distinct and autonomous complex subsystems. It would contradict the sociological core of the theory of communicative action. Yet something as radical as this is what Marx has in mind when he describes postcapitalist society, and this kind of transformation, of course, is rejected by Habermas.

This is despite the fact that Marx did distinguish what he called the "realm of necessity" from the "realm of freedom," and indicated that the former will always exist while the latter could only truly begin with "socialized man"—with the "association of producers" that will constitute postcapitalist society (Marx, 1959: 820).[13] For Habermas, the realms of necessity and freedom are metaphors in Marx for system and lifeworld, and critique in the latter is said to lead to the triumph of the lifeworld over the system of deworlded labor power (*TCAII*: 340). Marx makes the mistake, on the Habermasian view, of thinking that the rational direction of production through the abolition of classes (private property) is equivalent to the emancipation of human beings from the dominion of class-based production. By "dialectically clamping together system and lifeworld," Marx "does not allow for a sufficiently sharp separation between the *level of system differentiation* attained in the modern period and the class-specific forms in which it has been *institutionalized*" (*TCAII*: 340). For Habermas, a society largely free from reification and the pathologies associated with systemic colonization could exist today without the need for a revolutionary overthrow of the mechanisms of differentiation introduced and developed by capitalism. Progress toward such liberation is not achieved via a further rationalization of the system of production in the sense of the socialization of labor, but rather by the further rationalization of the *lifeworld*, which, being prior in principle if not in fact, will allow something of a pacification of the agitated demands currently made by capitalism. Again, under the Habermasian schema, the hope for a radically liberated or a de-differentiated condition of society is simply a false hope (McCarthy, 1985).

Against Habermas (and systems theory), however, alienation and fetishism cannot be neatly isolated as the products of such an 'economic sphere' because the abstraction of the modern economy is itself *part* of the phenomena of alienation and fetishism.[14] Likewise, the broader concept of reification does not simply designate an 'effect' or pathology of a social whole that turns back on itself in crisis, but rather designates a *condition* for the operation of that very same system that is said, on

Habermas's reading, itself to *produce* reification effects. Alienation and fetishism are aspects of the whole, not of its parts, of capitalist social production, not of any one moment of society that comes to dominate the others. This is why those such as Marx and Adorno refuse to see the fundamental distinction Habermas maintains between lifeworld and system. For the former, what Habermas calls the system is always already reproduced at the level of the lifeworld—and, vice versa, lifeworld spheres condition systems far more than simply providing their anchors.

It is not that lifeworld and system are thus dialectically clamped together but that to view these two spheres as constituted by quasi-ontologically distinct and exclusive rationalities is ultimately a false abstraction. One important practical consequence of such false abstraction is that the social basis of production—that is, the relationship between *need* and *social integration*—is lost from view.[15]

In a parallel to his reduction of capitalism to a singular aspect of the system, Habermas must also hold to a circumscribed concept of purposive-rationality to which he reduces concepts such as laboring activity and instrumental reason. Crucial to Habermas's concept of purposive-rationality are the delinguistified media of money and power through which purposive-rational calculations are made. But the idea of the delinguistified media themselves—the media that constitute a complementary advance to the rationalization of the lifeworld—is again an extension of Habermas's view of purposive-rational activity as a neutral affair when occurring in its designated spheres or extending only insofar as its mediatization does not overstep into colonization. These media do not produce reification in their systemic context because, for Habermas, instrumental reason only becomes reification as a phenomenon arising from an encroachment into the *lifeworld*, which is distinct in terms of the level of its communicative experiences. Hence money, for example, is not a representation of the reified exchange relation whose flows ought to be understood, monitored, and governed very carefully, but rather constitutes a generalizable code that allows an increase in purposive-rational freedom. Money, on the Habermasian reading, does not require a hermeneutic relation because it is a delinguistified medium of communication, an aspect of the "norm-free sociality." But this begs the question of critical theory's approach because such a critical-hermeneutic relation is just what *is* required of commodities: 'money' (as a unique representation of universal commodified value) needs to be deciphered from this appearance as a 'generalizable code' and revealed as a sign for the reification of value, the alienation of labor in class society, the suppression of incomensurability and difference. Habermas is willing to sacrifice any serious challenge to the operation of such reification in the interests of a limited democratic society. But, on the contrary, I think it very important to allow such challenge for the sake of a democracy capable of dispelling the mystification of domination that identical exchange reproduces.

It might help here to recall that Marx's theory of value is not concerned with determining what the 'true' or 'real' values of products are—he is not out to provide a theory that justifies the equivalence of exchange (for this is just what liberal political economy hopes to do for capitalism). Neither is he simply concerned with showing the institutional, and therefore historical, basis of money (in the gold standard or in state reserves) or property (in bourgeois civil law). Marx's theory of value is directed at root to the basic philosophical question of why there is value *at all* instead of an absence of value. Value itself is to be revealed as a social and political relation that, precisely because of this historical character, has no basis other than that established through the struggles, conflicts, and contradictions of a historical class society. Critical analysis inspired by Marxist insights turns us toward not just the perspective of labor or production but toward the question of *value* and its distinction from *wealth* in a much more emphatic sense than Habermas can acknowledge.[16] But it is here that Habermas's systems theory is supposed to pick up the slack in his social theory by isolating the material reproduction of the lifeworld objectified in the 'system.' Only by his recourse to a systems theory conception of delinguistified media that colonize lifeworld contexts can Habermas replace that contradictory relation—which in Marx is expressed through the theory of value—without blurring his own distinction between communicative and purposive rationality.

It is hence very important to draw a clear distinction between systems theory as systems-functionalism (Talcott Parsons/Luhmann) and a *critical* theory of the capitalist system. Habermas recognizes this difference but tends to present it only in terms of his own synthesis of lifeworld and system in the theory of communicative action. The two partial methodological strategies that Habermas associates respectively with the lifeworld and system perspectives are viewed as the 'disjecta membra' of the Hegelian-Marxist tradition. These dual elements, he contends, can only be recovered adequately via the theory of communicative action that does not finally rely on a social totality articulated through an aesthetic reason but on the coordinating power of reaching understanding and agreement in language. This distinction of levels is crucial when discussing the thesis of internal colonization, since it is capitalism as a functional system that, along with the process of bureaucratization, 'distorts' the lifeworld. Against this, I believe that a critical conception needs to maintain a grasp on the dialectical, contradictory totality in order to recognize reification adequately.

Habermas faces a very difficult task in satisfactorily redefining reification after so transforming—or, more accurately, rejecting—the critical idea of capitalist totality developed in the tradition of critical theory.

3.3. Real Abstraction and Ideology

In order to press my argument I would like to shift focus slightly in order to examine the concept of real abstraction (*reale Abstraktion*) in some detail. This will be revealing because Habermas himself believes he has contributed to a new understanding of real abstraction without the need to rely on something like Marx's theory of value (*TCAII*: 374). I would like to deepen the discussion of Habermas's distinction between lifeworld and system by exploring the socialness of exchange and real abstraction in a Marxist-inspired account. My account of real abstraction, which follows Sohn-Rethel's (1978) most closely, is compatible with Marx's account in the *Grundrisse* (1973) while not being identical to it.

The theory of real abstraction is supposed to explode the object's power over thought—that is, it exposes certain entities as abstractions and not as what they appear: natural things. But this is a theory of ideology that is not merely an unmasking, after which only an enlightened view of practice in capitalist society is possible. A Marxist-inspired ideology critique is not merely theoretical disenchantment, and those who continue to hold ideological beliefs in the face of critique are not merely chauvinistic or irrational but systematically deluded. It is rather a theory of why unmasking—or enlightenment—is *not enough* to overcome illusion.

The real abstraction of exchange society analyzed by Marx via the concept of commodity fetishism, and as described in Sohn-Rethel's (1978) account, is abstraction unlike the intellectual abstraction by which thoughts take their form. Abstraction is, according to non-materialist philosophical positions, an exclusively mental act: it designates the way in which *form* is recognized by the mind. For Marx also, abstraction is an act whereby we abstract (think) and it also refers to the concepts—abstractions—that we use to think, some of which are the ideological products of alienated society (Ollman, 1993: 26). But this kind of intellectual abstraction is contrasted by Sohn-Rethel to the real abstraction Marx identifies in the act of *exchange* (distinguished here from the *use* of the exchanged items themselves), which the former sees as the basis of civilized society. The reality of the exchange abstraction is precisely found in its independence from and obscurity to the minds of those exchanging:

Thus in speaking of the abstractness of exchange we must be careful not to apply the term to the consciousness of the exchanging agents. They are supposed to be occupied with the use of the commodities they see, but occupied in their imaginations only. It is the action of exchange, and the action alone, that is abstract. The consciousness and the action of the people part company in exchange and go different ways. We have to trace their ways separately, and also their interconnection. . . . One could say that the abstractness of their action is beyond realization by the actors because their very consciousness stands in their way. Were the abstractness to catch their minds their action would cease to be exchange and the abstraction would not arise (Sohn-Rethel, 1978: 26–27).

Hence the reality of the exchange abstraction derives from its *social* nature, but this very existence *depends* on actors repressing the consciousness of the socialness of their act. The social nature of exchange means that its reality exists only insofar as human society exists, and by virtue of it. For this reason the real abstraction or abstract objectivity of society (second nature) is different from the concrete, material objectivity of the natural world (first nature); the latter would, in principle, continue to exist without human beings to conceive of it. Real abstraction is Marx's attempt to get at the heart of the question of society, of the "social synthesis": that which simultaneously produces alienation—here individuation, difference—and identity or social cohesion. "The abstract and purely social physicality of exchange has no existence other than in the human mind, but it does not spring from the mind. It springs from the activity of exchange and from the necessity for it which arises owing to the disruption of communal production into private production carried on by separate individuals independently of each other" (Sohn-Rethel, 1978: 57).

The real abstraction of exchange is the condition for the formal abstractions of the theoretical consciousness. Thus the commodity-form, for example, is just that—a *form*—a form whose universality is not directly a product of the mind but rather owes its existence to a dialectical but repressed relation to the real abstraction of exchange. That the commodity-form is a *formal* abstraction means that the commodity can appear to the mind as a thing, independent of labor and exchange.

There is thus a compulsion to the illusions of social being in exchange society. It is demanded by the act of exchange. Exchange rests on a "social postulate" in which the use of commodities must be suspended until after the completion of the exchange, in which they are assumed to be of commensurable value when factually they are not, in which they exist only in terms of exchangeability (Sohn-Rethel, 1978: 68). The ability to make such formal abstractions regarding commodities is possible only by virtue of the *particular* logic of the abstract intellect, which emerges *because* it is cut off from its social origin (*ibid*, emphasis added). This necessity complements but is more than the pragmatic need for disseminating ideology that is intended to perpetuate class rule. For Sohn-Rethel, it is also a fault of the historical order of social existence causing it to be false (1978: 197–98). This is why such a Marxian concept of ideology can be regarded as symptomatic.

It is therefore possible to read the critique of ideology psychoanalytically, as is done in pioneering fashion by Frankfurt critical theory.[17] Moreover, according to Lacan, Marx thus "invented the symptom," a reading elaborated by Žižek (1989: 11–55). For Žižek, the social postulate identified by Sohn-Rethel functions as a certain "as if" that is implied by exchange:

> [T]he illusion is not on the side of knowledge, it is already on the side of reality itself, of what the people are doing. What they do not know is that their social reality itself, their activity, is guided by an illusion, by fetishistic inversion. What they overlook, what they misrecognize, is not the reality but the illusion which is structuring their reality, their social activity. They know very well how things really are, but they are still doing it as if they did not know. The illusion is therefore double: it consists in overlooking the illusion which is structuring our real, effective relationship to reality (1989: 18).

As he adds, "the fundamental level of ideology, however, is not an illusion masking the real state of things but that of an (unconscious) fantasy structuring our social reality itself" (32–33).

Such a reading of real abstraction posits a symbolic level below or beyond the abstract consciousness, which remains unconscious, but on which such consciousness nevertheless depends. By definition, such real abstraction cannot be brought to consciousness as *an abstraction*, for it is '*real*,' not formal or conceptual. Its reality is the condition of the exchanging actors' consciousnesses such that its 'ideality'—its representation—is prevented: "their very consciousness stands in their way." The reality of this abstraction is the object, nevertheless, of a critical *theory*.

What I would like to emphasize for our purposes here is the *way of thinking* that is required by Marx to conceive of abstractions adequately.

In stark contrast and opposition to the philosophy of the subject and consciousness philosophy, Marx's dialectical mode of thinking conceives of abstractions themselves as *relations*, the elements of which are *internally* related. The fundamental element of thinking is, therefore, not a single abstraction (or concept) but a relation. Ollman describes Marx's way of thinking by referring to a "philosophy of internal relations that gives Marx both license and opportunity to abstract as freely as he does, to decide how far into its internal relations any particular will extend. Making him aware of the need to abstract—since boundaries are never given and when established never absolute—it also allows and even encourages re-abstraction, makes a variety of abstraction possible, and helps develop the mental skills and flexibility in making abstractions" (1993: 36).[18] We cannot avoid abstraction for thought, but we must not remain content with *mere* or *reified* abstraction, for the abstraction is always internally related to something else that in turn reaches beyond itself again.

If we extend this conception to the previous discussion, then we can recognize that the real abstraction of exchange, the social act, is a fetishized relation established between actors, who must take up a peculiar, particular, objectifying, and instrumentalizing relation to each other in order for the abstraction to exist: "Nothing that a single commodity-owner might undertake on his own could give rise to this abstraction," Sohn-Rethel writes, "no more than a hammock could play its part when attached to one pole only" (1978: 69). But real abstraction appears not as the fetishization of the actors themselves (for they appear as individual egos, calculating their self-interest, and striking up relations with other such egos), but rather as the commodity form. Hence Marx speaks of the language of commodities brought to life, so to speak, in fetishism: "Could commodities themselves speak, they would say: Our use value may be a thing that interests men. It is no part of us as objects. What, however, does belong to us as objects, is our value. Our natural intercourse as commodities proves it. In the eyes of each other we are nothing but exchange values" (Marx, 1954: 87). Thus, in the context of capitalist society, the interaction of the objects of exchange provides the condition for the intersubjectivity of the human actors, rather than the other way around. This way of seeing things makes it impossible to isolate and analyze the economic system of exchange on its own without simultaneously reifying the exchanging actors in a new mystification.

Žižek argues that the main point of Marx's analysis of the commodity-form is that belief, rather than being an inner matter, is externalized in the activity of people—which we may understand as involving their suppressed internal relations—such that *"the things (commodities) believe in their place*, instead of the subjects: it is as if all their beliefs, superstitions and metaphysical mystifications, supposedly surmounted by the rational, utilitarian personality, are embodied in the 'social relations between things.' They no longer believe, *but the things themselves believe for them*" (Žižek, 1989: 34). This is a interesting formulation of the way in which this historical expression of intersubjectivity depends on a fantasized, but real, interobjectivity. It may be compared favorably with the Adornoesque view of intersubjectivity and interobjectivity that I introduced in section 2.2.

At this point, let us return to the issue of the analysis of real abstraction in Habermas. The essence of Habermas's reference to "real abstractions" turns on the argument that they can be analyzed as "an object domain for empirical inquiry" without using the theory of value or some such "translation tool" (*TCAII*: 375). Indeed, a central complaint of Habermas against Frankfurt critical theory is that for such theory, only instrumental reason found embodiment while "everything that existed was transformed into a real abstraction [that] escaped the grasp of empirical inquiry" (*TCAII*: 382). Leaving aside for now the question of whether or not this is true of Frankfurt theory, it is clear from our discussion of real abstraction above that it is impossible for 'everything existing' to be transformed into real abstraction. The real abstraction of exchange society is not identical to reification because it lies at a third level, as it were, distinct from the levels of formal abstraction and reification. The great expansion of the commodity-form that occurs in late capitalist society extends reification into spheres of life previously unsubjected to capitalist exploitation or rationalization. But the *real* abstraction is mystified through reified relations and itself becomes part of fantasized life, which then in turn assists this process. Habermas confuses two senses of abstraction that I maintain must be distinguished because he seems to see real where formal abstraction is the mode. Such a confusion is also indicated by the fact that Habermas never mentions real abstraction's opposite—formal abstraction—in his relevant discussions.

But Habermas is correct in his view that the real abstraction does not lend itself to positive empirical study—despite its designation as real. This, however, is not an indication of the concept's theoretical deficiency but a crucial sense of its meaning. If this level *were* open to *direct* empirical study, it would cease to be real abstraction and would not exist or would become something else—"Were the abstractness to catch [actors] minds their action would cease to be exchange and the abstraction would not arise" (Sohn-Rethel, 1978: 26–27). Hence the necessity of the theory of value or something like it. Habermas is aware of this need, and, as we saw, he cites the ability of the theory of value to explain the "translation rules" that govern movement from hermeneutic, lifeworld descriptions to objectivating, systemic descriptions as one of the theory's strengths (*TCAII*: 336-7). This immediately brings to mind the connection previously mentioned between systemic crisis and lived crisis, which Habermas views as so important to a critical theory. Yet we may see that such an interpretation of translation rules already assumes that the problem to be solved is how to render what is understood as real abstraction empirically serviceable. In my view, the point of the theory of value and the concept of real abstraction is to identify why such abstraction is *not* available to direct empirical investigation and even presents an extraordinary difficulty to the theoretical consciousness. But to admit this is not to admit thereby that real abstraction is permanently mystified. Rather, one has deconstructed the illusion of the subject as an autonomous, independent ego confronting a world of objects for itself and has presented a theory of the objectivity of subjectivity. To attempt to render the level of real abstraction (merely) empirically available is to become blind to the conditions of possibility of historical exchange society that the concept of real abstraction attempts to name.

Marx recognized this in the primacy of the production of value by social labor, for which the conditions of labor are themselves alienated and unrecognized by those involved. The following passage is worth quoting in full:

> The emphasis comes to be placed not on the state of being *objectified*, but on the state of being *alienated*, dispossessed, sold . . . on the condition that the monstrous objective power which social labor itself erected opposite itself as one of its moments belongs not to the worker, but to the personified conditions of production, that is, to capital. To the extent that . . . this process of objectification in fact appears as a process of dispossession from the standpoint of labor or as an appropriation of alien labor from the standpoint of capital—to that extent, this twisting and inversion [*Verdrehung und Verkehrung*] is a *real* [*phenomenon*], not a merely *supposed* one existing merely in the imagination of the workers and the capitalists (Marx, 1973: 831).

Marx did contend that this was a *historical* necessity associated with capitalist development and not with production in any absolute or transhistorical way. But his major point was that the (historical) mode of production and distribution itself conditions or posits the mystified objective and subjective reality in which individuals think and act. Changing this experience of thought depends on changing the conditions of social production, which is precisely what Habermas cannot recognize without abandoning his quasi-ontological distinction between lifeworld and system.

Reification, in Habermas's schema, is the "paradoxical" condition in which "systemic relief mechanisms . . . turn around and overburden the communicative infrastructure of the lifeworld" (*TCAII*: 378). It is a condition of surplus rationalization over and above a historical stage of universal development in which a level of basic rationalization may be identified (though the terms basic and surplus are not Habermas's own, they may be usefully applied to him, Horowitz, 1994: 197, and n.8, 217). However, reification conceived *merely* as systemic colonization removes the link between class domination and reification and replaces it with the paradoxical expression of a social rationalization that undermines its own achievements. The resultant appreciation of the class-unspecific effects of rationalization is, of course, a virtue of the theory of communicative action according to Habermas. But with this theoretical success, reification then becomes simply an experience of the anonymous effects of the generalizable codes of power and money rather than being *at root* an experience and product of *domination*. This is another reason why it is important not to abstract the system from the lifeworld in the way Habermas does. Not only does Habermas not in fact have an adequate concept of *capitalist* society, by extension he cannot have an adequate concept of *society* itself.

In the tradition of critical theory, rationalization is linked to reification historically, and no amount of reflection at the level of concepts can overcome it in the sense that Habermas claims is possible or desirable. This is why in the Marxist tradition so much emphasis is placed on *praxis* for transformative critique (in theory, the corresponding emphasis is on the *material*). Ultimately, no qualitative transformation is possible without the transition to a classless society that negates the social basis of domination and with it reification. Paradox is most definitely an important aspect of the phenomena of rationalization, but as a dialectically inspired concept it must be capable of reaching to a level inaccessible to Habermas's social theory. (See sections 4.4 and 4.5 for a discussion of Adorno's more promising notion of dialectical contradiction or paradox.)

3.4. Concluding Remarks

Among other things, dispensing with the need for a theory of class consciousness at the practical level is bound to cast doubt on the thesis that Habermas continues—albeit with different theoretical means— a critical project of liberation under (even further) changed circumstances

at the turn of the twentieth century. While the theory of class consciousness has tended to elevate the proletariat to the heady heights of a
Hegelian subject-object of history that would operate as the demiurge of
the revolution (as in Lukács, 1971), it was also intended as an attempt to
theorize a solution to the problem of reification that turned upon the
experience of reification-effects providing insight into their origins (see the
insightful discussion of Lukács' project in Jameson, 1988). Without a theory
of class consciousness—no matter how repressed or fragmented this
consciousness may be at present—the idea of reification itself would
seem to be diminished as a critical concept and the notion of democracy
limited. Class itself, however, if it is not to be hypostatized as Spirit or
Macrosubject and thereby ontologized in theory or epistemologically
privileged in historical analyses or practical politics, must be thought
negatively, as a negative or critical category. For class, at root, is always
a relational concept that includes and excludes within a social context.
Class is precisely a concept of identification and abstraction that is always political in human social relations. Within a theory that recognizes
reification and fetishism, the concept of social class highlights the domination of identifying thought as it pertains to the production of intellectual and material products (which are immanently intertwined). One
ought not to foreclose theoretically on social challenge and opposition to
capitalist reification and fetishism, for the possibility of such challenge is
central to any adequate notion of democracy.

What a critical theory requires and hopes for is a new way of
thinking *about* production that is dialectically related to thought's own
material conditions of existence. This allows new thinking about *what* is
produced as well as the internal relations between social actors who
produce, exchange, and think. A contemporary historical and materialist
conception of production—production of goods as well as of ideas, intellectual products—focuses on the critique of the capitalist experience of
alienation and commodity fetishism as aspects of a social totality in which
the socialness of the exchange form is repressed yet compulsively present
in objects of consciousness. The political response to such a condition is
not to call for the act of exchange to be abolished (since we already have
non-reified relations of exchange in, for example, the act of gift giving),
but rather to call for its mystifications to be done away with, mystifications that are bound up with the domination of the many by the few but
that operate to dominate all.

4

FROM THE PURSUIT OF TRUTH TO THE
PARADOXES OF APORIA AND CONTRADICTION:
HABERMAS AND ADORNO

"For the bourgeois form of reason must lay claim to universality and at the same time set forth limits to it."

—Horkheimer and Adorno

Habermas's turn to linguistic or communicative philosophy has taken place in the context of a dominant philosophical concern with language in the twentieth century. Various major lines of thought on the analysis of language in this century can be traced from such figures as Saussure, Wittgenstein, Heidegger, Austin, and Peter Strawson. Other figures—for example, Apel, Paul Ricoeur, and Richard Rorty—have made the so-called linguistic turn explicit in distinctively critical ways that parallel Habermas's effort. Habermas's use of the phrase *linguistic philosophy*, which he contrasts paradigmatically with consciousness philosophy, provides a useful general characterization of the new and central significance of language in his critical theory. But it would be more accurate to say that Habermas makes a pragmatic turn *within* the more general linguistic turn in philosophy and social theory. Habermas approaches language via a universal pragmatic theory of speech action and translates many central problems in social and political theory onto the plane of language-in-use. This approach draws explicitly from the theory of speech acts (Austin and Searle) and transcendental-pragmatics (Apel), as well as from other sources such as Chomsky's structural theory of generative grammar, G. H. Mead's symbolic interactionism, and Parson's systems theory.

In the first half of this chapter we examine Habermas's communicative theory in detail, focusing on a constellation of issues relevant to the key socially binding and bonding nature of communicative rationality. We then turn to Habermas's critique of Adorno, which is cast here primarily as a critique of performative contradiction.

4.1. The Primacy of Language-Use

Unlike many other anthropologists and sociologists, Habermas is interested only in the social and political significance of *linguistic* communication (with respect to social integration in the lifeworld), which the latter regards as uniquely and properly human. Language, for Habermas, does not merely represent or express states of mind or the ideas of the communicating subject nor does it merely represent an objective reality to the comprehending subject. Consciousness philosophy, which emphasizes the productivities that the subject invests in its symbols, views language in these kinds of terms as expressive representation. The subjective bias characteristic of this paradigm is evident in the way in which language tends to be regarded unproblematically as a tool either for representing an objective reality to the mind or for bringing forth into the world an actor's subjective intent or inner states. Philosophers of consciousness, Habermas argues, peer "right through language as though it were a glassy medium without properties" (*PT*: 161).

In the positivist vein, the rationality of language can be regarded as that which guarantees the adequacy of the relation between the object that is perceived or intended to be known and the sign by which this object is represented to consciousness. This process as representation is naïvely conceived as a relatively unproblematic translation of sensory perception into cognitive signification. Scientistic approaches like logical positivism conceive language in this strictly objectivistic way, as the medium forming the cognitive correlation between reality and its signification. Such relationships between sign or symbol and natural or original experience are false because they overlook the fact that the *medium* of language affects the original perceptive experience that is supposed to provide the unconditioned data. The Habermasian move to the primacy of language-use is intended to circumvent the apparent intractable opposition between idealism and realism by calling attention to the medium in which linguistic or conceptual representation occurs. If the operation of language is also determinant in perception, then it requires its own theory.

Any kind of original or transparent perceptive relation is in principle possible only *prior* to the formation of an autonomously acting subject within a culturally distinct lifeworld, that is, prior to the very hominization of the species. In such a case, however, the experience would not be of an independent *representation* but would involve some other kind of mimetic relation whose immediacy we, who understand through language, cannot conceptualize or comprehend in any straightforward way.

What is important for Habermas with respect to the question of subjectivity and action is the way in which he conceives the relations between inner life, intersubjective life, and our life in the objective world through language-in-use. Individual autonomy is acquired in the first place only by a subject who exists within, and acts in relation to, domains understood as independent from the subject. But, for Habermas, it is only possible to achieve the experience of such objectivity by virtue of the communicative relation established between such a subject and other subjects, and only then within a sufficiently developed, linguistically mediated culture that is distinguished from nature. The autonomous subject, for Habermas, is not constituted monologically (solely in relation to an objective environment), pre-socially, metaphysically, or transcendentally with essential 'natural' human capacities and characteristics (as in, for example, religious-metaphysical conceptions, or in Hobbes, Descartes, or Kant). Rather, the autonomous subject emerges only by growing into a social world that involves him or her in constant and constitutive linguistic and intersubjective relations that endow the individual with capacities and competencies for using language in social life.

However, it is equally important for Habermas to conceive of a *progressive* history that expresses the development of social structures, language-use, and social subjects. This is important, as we saw in Chapter 3, in order to discern the unique communicative principles that emerged with modernity in an evolutionary fashion. Indeed, one of Habermas's central philosophical claims in his work from the 1970s about the evolution of society and its communicative structures is that there is a *homology* between development at the level of stages of individual communicative consciousness and at the level of structural social evolution. Thus human maturity (*Mündigkeit*) in individual communicative competence can be loosely mapped according to the historical institutionalization of communicative social structures (see Habermas, 1979).

The hermeneutic circle that traps the interpretive sociology of meaning within the relativism of context can only be transcended by a reconstruction of the *pragmatic* presuppositions of language itself as the medium of interpretation.[1] Likewise, the conceptual pair of contestableness and consensus that define the practice of Discourse, if viewed as ontological limits to theory, constrain reason within a circle that tends to undermine any notion of cultural progress. The work of Kuhn (1970), who analyzes scientific revolutions in terms of the incommensurable substitution of 'paradigms,' serves as an example of such a non-cumulative conception of the development of scientific discourse. But also Foucault's (1973) analysis of discourse, whose notion of the episteme functions as an equivalent to Kuhn's 'paradigm,' rejects any sense of the cumulative acquisition of truth in the human sciences. From the Habermasian perspective, discourse theory can escape its circle only by a switch to the pragmatics of discourse, that is, of argumentative speech that the theory of communicative action can provide (though the proponents of discourse theory may not recognize Habermas's criticism as constituting a problem).

When Habermas refers to language, he means the strict sense of grammatical language expressed in speech and writing rather than a more encompassing notion that might include other forms of patterned communication. The basic elements of Habermas's concept of language are, following Wittgenstein, sentences that can be abstracted in propositional form rather than individual signs or words. Language, in this sense, has developed beyond the situated, narrative structures of oral cultures and achieved a certain autonomy from its context and referent. Pre-linguistic forms of symbolic communication may still involve words and primitive grammar. But at this level the crucial Habermasian roles of speaker and hearer, along with what Habermas describes as the three differentiated worlds or domains of experience, are not yet sufficiently developed and distinguished to warrant the description of an autonomous language. The abstraction and formalization allowed by a written language based on an alphabet and its expression through a differentiated grammatical structure, which are distinguished from the writing of pictograms or hieroglyphs, have, in Habermas's eyes, many advantages over previous forms.

Yet Habermas does not want to abstract language *completely* from context, for this would excessively reify its form and would instead resemble an artificial rather than a natural language (for example, the instruction 'language' written for communication with and between computers). What must be stressed is that communicative action is an *interpretive* action whose unique mode aims at reaching understanding and agreement. This effort relies on a special relation to context in which a speaker and hearer both have reciprocal expectations with respect to the use of symbolic expressions and an assessment of their *appropriateness* in a given context is required (*TCAII*: 17–22). The crucial achievement of *sameness* in meaning occurs only with the ability to follow a rule (according to Wittgenstein), which depends on intersubjectively established meaning contexts.

Once it has become possible to use symbols with identical meanings, the extra-linguistic context of motivations and behavioral dispositions themselves become permeated by language. With the creation of the subject of linguistic utterances, the instinctual behavior that was the origin of gestural communication itself is transformed and removed from immediate experience. The subject of language reflects on the inner natural world of instinctual desire and need, on the one hand, and 'subjective' selfhood, on the other, in the same linguistically mediated way in which reflection is undertaken on the 'objective' world of external nature and the shared 'social' world of the cultural tradition.

But 'language' nevertheless has a number of senses in Habermas's schema. His use of the term is ambivalent despite his close attention, which has led some to cast doubt on the success of the paradigm shift from consciousness philosophy itself. With Habermas's efforts to clarify his central conceptions of language, communicative action, and rationality in several texts following *Theory of Communicative Action* (*PDM*, *MCCA*, and *PT*), he has stressed the *pragmatic* dimension in his approach over the hermeneutic or functional. For it is by virtue of the pragmatic, *performative* nature of language-in-use that Habermas abstracts the constitutive presuppositions of linguistically mediated social action. Notwithstanding this effort, however, Habermas's theory remains far more concerned with the functional, coordinating aspects of communicative action than its critically and hermeneutically important world-disclosive aspects, even while the pragmatic nature of language is stressed. In the course of this chapter, I will endeavor to show how decisive this is for understanding his position.

4.1.1. Pursuing Truth as Social Coordination

From Habermas's ongoing critique of philosophical hermeneutics, which he regards as still trapped by the premises of metaphysics, he concludes that the context of intersubjective relations is coterminous or equiprimordial with the subjects who act within it (for a summary of the earlier Habermas-Gadamer debate, see Misgeld, 1977). Language, he writes,

sets itself off from the speaking subjects as something antecedent
and objective, as the structure that forges conditions of possibility. On the other hand, the linguistically disclosed and structured
lifeworld finds its footing only in the practices of reaching understanding within a linguistic community. In this way, the linguistic formation of consensus, by means of which interactions
link up in space and time, remains dependent upon the autonomous 'yes' and 'no' positions that communication participants
take toward criticizable validity claims (*PT*: 43).

This equiprimordial or simultaneous existence of subjects and
language is necessary in order to avoid a metaphysical conception of
either. The intentional action of subjects in the modern world is found in
the autonomous choices of the yes or no positions they adopt toward
validity claims, choices that cannot be avoided in any linguistically
mediated action. The assumption of such autonomy to accept or reject a
validity claim is logically necessary in order to make sense of the democratic idea of a *valid* consensus.

In propositionally differentiated speech, reaching understanding
(*Verständigung*) means more than just acquiring an understanding
(*Verständnis*) of the meaning of an utterance. Rather, it requires that an
agreement (*Einverständnis*) be achieved between (at least two) communicating subjects with respect to the meaning of the utterance. *Verständigung*
has a threefold meaning for Habermas: with an utterance, a speaker
assumes that he or she utters it in the *right* normative context that establishes a *legitimate* intersubjective relationship between speaker and hearer,
that the speaker makes a *true* statement that will be accepted as knowledge by the hearer, and that the speaker expresses his or her beliefs,
intentions, feelings, and so on, *truthfully*, such that the hearer will give
credence to what is said (*TCAI*: 307–8). Speakers and hearers thus take
up relations to the three worlds of experience and the three corresponding validity claims *simultaneously* with every communicatively oriented
speech act. The concept of communicative reason cannot be identified
with just one kind of rationality or one sphere of experience, as in scientific reason. Nor should this communicative reason be understood as
strictly formalized, as an abstract structure, for it invokes a practical form
of life (intersubjective pursuit and reproduction of consensus) that is
incomplete without specific content and particular experience. While it
need not specify this content, it does suggest a form of political life
inconsistent with, for example, widespread deception, the exclusion of
relevant and important knowledge from public scrutiny, or autocratic

governance without opportunities for seeking agreement or consensus from those affected.

Communicative action designates interaction in which all participants pursue aims oriented toward furthering intersubjective relations. It names a cooperative activity aimed at mutually affirming the goals of reaching understanding and agreement, and as such requires a special kind of recognition and action. These achievements enhance and develop communicative relations that are outside formally constituted communicative actions such as those in religious rituals or legally established relations. By contrast, action that aims to achieve effects on the hearer that lead to the speaker's strategic or instrumental goals do not *enjoin* the hearer in a communicative relation. Instead, the speaker seeks to influence the hearer according to the speaker's will rather than according to the validity of what is said. A speaker may aim at such effects openly or these aims may remain hidden, in which case a speaker feigns a communicative intention while masking his or her actual strategic goals. When actors engage in such deception with their speech acts, the communicative, 'illocutionary' element drops out of their action despite the fact that the speaker may *ostensibly* be aiming at goals of mutual understanding and agreement. In these cases their speech acts are oriented strategically, toward instrumental success. Speech occurs simply in order to achieve an effect upon the hearer, or to get the hearer to do or not to do something (see *TCAI*: 294–95). This kind of manipulative action must, presumably, involve deception or false representation for otherwise people would need to agree that they were saying and doing the things for the same reasons, which would require a mutually recognized claim to validity (see *PT*: 82–83).

This does not, of course, discount situations in which actors accept validity claims, act accordingly, but are nevertheless mistaken regarding their own or another's interests. Such situations would count as simple mistakes or, in the language of ideology critique, would constitute an instance of distorted communication structured by systematic operations occurring behind the backs of participants. Actors may make erroneous interpretations, not realizing that the claims they accept would not receive such general assent if all relevant knowledge were available. It may be the case that no one is consciously deceived, but rather that structural constraints prevent a speaker from recognizing his or her own interests or the general interest that is at stake.

Hence, for Habermas, to act communicatively is to act reflectively and rationally, that is, autonomously and freely, which assumes a *responsibility* that is built into communicative action. Communicative actors who raise and redeem validity claims must be prepared to offer reasons for a claim in the event it is criticized. A *reflective* speaker is able to place himself in the position of the potential hearer of his utterance and take up the hearer's perspective on himself as the utterer of validity claims. From the perspective of the hearer the speaker can anticipate a negative response to the claim he raises and be prepared to argue. By internalizing this relation, the speaker becomes capable of self-criticism, of knowing that he does not know, which is a condition that has, since Socrates, been the basis for self-knowledge (*TCAII*: 74–75).

The *illocutionary force* of an utterance, the operative rational constraint Habermas is most interested in, is hence contained in the claim to *validity*. This rational 'force' is to be distinguished fundamentally from the force of a *power* claim, just as the goals of communicative action are fundamentally distinguished from those of strategic or instrumental action. Power claims achieve action coordination based on *empirical* rather than *valid* reasons. Threats or rewards induce a willingness to accept claims and to bring one's action into line with another's, but they do not require justification and neither do they involve mutual understanding and agreement. "Sanctions belong to a class of actions that ego threatens for the sake of their impact, or when they are linguistic, for the sake of their perlocutionary effect" (*TCAII*: 279). *Rational* motivation, by contrast, relies on the special force of validity. The condition for claiming validity, Habermas argues, is that reasons must always be able to be given that *demonstrate* the validity of a claim to the satisfaction of all concerned. Acceptance of a validity claim is thus an acceptance that valid reasons *can* be given, and further, that both speaker and hearer *can* and *will* agree that these conditions for a claim's validity have been satisfied. This is how communicative action can be said to *bind* speakers and hearers rationally:

> . . . a speaker can *rationally motivate* a hearer to accept his speech act offer because—on the basis of an internal connection among validity, validity claim, and redemption of a validity claim—he can assume the *warranty* [*Gewähr*] for providing, if necessary, convincing reasons that would stand up to a hearer's criticism of the validity claim. Thus a speaker owes the binding (or bonding: *bindende*) force of his illocutionary act not to the validity of what is said, but to *the coordinating effect of the warranty* that he offers: namely, to redeem, if necessary, the validity claim raised with his speech act. In all cases in which the illocutionary role expresses not a power claim but a validity claim, the place of the empirically motivating force of sanctions . . . is taken by the rationally

motivating force of accepting a speaker's guarantee for securing claims to validity (*TCAI*: 302).

Both speaker and hearer engage in *communicative* action *only* with the assumption that an agreement based on mutual assent is possible in principle. The orientation toward mutual understanding and agreement is thus said to be an unavoidable presupposition of communicative speech action. On the face of it this model appears most appropriate for more abstract and rigorous academic discourse or debate. But the principle of communicative action is not intended to apply only to specialized argumentative discourses in the intellectual disciplines. It is, for Habermas, a principle that is operative in the presuppositions of speech itself all the way down to the level of the everyday. Everyday communicative action assumes the same presuppositions of speech and entails mutual understanding and agreement in basically the same way as the most refined form of argumentative discourse. For what Habermas's theory of linguistic communication hopes to identify is the way in which all communicative speech action relies on establishing mutually recognized agreements regarding truth-in-the-world that necessarily *enjoin* communicative participants in a continual renewal of their sociality, their cooperation and coordination.

A criticizable validity claim also expresses most centrally a claim to *truth*. The concept of *truth* is bound up with the idea of validity; the concept of *validity*, in turn, provides strong normative connotations. This entwinement evokes the universality of communicative speech Habermas is getting at. Each validity claim is *analogous* (but not identical) to the truth claim of assertoric sentences (propositions about true states of affairs in the objective world), which he believes is supported by the fact that all normative and expressive statements can be expressed in assertoric form without loss of meaning (*TCAII*: 66). Yet assertoric, as well as expressive speech acts, contain an *illocutionary* content without which they could not be said to *force* participants into taking a critical attitude to a particular truth claim. Thus the claim to validity of a *norm* is the model of the performative speech act—the illocutionary act. Yet propositional assertions and expressions must seemingly be made independently of a prior normative context that provides their validity (*TCAII*: 69). The criticizable validity claim thus cannot be completely identical to or subsumable under either claims to normative validity or objectively valid truth. Instead it combines the sense of both and exists only in conjunction with the active participation of speakers and hearers reaching a rationally motivated understanding.

Habermas thus conceives of truth as the historical achievement of a consensually oriented discursive process that cannot be abstracted from its performative action. Participants in a discourse or language community recognize truth precisely by reproducing agreement and consensus. This means that in order for either an objective proposition, a moral-practical prescription, or a public expression of personal fidelity to be described as *true*, it must, in principle, receive assent from an *interested* community. This implies a substantive need for recognition that, at least in principle, aims beyond merely representative or 'theoretically' determined interests. Since truth acquires its meaning from such practical intersubjective recognition, it follows that no one who is potentially affected by the social or political legitimization of what is to be recognized as true or valid should be excluded from this activity of assent and consensus building. That is, for all statements that are intended to acquire normative status (for example, in law, public policy, or even in common informal ethical relations), recognition (or contestation) should thus be sought from all those who have an interest in such claims to truth (validity). This suggests clear principles, procedures, and ethical conditions for arriving at a consensus if the product of such a process is to be called true in a meaningful way. This is partly why Habermas refers to his conception of ethics as a *cognitive* discourse ethics—it relies on positive knowledge and strong sense of comprehended recognition and understanding.

It is clear, then, that the general orientation toward truth, which for Habermas constitutes the universal feature of human understanding reaching back through archaic, mythic cultures, is not simply a cognitive idea reserved for modern science. This effort at once to moderate scientific-technological reason's dominance as well as extend institutionalized truth-seeking to the moral-practical and expressive realms, if successful, would appear to offer substantial benefits for modern differentiated societies seeking to promote a democratic culture amid a permanent diversity of identities and conflict and struggle over law, rights, distribution and use of resources, etc. But Habermas rejects the conclusion that such a condition would usher in a transparent society (Habermas, 1986a), despite his belief that we should and must all be honest and sincere in our communications. His model of the ideal conditions of reaching agreement and understanding serves as a regulative ideal not a utopian vision. As such it has a counterfactual status since actual discussions, deliberations, and consensus formation can never match such conditions completely or even predominantly. Complete transparency, as I mentioned at the outset, is really beyond a life mediated by language. Nevertheless, these ideal conditions of speech necessarily serve as presuppositions for all communicative action and he believes they cannot be denied or abstracted away.

4.2. VALIDITY AND THE ETHICAL FORCE OF LANGUAGE-USE

Communicative action thus does not simply designate the linguistic form of communication, but the *kind* of action that is entailed by a fully developed language. "For the communicative model of action," Habermas argues, "language is relevant only from the pragmatic viewpoint that speakers, in employing sentences with an orientation to reaching understanding, take up relations to the world . . . in a reflective way" (*TCAI*: 98). Language is the medium in which interpretive acts oriented to reaching understanding about the world occur, but the communicative *action* embodied in this entails that subjects reciprocally raise and redeem validity claims. A communicative act is successful, in this sense, when the partners in dialogue achieve an *intersubjective recognition* of validity with respect to the claims raised in speech. This intersubjective recognition only makes sense for the speaker and hearer *together*; it cannot be achieved only by one party.

In Habermas's social theory, the classic problem of the relation of the individual to the collectivity is solved through the analysis of linguistically mediated action. Language, as a medium of communication, entails that speakers and hearers follow and comprehend a set of grammatical rules, but it also entails a special intersubjective relation between a speaker and a hearer that is absent in less developed symbolically mediated communication. A linguistic utterance contains a claim or claims to validity, to which the addressee of the utterance can respond by accepting, rejecting, or leaving undecided the claim in question. But in assuming this relation, the hearer of an utterance can always criticize the claim to validity, for otherwise the hearer could not be said to have the ability to accept or reject the claim.

This does not necessarily mean that a norm underlying a validity claim *itself* is criticized if a hearer rejects the validity claim of the utterance. For example, traditional norm-consciousness does not as a matter of course allow the norms that coordinate action to be brought into question themselves. The predominant question for traditional norm-consciousness instead concerns the appropriate context of applicability for the given norm. On *this* question challenge, discipline, and enforcement are nevertheless essential in traditional societies. Another example is found in scientific discourse, in which a claim to truth about the objective world may be rejected for not matching the available evidence without thereby rejecting the causal theory that gives sense to the claim. In these cases the illocutionary force of the utterance has still enjoined the disagreeing party in the speech action. In fact, Habermas argues, being able to say 'no' to a validity claim is essential for hearers to be 'bound' by speech act offers because they are permitted to reject them only on account of *reasons* (*TCAII*: 74).

Thus the claim to validity is not quite identical to this enjoining, practical force (the illocutionary force) immanent to the performance of an utterance, but is rather its medium of operation. The cognitive orientation of Habermas's theory, combined with its view of the pragmatic presuppositions of speech, enable him to move beyond the opposition of objectivism and relativism. By virtue of the fact that the intersubjective communicative relation requires the act of interpretation and the possibility of criticism but also mutual understanding and agreement with respect to relevant meaning, it presents a picture of communicative life that is relatively fluid and indeterminate but at the same time grounded by universal-pragmatic presuppositions of speech. The condition of contestableness, which for Connolly (1983), following J. B. Gallie, is so essential to the concepts of political discourse, is turned into a principle that for Habermas *guarantees* the orientation toward consensus.[2] Neither aspect of communication should be seen as elemental nor should each be seen as mutually exclusive. Both the contestableness of validity claims and the reproduction of a consensus about them are reciprocally related.

Yet it is only with the development of post-traditional norm-consciousness that we can truly speak of the *criticizable* validity claim with respect to normative discourse. Here the conditions of legitimate argumentation that the modern world has developed apply in their respective ways to claims in different domains of the experiential world. Norm-coordinated action in modern society occurs against a background that is to be sure still unproblematic in many respects, but there is here always already the assumption that any norms could in principle be justified rationally. Indeed, the institutional form of post-conventional morality—modern positive law—requires a matching institutionalized form of rational justification. In nineteenth- and twentieth-century liberal-democratic theory, this is what is supposed to be embodied in the legitimate process of democratic will-formation in the democratic-constitutional state. In this respect, what Habermas would like to do is provide a better, more secure theory of democracy than has so far been managed in the liberal tradition.

The development of language in the full sense occurs when the process of reaching understanding is separated from the individual and society through the speech action of raising and redeeming validity claims. The concept of the speech act contains both the notion of linguistic meaning and the pragmatic element arising from one subject acting in relation to another. The act of raising and redeeming validity claims orients participants in speech to the expectation of reaching a *rationally* motivated agreement, an expectation which lifts their action coordination out of the spheres of mere caprice, conditioning, imitative behavior, or mere response to threat or reward. The structure of speech thus takes on its own logic and systemic existence independent of natural behavior and needs. Since the conception of communicative rationality is thus central to Habermas's theory of democracy, I would like to pursue further his idea of the new sociality immanent to the 'enlightened' (rationalized) world in the following two sections.

4.2.1. A Happy Evolution to Modernity

From the vantage point of the most common modern perspectives on archaic societies, Habermas argues, mythical interpretations of the world seem to confuse the realms of nature and culture such that a clear categorical distinction cannot be made between manipulatable objects and the subjects who speak and act. This further signifies a lack of differentiation between, on the one hand, *language* and the relations of meaning, and on the other, the objective world that exists in terms of physical cause and effect (*TCAI*: 48–49). In myth, Habermas points out, the interpretation of the world cannot be identified *as* an interpretation, traditions are not recognized *as* traditions. In such an undifferentiated worldview, "concepts of validity such as morality and truth are amalgamated with empirical ordering concepts such as causality and health" (*TCAI*: 50). There is thus very little possibility for individuals to challenge the validity of mythical interpretations of human relations or natural phenomena since these meanings are bound up with the very well-being of the individual and his or her group. Such challenge is literally unthinkable because it would undermine the basis of the lifeworld in which the individual and group exist. One need not argue in order to establish the validity of mythic views or interpretations; consensus is secured and reproduced independent of the need for justification. Hence Habermas describes mythical worldviews as "closed"—closed to world-differentiation and to a reflexivity that would allow rational challenge and revision (*TCAI*: 52–53).

It is only when nature and culture, language and world, are properly differentiated that the *validity* of an interpretation *about* a state of affairs can be brought into question. But it is not so much the distinction between nature and culture that makes for the essential transformation from mythic to modern worldviews. It is rather the desocialization of nature and the denaturalization of culture whose dual process results in the differentiation of an external world of objective nature from a socially constituted world of norms and conventions. At the same time, a third world of inner, personal existence crystallizes in contrast to objectified nature and group relations and identities. For an *external* world and an independently *shared* social world only make sense in relation to an *internal* world of subjective experience that is not 'out there' but neither is it shared with others.

This differentiation requires, for Habermas, that three formal world-concepts be distinguished that refer to exactly three intersubjectively recognized domains. These domains constitute three worlds about which statements can be made that can receive intersubjective agreement. That is, all communicative subjects must recognize that these domains *exist*, and that they can take up relations toward each of them by making *claims* about something existing within them. It is only with such a differentiation that the individual is freed from the constraints of mythical worldviews and required to exercise a certain intersubjective autonomy of his or her own.

The relations to the world that the communicating subjects must take up consist of interpretations that then constitute the shared lifeworld of participants. Habermas differentiates three basic world-relations that may be thematized with utterances—that is, brought into specific focus in a cognitive orientation. These relations hold between an utterance and "the objective world (as the totality of all entities about which true statements are possible); the social world (as the totality of all legitimately regulated interpersonal relations); and the subjective world (as the totality of the experiences of the speaker to which he has privileged access)" (*TCAI*: 100). The interpretations relating to each world of experience entail raising *validity claims* about each domain. Thus one makes a *truth* claim when one makes a statement about an objective state of affairs, a *normative* claim when one makes a statement about legitimate or right social relations, and a claim to *sincerity* or *truthfulness* when one makes a statement about what one feels, desires, intends, and so on. Specific modes of assessment can then correspond to these discrete validity claims.

For Habermas, the enlightened reason of claims to validity is the crucial achievement of emancipation and autonomy from myth and nature. The rationality of the orientation to differentiated worldviews, Habermas argues, can be measured in terms of the formal-pragmatic basic concepts they place at the disposal of individuals for interpreting their world (*TCAI*: 45). Individual autonomy grows as society becomes more differentiated (and appropriately rationalized). Likewise, following Jean Piaget, "Cognitive development signifies in general *the decentration of an egocentric understanding of the world*. Only to the extent that the formal reference system of the three worlds is differentiated can we form a reflective concept of 'world' and open up access to the world through the medium of common interpretive efforts, in the sense of a cooperative negotiation of situational definitions" (*TCAI*: 69). But as decentration and differentiation increases, the content of the lifeworld—as the totality of cultural knowledge and the 'background' against which human action occurs—loses the overwhelming givenness it had in its mythically and traditionally defined forms.

> The more the worldview that furnishes the cultural stock of knowledge is decentered, the less the need for understanding is covered *in advance* by an interpreted lifeworld immune from critique; and the more this need has to be satisfied by the interpretive accomplishments of the participants themselves—that is, by way of risky (because rationally motivated) agreement—the more often we can expect rational action motivations (*TCAI*: 70, translation altered).

The enlightened society is distinguished from mythical or archaic society by virtue of the possibility of, and increasing need for, reaching a rationally motivated agreement about intersubjectively raised claims to validity. By virtue of the fact that, in contrast to the mythic, the modern understanding of the world contains the structural possibility of questioning the interpretations of worldviews, Habermas calls the latter "open."

But all this is not to say that myth is thereby completely irrational. Habermas wants to defend a *universalizable* concept of rationality whose contours could still be found in myth. Despite the narrative limits to the mythical worldview and the impossibility of challenging interpretations within the formal structure and discourse of myth, what is nevertheless universal even in myth, according to Habermas, is the claim to truth itself. If Horkheimer and Adorno recognized an (ambivalent) enlightenment rationalization in myth, Habermas sees instead the universal orientation toward truth. Language, in the strict sense, always presupposes the universality of truth, but truth can only arise *within* language, as an (essential) element of language-use. Notwithstanding the confusions of myth, the rational assumption of its participants is nevertheless that it is *true*. This is truth's relation to human action in the world. "Whatever language system we choose, we always start intuitively from the presupposition that truth is a universal validity claim. If a statement is true, it merits universal assent, no matter in which language it is formulated" (*TCAI*: 58). Hence the rationality of mythic cultures should not be measured against the dominant modern standard of scientific rationality. Science, for example, would contend that since the belief in witches and magic is scientifically unverifiable and objectively untrue, mythic cultures are to that extent *irrational*. But neither should one hold the opposite position (for example, as Peter Winch does) that worldviews (mythic and modern) present incommensurable concepts of rationality and hence cannot be theoretically compared from the modern perspective. On the Habermasian view one should instead note the undifferentiated condition of myth, which nevertheless orients its subjects toward existent truth, and also recognize the one-sidedness of modern rationality that tends to subjugate all rationality to its scientific form.

In contrast to either archaic blind obedience or empirical force, in modernity it is now the orientation toward the claim to validity that secures social interaction. The interrelationships of understanding that bind individuals and society together in prelinguistic communication are transformed in the transition to speech action. Speech acts constitute a new and fundamentally different sociality that is reproduced through the 'binding/bonding' (*bindende*) effect of raising and redeeming validity claims. The will of a responsible actor is *bound* by the illocutionary force of the speech act: one can only respond rationally to a claim to validity with a yes, a no, or a deferral based on the claim's present undecidability. Once agreements are achieved communicatively, they are said to be achieved rationally: any additional coercion or co-optation is unnecessary. The orientation toward mutual understanding and agreement enables a new mechanism of social coordination to take effect based on rational motivations.

At this stage in the discussion we begin to see Habermas's strategy for denying the binding nature of what Horkheimer and Adorno call the dialectic of enlightenment. The quasi-transcendental status of the orientation toward truth (one of the presuppositions of speech) guarantees a sphere for reason free from the dominative dictates of self-preservation and the capricious force of self-interest. For beyond cognition (identification) and action (control, intended intervention in the world) is *understanding*, which enjoins others for the sake of mutual recognition and agreement. Simple symbolically mediated communication or natural adaptive behavior cannot *enjoin* its participants in an action outside of specific contextualized relations or instinctual motivations. By contrast, formally differentiated, linguistically mediated communication is said to depend on just such universally enjoining action, and it is this ethical content that makes it politically important for a free, democratic politics in a modern society.

Under pressures of disenchantment and rationalization, interpretive reason has necessarily expanded further into society to allow mass enlightenment possibilities. The idea of democracy is inherently bound up with this process that extends the interpretive need for reaching mutual agreement. While disenchantment and rationalization destroy previously unquestioned ethical formations based on religious or metaphysical justifications, this process frees the subject from the domination of myth by opening operative consensuses to the *processes* of reaching rational agreement. The principles of free argument and open discourse, central pillars of democracy, come to undergird the *practical* ways in which an absent or disrupted consensus is reestablished in differentiated and complex modern society.

If norms are called into question in modern society, then the problems raised by such challenge should, however, only be settled in a practical discourse if the power of free social bonding is to be balanced with the free strategic and instrumental actions of individuals in the parallel spheres of economy and administration. This does not mean that all post-traditional norms and claims will thereby *become* criticized or available for criticism. As I discussed in Chapters 2 and 3, there are many reasons why the normative background to action remains unexamined or underexamined in modern capitalist society, just as there are reasons why unequal and hierarchical relations have been unproblematically legitimated in past societies. Nevertheless, the structure of the decentered modern self, with its post-traditional forms of consensus, allows, at least in principle, for challenge and criticism of all consensually held practical knowledge within the respective speech community that Habermas believes is the natural partner of the rationalized and instrumentalized spheres in which the self also operates.

Argument, truth-seeking, and freedom are thus for Habermas not only immanently related in democratic life, they are also most appropriate for the particular modern form of society. Although all societies are constituted on the basis of the orientation toward truth, this can only finally be seen from the differentiated perspective afforded by modernity. The idea of the truth-claim, which is bound up with the *telos* of communicative action (mutual understanding and agreement) is understood to be a presupposition of language-in-use that has universal application. As we saw earlier, what Habermas is ultimately aiming at with the ideas of the criticizable validity claim and the orientation to mutual understanding and agreement is a conception of the speech-pragmatic presuppositions underlying communicatively achieved social integration. Indeed, it is Habermas's theory of universal pragmatics that provides the philosophical core for much of his social theory and it also constitutes the most significant moment in the shift in focus inaugurated by the paradigm shift.

The pursuit of valid knowledge, for Habermas, is conceived as immanent to society itself, that is, to its reproduction through communicative interaction, since social interaction *depends* on raising and redeeming validity claims. For this argument, Habermas draws on Michael Dummett's 'truth-conditional semantics' that emphasizes the dialogical (rather than the monological) element of truth-claims. "It is part of understanding a sentence," Habermas explains, "that we are capable of recognizing *grounds* through which the *claim* that its truth conditions are satisfied *could be redeemed*" (*TCAI*: 317). Unless we raise truth-claims and pursue truth, speech capable of possessing meaning and coordinating action would be impossible. Socialization and social integration can occur only through the medium of action oriented toward mutual understanding—and thus, for Habermas, we are drawn to a theory of communicative action. Communicative rationality is universal and a foundation of sorts, which cannot be opted out of by a communicating social subject without the risk of self-destruction. He or she who abandons speech abandons human society.

Habermas believes he has thus found in the unavoidable presuppositions of communicative action the quasi-transcendental conditions of free, rational sociation. To deny these presuppositions is to deny one's own identity (individuation) and social being as a communicating self—the very conditions that enable one to utter such a denial. Hence for Habermas, the arguments of a radical skeptic or relativist, who denies that a universal concept of reason or truth can be discovered, are undermined by the universal-pragmatic presuppositions he or she is nevertheless forced to make in uttering such claims. (I will examine this criticism as it is leveled at critical theory's 'totalizing' critique of modern reason in section 4.3.) These presuppositions are not merely formal, they do not merely exist at the level of individual communicating subjects, but rather operate as conditions of individuation and sociation simultaneously.

The notion of the speech community represents an ethical whole that stands behind such mutual relations of individuation and sociation, but this totality is supposed to be open rather than closed, liberatory rather than repressive. Membership in any particular speech community is grounded in the possibility of the speech act and cemented through the ongoing processes of raising, criticizing, and redeeming validity claims. Actors are social and bound together insofar as they must speak within an existing context of concrete intersubjective relations, but they must raise and redeem validity claims in order to be individuals and to act at all. These conditions of modern sociation cannot be systematically avoided or suppressed without producing pathological side effects, a proposition that Habermas believes can be confirmed empirically at the individual, social, and political levels. The speech community projects a horizon beyond which it is impossible for a speaker to go without risking mental instability or illness. One may, for example, point to such pathologies as megalomania and paranoia as examples of behavior that is characterized by a suspension or rejection of constitutive relations with others, a decline into delusional self-reference.

4.2.2. Linguistification of the Sacred

Habermas backs up these universalizing claims by tracing the genealogy of the concepts of truth and validity back to archaic and anthropological origins. For this he draws on Durkheim's sociology of religion, which represents an attempt to discover the origin of the binding power of morality in the authority of the sacred. Habermas's intent is to reach a Weberian conclusion concerning the rationalization of the sacred, but, contra Weber, to find the energies of the solidarity of the holy not dissipated and lost in the modern but transformed and reproduced in the communicative practice characteristic of modern discourse. Although modern rationalization destroys the senses of identity, belonging, and solidarity found in the sacred worldview, as well as its authority, these losses are replaced with identities, a solidarity, and a form of legitimate authority that have more explicit rational bases. Weber's suggestion that only essentially irrational phenomena—such as charisma—can replace these losses of meaning produced by modern rationalization is rejected by Habermas. Instead, Habermas wishes to identify the precise ways in which the lifeworld processes of identity and meaning formation, the reproduction of social solidarity and legitimate authority have themselves been rationalized under the development of *communicative* rationality.

The orientation toward validity and truth are central to Habermas's account concerning all domains of communicative rationality. I would like to continue my focus here on the ethical dimension of communicative action, exploring the way in which Habermas theorizes the new sociality of the modern lifeworld in contrast to premodern forms. Weber's concept of value rationality (*Wertrationalität*), which he contrasts with purposive-rationality (*Zweckrationalität*), is inadequate to capture this dimension of modernity. Its focus on the subjective relation to *values*, one might note, is the kind of idealist relation characteristic of the philosophy of consciousness.

The concept of the criticizable validity claim is not seen by Habermas as entirely limited to rationalized and secularized modernity although it is here that it reaches its autonomous form. Such a concept already identifies a fundamental feature of emerging civilizations based on religious worldviews. The religious worldview, in contrast to the consciousness of animism or the sacred totality of the primitive tribe, crystalizes only after sufficient differentiation of grammatical language that allows for individuated speaking and hearing subject positions. It is subject to the rationalization introduced through linguistic mediation in the more developed sense discussed earlier. The religious worldview self-consciously sets itself off from previous sacred forms and thus achieves a certain reflexivity that understands itself as a cultural tradition. As such, the religious worldview is in need of processes of communicatively achieved interpretation and consensus. For Habermas, it is only through the "feedback" processes of reaching understanding that a cultural tradition—in the form of *cultural knowledge* that is based on both cognitive and socially integrative experiences—can be reproduced (*TCAII*: 56).

Following Durkheim, what interests Habermas most about the authority of the sacred is the way in which social solidarity is secured. The distinction between the sacred and profane or between the moral and non-moral, which admit of certain structural analogies for Durkheim, are ultimately derived from the individual's solidarity with the group. But the belief in the normative authority of the sacred cannot be explained simply by reference to a higher order set of beliefs or values, for that is the recourse of the philosophy of consciousness and would be unavoidably circular. Obedience to and respect for norms needs special motivation, a motivation that stands *behind* the awe-inspiring force of specific normative beliefs and values.

Giving his own pragmatic spin to Durkheim's theory, Habermas argues that it is not religious beliefs or representations themselves that are important for establishing normative authority in primitive or civilized societies but the *form* of religious symbolism and the *way* these symbols are developed and reproduced. The existence of the symbolic form of the sacred depends, even in its primitive identification, on a prelinguistic element of communicative action achieved by the collectivity. This element is what Durkheim calls the *conscience collective* of the group, the normative consensus on the sacred, that is reproduced through ritual practice. The individual achieves a 'mechanical' identity with the group by reproducing the normative consensus through simple ritual practices in which sacred objects are collectively recognized and distinguished from the profane. What is important for Habermas is the way in which a primordial orientation toward validity and truth is to be found in the analysis of religious paleosymbols: "The normative consensus that is expounded in the semantics of the sacred is present to members in the form of an idealized agreement transcending spatiotemporal changes. This furnishes the model for all concepts of validity, especially for the ideal of truth" (*TCAII*: 71). The individuated subject is *required* to orient him- or herself toward truth if belief in and experience of the authority of the sacred *and* membership (individuation) are to be maintained.

In Durkheim's theory of the authoritative power of the sacred, the idea of truth derives its structure ultimately from the idealized agreement inherent in this collective identity. For Habermas, by contrast, it is not ultimately the power of the sacred nor strictly the form of the valid norm that produces the *criticizable* validity claim, but rather the integration of the authority of an idealized collective agreement *and* the objectivity of experience of the world:

> The idea of truth can get from the concept of normative validity only the impersonality—supratemporal—of an idealized agreement, of an intersubjectivity related to an ideal communication community. This moment of a 'harmony of minds' is *added* to that of a 'harmony with the nature of things.' The authority standing behind knowledge does not coincide with moral authority. Rather, the concept of truth combines the objectivity of experience with a claim to the intersubjective validity of a corresponding descriptive statement, the idea of the correspondence of sentences and facts with the idea of an idealized consensus. It is only from this *combination* that we get the concept of a criticizable validity claim (*TCAII*: 72).

The universal-pragmatic presuppositions immanent in language in the full sense finally emerge in conjunction with this 'linguistification of the sacred'—the transition from symbolically mediated to linguistically mediated communication. This describes a general rationalization of worldviews in which a communicatively achieved religious authority emerges from the collective authority of sacred symbolism. The rationalization of communicative action gradually replaces the total, cosmological authority of the holy, in which the authority of the idealized collective agreement is merely recognized through ritual, with the authority of an *achieved* consensus. This frees communicative action from the unreflective power of the sacred by translating sacred collective authority into normative consensual recognition. "The aura and terror that emanates from the sacred, the *spellbinding* power of the holy, is sublimated into the *binding/bonding* force of criticizable validity claims and at the same time turned into an everyday occurrence" (*TCAII*: 77).

But this story of disenchantment, while not a 'liberation' in the critical sense, is not as progressive or unequivocal as Habermas seems to imply. For the new openness and freedom is gained only at the price of introducing new constraints imposed by social relations, which are viewed as unproblematic in Habermas's theory. Operating within these new constraints, the enlightened rational actor *must* now be oriented toward claims to validity and be willing to comply with 'the force of the better argument'—the truth claim of validity—on pain of social irrelevance or dysfunction.

It has been observed in this respect that the force of the claim to validity, while meant as a progressive, liberating force, is still nevertheless a *force*. But what kind of force could operate as the guarantor of the rational or ethical form that could be *embodied in* the notion of validity rather than coming to it from the outside? The 'force' of the better argument is not equivalent to the argument itself, that is, to its specific expression or formal rational structure, but is somehow present in it or behind it in the properties that allow the 'betterness' implied by validity to be recognized in the first place. Force, by definition, cannot stand at the level of ethics or pure rational justification. It is, as a matter of course, distinguished as antithetical to the freedom assumed for responsible ethical or moral action. Coercive influence on a subject invalidates a subject's moral action, such as when a prisoner signs a confession to avoid another beating. This sort of empirical force cannot, of course, be the kind of force that stands behind validity, indeed it is exactly empirical force that Habermas is out to replace with the force of the better argument. Can we properly distinguish force in such ways? If validity refers to a benevolent force of the lifeworld (a 'good' sociality) that deserves recognition, then one would seem to require a further standard to judge benevolent from malevolent forces—which is just what this specifically *rational* force is supposed to do.

We do, however, quite naturally acknowledge the force of an argument yet do not bristle with indignation at the thought of being coerced. Rather we respect it in the absence of a compelling counter-argument. This respect is immanently tied up with the sense of obligatory force we associate with the recognition of validity, which Habermas sees as the modern sublimation of the respect and reverence of the sacred. But the question remains how our respect for the reason of an argument can be separated from this sense of logical force. For if the force has meaning only in conjunction with respect for the binding power of validity, then it is not an independent manifestation of force but already an ethical construction. Perhaps the Habermasian use of the term *force* is a metaphorical description of some other sense that we intuit more than anything. But such a recourse could not finally satisfy the Habermasian position, for the appeal to intuition is a characteristic of the philosophy of consciousness and suggests a 'bad' metaphysics. The meaning of validity cannot be beyond theory itself for this would imply just the kind of problematic gesture Habermas criticizes in Horkheimer and Adorno. Yet it is equally clear that Habermas cannot tolerate a condition in which force and domination are primordial, in which violence is, as Horkheimer and Adorno recognized, at the core of reason and must be acknowledged as such in order for thought to move to a new level at which freedom and rational understanding might be more genuinely reconciled.[3]

It would appear that there is no a priori reason why the force of the better claim to validity takes priority over, say, the force of the better emotion or the more intense pleasure, except insofar as a life that respects orderly and open discussion among interested parties is preferable to a life in which, for example, people merely choose and follow charismatic, telegenic sets of leaders, content themselves with the substitute gratifications that consumerism provides, or remain observers of the spectacle and sheer contestation of politics. There may be quite clear political dangers in simply affirming emotional or pleasurable forces over the force of validity, which can easily raise the specter of aestheticized politics. But only a *judgment*, which is itself ungrounded but may nevertheless have a very strong and reasonable ethico-political content, can decide such matters. Perhaps few today would disagree that a reasonable democracy is preferable to consumerist stultification, passive spectator politics, or the dangers of aestheticization of politics (and arguably our politics has already become aestheticized to a large extent via its televisual mediation). I do not wish to imply that I disagree that a reasonable democracy is preferable for practical reasons to (at least) these alternatives. What I contest instead is the possibility of philosophically grounding such a form by reference to the force immanent to the presuppositions of communication itself. Whether the validity of *logos*, the rationality of order, or the social need to maintain a certain kind of life rather than others, etc., is preferable to the particular 'validity' of emotions or pleasures is itself a question of judgment. There can be no final philosophical justification for this force in the formal, universal, and unavoidably rational sense Habermas (and others such as K. O. Apel) would like recognized. No such justification, that is, without a certain suppressed circularity, as I will argue shortly.

However, it is precisely the aim of all foundational transcendental or quasi-transcendental arguments to give such an account of why this force *must* be recognized. Habermas's consistent response to all such objections as those I have just outlined is to invoke the performative logic of the pragmatics of speech that is grounded in his account of the rational form of language itself. As we will see, Habermas is drawn to quasi-transcendental conditions of possibility in order to justify the force attached to the theory of communicative action, for without such appeals Habermas's crucial distinction between power and validity could not be so sharply maintained. These conditions involve fundamental philosophical and ethical constraints that can, Habermas believes, only be denied by social actors at their own existential or political peril. This is the ethico-philosophical equivalent to the social-theoretic compulsion laid out in Habermas's theory that I contend, in the last analysis, mirrors the constraints and requirements of social functionality or socially useful coordination pressures. This is the point at which the present argument links up most closely with the one in Chapter 3, which focused on the functionality accorded to the 'economic sphere' at the expense of a more critical concept of capitalist society.

Habermas's theory of communication cannot be grounded universally in the ethical way he claims for again it is precisely this very functionality that is to be opened to reflection and criticism. In the remaining sections of the present chapter, I consider Habermas's critique of Adorno with special attention to the charge of performative contradiction while drawing on Adorno's own radical critique of reason in order to reveal more of the limits to Habermas's theory. My continued reflection on Adorno's position allows us to contrast Habermas's theory against the tradition of critical theory in a most fruitful way.

4.3. The Performative Contradiction in the Radical Critique of Domination

Habermas faults Horkheimer and Adorno for the way in which they develop the concept of reification drawn from Lukács by way of a transformation of the Weberian thesis of rationalization. The subjugation of value rationality to the dictates of purposive-rationality analyzed by Weber is taken up by Horkheimer and Adorno in their theory of the tendency toward total reification in the "administered world" (*verwaltete Welt*). Habermas contends that the expansion of the exchange relation via the commodification of culture—a process Horkheimer and Adorno are said to explain through the domination of instrumental reason—cannot be complete in any *total* way because *socially* integrative action does not occur simply according to the logic of purposive rationality. Commodification cannot *completely* dominate culture because social integration achieved through the mechanism of language, in the differentiated form it takes in modern society, relies on the special communicative achievement of reaching understanding and agreement. The philosophy of consciousness misses this crucial linguistically mediated moment. Hence, the thesis of the total bureaucratization or administration of society, which becomes merely a trivial methodological presupposition for contemporary systems functionalism but which was for Adorno "a vision of complete horror" (*TCAII*: 312), is inadequate.[4] It is inadequate because it holds that modern social integration (albeit a dehumanized, one-dimensional integration) in fact *can* be achieved through totalizing extensions of purposive rationality (which is precisely the threat), that actual reason has become wholly manifest as *Verstand* and has obliterated *Vernunft*.

Habermas remains unconvinced that critical theory can extract itself from the aporia of the radical critique of society derived from this critique of instrumental reason. During the period in which the program of critical theory was being developed, Habermas contends, the metaphysics of universal reconciliation in the "great" philosophical tradition that culminated in Hegel "perished together with metaphysical world views." At the same time, however, the historical moment of "realizing philosophy" in the revolutionary praxis posited by Marx's theory had also passed (*TCAI*: 377). Given Adorno's abandonment of the classic Marxist theory of revolution, a different relationship to praxis and to social movements is apparently required by his theory.

But a contradiction is thus said to arise between the two theoretical consequences of the radical critique of instrumental reason. On the one hand, there is the Hegelian-Marxist desire to realize as freedom some form of "reconciliation" (*Versöhnung*) between subjective reason and the alienated, hostile, objective whole, which Habermas contends animated Adorno's theoretical efforts throughout his life. This model of the reconciliation of universal and particular in Adorno, Habermas argues, is still

formulated along the axis of subject and object characteristic of the philosophy of consciousness that produced the critique of ideology. On the
other hand, there is the prohibitive impossibility of theoretically representing this reconciliation in the face of thoroughly reified subjective
consciousness and the alienated whole that is in totality "untrue." That
is, the normative ideal of reconciliation cannot receive *explicit* theoretical
expression for Adorno except in false metaphysical form. This alleged
"Weberian thorn" (*TCAI*: 378) in the side of critical theory prohibits any
recourse to a renewed metaphysics of reconciliation, while at the same
time, Habermas argues, Horkheimer and Adorno are unable to break
with the theoretical path dictated by their commitment to some kind of
philosophy of reconciliation.

Instead of looking to the intersubjective conditions of communication, which, according to Habermas, would have allowed a reconstruction of rationality free from the dictates of instrumentality, Adorno turned
to the communicative sphere of art and aesthetic production. Adorno
meets the demand for a practically interested theoretical critique with the
concept of *aesthetic mimesis*, which is to take the place of reason conceived
as critical enlightenment (I will explore the ethical and political content
of Adorno's view of art and aesthetic mimesis in more detail in section
5.3). The mystical and politically debilitating result, on Habermas's reading, is that the critical concept of aesthetic mimesis to which Adorno
appeals as the final hope for truth remains forever beyond *cognitive* grasp
and, arguably, without a relevant historical purchase on social movements. The experience of aesthetic mimesis in the production and reception of art escapes the domination of instrumental reason, but, for
Habermas, it can by definition have no practical relation to the world—
the world that needs to be changed—for that would transgress its principle. This aporetic situation is thus said to leave Adorno mute with
regards to the original transformative aims of critical theory that were to
be achieved via ideology critique.

The assumptions behind Horkheimer and Adorno's analysis of
modern society, Habermas argues, are located in their conception of social evolution developed under the title of the dialectic of enlightenment.
The major dialectical thesis of the book by that name—that "myth is
already enlightenment and enlightenment reverts to myth" (*DA*: 6/xvi)—
is developed in a critique of enlightenment thinking that reaches, according to Habermas, into the very core of the reason that establishes it (for
my discussion, see section 2.2). The argument in *Dialectic of Enlightenment*
is, on Habermas's reading, that "*from the very start* the process of enlightenment is the result of a drive to self-preservation that mutilates reason,

because it lays claim to it only in the form of a purposive-rational mastery of nature and instinct—precisely as instrumental reason" (*PDM*: 111). Institutionalized domination is coupled with the technical mastery of nature and secures the independence of the rationality of domination from the self-reflection of the species that has reached pathological levels. For Habermas, Adorno describes a "self-assertion gone wild" (1983d: 101).

Following this preoccupation with self-preservation, Habermas contends, Horkheimer and Adorno continue to rely on the twin 'models' of the epistemological subject associated with the philosophy of consciousness—representation and action. This is demonstrated, among other things, by the way in which rationalization is conceived overwhelmingly as increasing instrumentalization. With the philosophical destruction of objective reason and the erosion and replacement of metaphysical-religious worldviews, knowing and acting for an end are transformed into functions in order to "reproduce a 'life.' This 'life' is characterized by the knowing and acting subject's devotion to a blind, self-directed, intransitive self-preservation that is his only 'end'" (*TCA I*: 388). According to Habermas, Horkheimer and Adorno thus equate subjective reason with instrumental rationality, which is then generalized via a parallel relation between society's relation to nature and the individual's relation to objects. The reproduction of society is achieved through the societal subject's instrumental relation with external nature: the "structure of exploiting an objectivated nature that is placed at our disposal repeats itself within society, both in interpersonal relations marked by the suppression of social classes and in intrapsychic relations marked by the repression of our instinctual nature" (*TCA I*: 389).

One of the most important theoretical difficulties brought forth by allegedly remaining within the dual relation of the subject's objectification is, on the Habermasian reading, that Horkheimer and Adorno cannot explicitly say how social subjects reproduce the social bond or even what a worthy conception of sociality might be. That is, the destruction of forms of life under instrumentalization is wholly one-sided from the perspective of the critique of instrumental reason. It is 'subjective' in a radical way since the viewpoint of the perceived and manipulated object can receive no expression: thus Horkheimer and Adorno's "appeal to social solidarity can merely indicate *that* the instrumentalization of society and its members destroys something; but it cannot say explicitly *wherein* this destruction consists" (*TCA I*: 389). Adorno cannot say exactly *what* has actually been repressed except, on Habermas's view, that it is some essential element of subjective and/or objective nature. The theory of communicative action, Habermas argues, is hence superior to the critique of instrumental reason on this point since it enables an explicit and immanent account of this solidarity and the ways in which it is destroyed. As we saw in Chapter 3, what is lost, or rather instrumentally transformed in administrative and capitalist domination, are the communicatively achieved identities, solidarities, meanings, and freedoms that compose the lifeworld resources of society and its communicative subjects. Reification is understood as a systemic colonization of these lifeworld spheres for the purposes and needs of systems functions. Communicative action thus identifies the immanent binding/bonding effect of speech acts as the key action foundation of social coordination and solidarity, which also gets Habermas beyond what he sees as the one-sided accounts characteristic of the philosophy of consciousness.

Habermas's effort here is consistent with modern critical traditions that have recognized the importance of theorizing an alternative relation to the other and to otherness distinct from the cognitive-instrumental. To recall our discussion from section 3.1, this is a crucial aspect of Habermas's stress on the uniqueness of intersubjectivity and the communicative relation since what is generated is a knowledge of ourselves that he distinguishes starkly from a knowledge of nature or objects in the world.

Habermas's distinction between communicative and purposive-rational action thus also allows him to fault the related psychological model that Horkheimer and Adorno employ. The Freudian thesis of repression is assumed by Horkheimer and Adorno to operate via the internalization of the social domination of nature. But the Habermasian contention is that social domination of external nature must be distinguished in form from the psychic domination of internal nature. The latter is, by contrast, a matter of intersubjective, social relations of communicative learning rather than the domination characterizing subject-object relations since the individual internalizes not only authority but a variety of social roles constituted by interpretive efforts that require communicative relations with others. The acquisition of these social roles thus relies on achievements of communicative interaction through linguistic mediations that produce consensually achieved 'domination' at a different level from the domination of nature. Hence Honneth contends that "Adorno and Horkheimer are so strongly fixated on the model of the instrumental control of nature, which is the real interest of their philosophy of history, that they also want to conceive the manner of functioning of intra-social domination according to this model" (Honneth, 1991: 52; see also 1995b).

However, as I argued in Chapter 2, critical theory recognizes an indelible natural element in human society and history that cannot be abstracted out for the purposes of isolating an ahistorical socialness. But it is not that social functionality is thereby elevated to a totalizing category that can then no longer be distinguished from an amorphous concept of domination. Distinctions can still be made between functional or instrumental relations and those that invite understanding, love, or that generate true rather than false happiness, as we will see with more clarity in Chapter 5. However, the possibilities of such non-functional or non-instrumental relations are immanently *political* possibilities that cannot actually coexist with the current overwhelming and expansive domination of nature and the domination of the vast majority of people. A system that permits understanding and agreement among people while extending reification in a totalizing manner partly as a condition of *producing* that understanding and agreement, a system that obliterates dialectical thinking under identity thinking and thereby violently closes off access to the nonidentical basis of identities, cannot be said to generate true or genuine understanding or agreement. There is a contradiction at the core of any such notion of consensus that does not recognize that the suppression of the non-identical is a partner to the political repression of class society, especially, as well as the multiple oppressions of race, gender, sexuality, and age that also attend social domination.

For critical theory, the effort of understanding others and the freedom of each to reach agreements with one another, which would as a whole constitute a utopian vision and project a powerful socially bonding force, is possible only if none are first damaged and mutilated by the social domination that is bound up with the domination of objects in the world. The monadic subject is a product of domination, discipline, and reification—self-domination as well as social discipline under conditions of multiple social dominations—and these constitutive relations cannot be bracketed out for the purposes of entering political discourse and reaching consensuses. They are instead centrally relevant to the very possibility of such free intercourse and sociability between human beings (as well as for the rather different communicative possibilities between human beings and their others among the non-human world).

Likewise in Chapter 3 I contended that neat separations of the levels of lifeworld and system that are required in order to theorize communicative as distinct from purposive actions must in turn deny that there is a constitutive relation between the interaction of quasi-natural entities such as the commodity and the social interaction of communicative human beings. It is not that those such as Horkheimer and Adorno fail to recognize the level Habermas wants to single out with the concept of intersubjectivity, but that they account for social interaction in critical and political ways that demand the reconciliation of society or civilization (Kultur) with the life of nature, a nature that is already damaged, deformed, and repressed within the social forms themselves. For Horkheimer and Adorno, the domination of nature and the social class forms representing it are always already entwined such that the projection of freedom—which Habermas wants to identify solely as the condition of rational deliberation and discourse oriented to achieving agreement—requires liberation from class society at the same time as it demands a new, non-dominative human relationship with nature. This theorizes a deeper meaning to the reconciliation of culture with nature that simply cannot be recognized by Habermas, hence his frustration with Horkheimer and Adorno's unwillingness to name the sociality of communicative freedom explicitly. Habermas's paradigm shift that identifies the essential socialness of society distinct from the social relations with and within nature is again revealed not as a paradigmatic shift within the tradition of Frankfurt school critical theory but rather amounts to the affirmation of a completely new set of philosophical premises.

To recall our discussion in Chapter 2, ideology critique is not supposed to represent a competing theory but rather a reflexive method for exposing the untruth in theory and in ideas that are produced through enlightenment. In showing how a suspected theory does not live up to its claims, ideology critique holds out the possibility of overcoming the myth of the false conception by ushering in an enlightened knowledge of the phenomena. The dialectical aim is not simply to replace but to preserve and transcend the progressive, enlightening aspects of, for example, bourgeois philosophy, without the myth, which thereby allows the fulfillment of its hopes. This 'good' dialectic of reason, aims (via praxis) to produce a truth, a cognitive vision, through which the individual may relate to society under conditions of substantial transparency. Once the productive bases of class domination in capitalism have been abolished, reification, the fetishism of commodities, and class ideologies will presumably fall away under the conditions of liberation. Adorno, like poststructuralism and post-Marxism, rejects the theoretical confidence and ethical hope evident in this 'good' dialectic, for such transparency, stable presence, and perpetual peace are, finally, impossible given the indelible entwinement of reason and reification. The dark and apparently irresolvable problem, according to Habermas, is that Horkheimer and Adorno take an additional radical step by criticizing the bourgeois reason of modern society itself as unreason. They thereby call into question the very basis of theory production itself and the possibility of progressive enlightenment.

Hence the progressivism attached to the fulfillment model of ideology critique is implicitly denied by Horkheimer and Adorno, which is one of the sources of their alleged pessimism. Once society becomes totally rationalized, reason becomes a parody of its former self, and as a consequence its substance cannot be fulfilled by immanent critique. Notwithstanding this, Horkheimer and Adorno maintain that their task is in fact progressive—they hope not for the conservation of what has been lost of the past, but instead for the "redemption of the hopes of the past" (*DA*: 5/xv). Their rejection of (bourgeois) reason is an attempt to face up to and get beyond the historical *failures* of this reason by recognizing its theoretical *and* practical-political limits. But Habermas contends that, without the paradigm shift he has achieved, the only solutions to be derived from Horkheimer and Adorno's critique of the historical failures of reason are aporetical and self-defeating.

The paradoxical result of calling into question the very basis of theory production, according to Habermas, is that "ideology critique *itself* comes under the suspicion of not producing any more truths," and Horkheimer and Adorno are forced to render critique "independent even in relation to its own foundations." Since ideology critique, as a reflexive method, found the rational standards of its own criticism already given in that which it criticized and simply took ideology "at its word" (*PDM*: 116), the critical action of undermining the reason inherent in the thinking of ideals and of bourgeois theory leaves no 'theoretical' reference for critique. The most important consequence of this, according to Habermas, is that the concept of reason thus becomes "blurred" when the distinction between power and validity in reason is erased (for Habermas, ultimately due the influence of Nietzsche). This effacement of reason undermines the very possibility and logical existence of critical theory.

In *Negative Dialectics*, Habermas argues, the paradox of the aporias of critical theory is played out via the "performative contradiction" of holding onto the aim of critical unmasking—or at least producing its effect—while simultaneously declaring critical reason to be dead (*PDM*: 119). The radical critique of reason is necessarily performative contradiction. Habermas uses this analysis to level the charge of incoherence at the critiques of modern rationalization and reason that are found, on the one hand, in Adorno in the tradition of Frankfurt critical theory, and on the other, in more recent deconstructionist and poststructuralist positions.

As Habermas presents it, Adorno is required to keep circling within the performative contradiction produced by the negative dialectic in the hope that the paradox will open upon a "magically invoked" mindfulness of nature in the subject (*PDM*: 117–18). This experience will then disclose a (possible) path to a reconciled reality. For Habermas, the sincere *self-consciousness* of this contradictory performance marks Adorno's essential difference from other contemporary post-Nietzschean radical critics of reason and language because the latter nevertheless deny the binding nature of their performative contradiction.[5] This alleged Nietzschean destruction of reflection in the collapse of power and validity has drawn essentially the same charge of irrationalism from Habermas since the 1960s. The disavowal of reason can in the end be suppressed by those who hold to it only by some kind of mantra: "The ironic contradiction of a self-denial of reflection, however, is so stubborn that it cannot be dissolved by arguments but only appeased by invocations" (*KHI*: 299). Yet while Adorno did not follow Nietzsche in this final step, he remained far too influenced by the former, according to Habermas. For the practice of the negative dialectic, which allegedly cannot be *theory* at the same time that it is performative contradiction, is, in its blindness to the rational potentials in communicative action, also "like an incantation" (*PDM*: 128). Habermas can see only a helpless circling in the operation of the negative dialectic, a non-systematic "exercise" or "drill" (*TCAI*: 385).[6] For the special, non-dominative capacity of *mimesis*, which is somehow *before* reason (as it must be, on Habermas's reading, because he interprets Adorno's thesis of totalizing rational domination literally) and to which Adorno appeals as the basis for a reconciled society, is inherently incapable of being clarified—which means it cannot be *theorized* (*TCAI*: 382).

The denouncement of reason and enlightenment for 'becoming totalitarian' is paradoxical from the Habermasian perspective because it proceeds only by way of the 'tools' of that very self-same reason. For Habermas, the critique of instrumental reason is a totalizing critique of reification and commodification in which "the instrumental reason of a purposive-rationality puffed up into a social totality" overwhelms and buries "everything once meant by reason (*Vernunft*) under its debris" (*PDM*: 118, 68–69). The radical critic, like the radical skeptic, would seem to be condemned to a quietism since every positive specification would itself be suspect (McCarthy, 1978: 108). The charge of performative contradiction is leveled at Adorno since one allegedly cannot criticize reason itself without having already some notion of reason that escapes the totalizing instrumentality. Yet it is strange to refer to Adorno's use of the tools of critical reason because critique is anything but an activity of tool-using, and Adorno adamantly resists and challenges all attempts to instrumentalize theory.[7] Instead, he recasts theory as a form of praxis—

"the morality of thinking" as Rose (1978: 148) describes it. What this identifies is the *performative* or *aesthetic* aspects of thinking with which self-reflection (critical theory) is always involved. This orientation, one might suggest, keeps faith with the old Marxist notion of philosophy becoming practical in a rather more substantive way than is implied by the Habermasian call for the political institutionalization of the norms of free and open discourse. But leaving this issue aside for now, let us reconsider Adorno's formulation of the theory of contradiction as a way of assessing Habermas's critique.

4.3.3. Adorno's Negative Dialectic: A Recapitulation

Adorno's conception of genuine critique as a negative dialectic is arrived at through the critique of identity thinking, which we introduced in Chapter 2. The term *identity thinking* stands for any view that equates the concept with the concept's subject-matter (*Sache*). This is the classificatory consciousness of subsuming the particular under the universal, of grasping the fact of immediacy independent of what might be occurring in and through the mediation of conceptual thought. The formalism of mathematics expresses this kind of thinking most abstractly, but it reaches through science all the way down to the positivistic ideology of the everyday. Cognition believes through its own concept that it can subject existence to itself and thereby achieve control over it for itself, but the more it does this the more it becomes blind to the process by which this existence is mediated for the enlightening consciousness itself. Such cognition or knowledge more and more becomes blindly resigned to the way things are or seem, their identity in the immediate, which obscures the historicity of current social arrangements and their systems of domination under which this knowledge is produced. The absence of a historical dimension to practical acts of thought severely limits the thought that social arrangements could be radically different than they are.

But more than this, the alien and hostile appearance of things and others—the non-identical 'other' of subjectivity—is domesticated for identifying thought. This is not simply for the sake of grasping the alien, the other, but is necessary if the *subject* is to have control over *itself*. Instrumental reason serves to discipline the self through the specific rational control required for the domination of its other. The advance of an instrumental reason that serves the self-preservation of the subject consequently treats otherness and non-identity as that which can be made rational and identical, and thereby like itself. In the process by which all things are subjugated to subjective, identifying reason, the sacrifice of subjectivity for the sake of subjectivity (class society) becomes the dominant social logic and men and women pay for their increased power by increased psychic and social repression (see section 2.2).

If assimilation proves impossible (under the given existing conditions), then this material remains alien, hostile, and irrational, which for the identifying consciousness means that it must thereby be excluded from social life, even destroyed or repressed into non-existence.

Western (European) imperialism, for example, was successful not simply through superior technologies of war and administration, though these were clearly important, but rather through its ability to assimilate alien identities and cultures into subjugated positions within its own system of self-discipline and domination. The missionary or millennialist motivation of Christianity was a key ideological partner to European imperialism, since its central aim was to convert the pagan peoples of the world in order to prepare the world for Christ's Second Coming. Christianity's totalizing ideology (which is only one aspect of the Christian religion, it should also be noted) later matched European global political ambitions and the emergent need of imperialist capitalism to assimilate more of the world within specifically capitalist social relations in order to reproduce accumulation on a world scale.

In the new phase of globalization in which we currently exist, the vast areas of social life in colonized societies that were left largely outside the imperialist system—areas that served the material reproduction of the new labor force, for example, or provided 'distraction' such as festivals—have now become sources for further system expansion. This time, however, following the struggles of decolonization during the twentieth century, there is little opportunity but also little need for the direct political domination that guaranteed earlier compliance to imperialist demands. Discipline is still nevertheless required by multinational capitalist interests, but it tends to be exercised indirectly through the NGO organizations associated with international finance capital and trade organizations such as the IMF and the World Bank. International agreements and associations such as GATT, NAFTA, the EU, and the planned MAI facilitate the required disciplinary and regulatory regimes at the level of international political economy (see, for example, Gill and Law, 1988).

At the level of the culture industries, the commodification of difference, rather than the direct assimilation of the other to a Western (Christian) identity, now allows for the safe encounter of the alien and the different via the consumption of goods and 'experience.' Today, tourism, and more recently, eco-tourism, constitute the new form of imperialism as formerly colonized countries on the periphery gear themselves more and more to catering to the leisure and adventure needs of vast numbers of people in the centers. Nature and cultures alike are commodified for the cultural consumption of the privileged; the otherness of nature and the alienness of foreign cultures are once more rendered unthreatening to the integrity of the self-identifying subject. They may thus be encountered freely without the risk that the non-identical basis of Western subjectivity—its historical domination of all that is other to it—will present itself to the consuming subjects.

Identity thinking is never in itself merely or purely thought since all thinking entails a determinate relation to its social context and therefore implies something more than its own thought content. It is not merely that facts and values cannot (or should not) be separated as they are absolutely in the positivist view. Identity thinking always expresses a particular, historical interest in domination that benefits the status quo ruling class. But the domination over inner and outer nature that establishes subjective reason also establishes the identity of concept and thing (*Sache*), for without such identity the discipline necessary for subjectivity itself could not exist. For Adorno, however, subjective reason and identity thinking thus arise with and are coextensive with the very hominization of human beings. While Habermas understands this argument of *Dialectic of Enlightenment* as an *ontological* claim, it is instead a *historical* one. Horkheimer and Adorno do not, as Habermas claims, "anchor the mechanism that produces the reification of consciousness in the anthropological foundations of the history of the species, in the form of *existence* of a species that has to reproduce itself through labor" (*TCAI*: 379, emphasis added). Such an ontological claim may very well produce a despair that finds itself in aporias and dead ends as Habermas believes. Horkheimer and Adorno *do* want to claim that the domination of identity thinking and subjectivity (which is not the same as reification) historically predate capitalism and class society, and that such domination has been a constant characteristic of civilization in varying strengths. The history of this domination can be traced in principle from the beginnings of the human species to the present. But this does not mean domination cannot be resisted effectively or even abolished in its extravagant forms and considerably reduced to socially necessary and sufficient levels. Under the conditions of primitive human existence domination is at a relatively low level (but it is still present). With the appearance of class society social domination increases markedly. Domination will thus not completely disappear in a post-capitalist classless society, but the level and experience of such domination would be considerably less than that under capitalist society. The role of utopian thought is to envision the kind of social relations that would be required so that a reduction in domination is possible. The critical theory analyzes the historical impediments to such a development under current conditions. Thus the *historical* critique of subjective reason criticizes the present with an eye to its own future, its present *possibilities* for reducing domination.

The origin of specifically *class* domination, for Adorno, lies in the separation of intellectual (*geistige*) and manual (*körperliche*) labor and the subjugation of the latter to the former:

> Ever since intellectual and manual labor were separated in the sign of the domination of *Geist* and the justification of privilege, *Geist*, thus separated, had to vindicate each claim to domination with the exaggeration of a bad conscience, which it derives from the thesis that it is First and originary, and it must strain to forget from where its claim originated, unless this claim should lapse (*ND*: 179/177).

With the advent of the capitalist mode of production and the triumph of the capitalist principle of exchange, identity logic achieves a new independence in a new form of totalized identity:

> The exchange principle, the reduction of human labor to the abstract universal concept of average working hours, is originally akin to the principle of identity. The principle of identity has its social model in exchange, and it would not exist without it; through exchange non-identical individuals and performances become commensurable, identical. The spread of the principle imposes on the whole world an obligation to become identical, to become total (ND: 149/146).

To become self-identical is to become total, a self sealed off from its non-identical history and thus from its ability to recognize itself in the world and in others.

Following Hegel and Marx, Adorno conceives of the actual constitution of the individual—of the knowing and acting subject—as, to its core, a product of society; and this modern, bourgeois society is antagonistic and conflictual, at odds with itself, in *contradiction*. Class domination ensures that contradiction and antagonism rend the social whole. Unlike Hegel, however, Adorno is not willing to resolve these contradictions and antagonisms in a dialectical movement of the Concept, for the Absolute cannot be arrived at *at all*. Where Hegel refers to *Geist* Adorno sees society; but this society, because it is *class* society governed by the principles of exchange and domination and characterized by identity thinking, is a whole that is fundamentally *un*true, and as such does not have the reason aspired to by its concept. It follows that it is this untruth that actually constitutes the subjects who make it up; their immediate experience is the experience of the reified, antagonistic whole because they themselves are mediated by its functioning.

At the same time, however, society is not to be hypostatized—the individual as the mere agent of his or her function in the social process is the irrational perspective of the system itself and not Adorno's. Individuality, on the other hand, is already shot through with alienation, and this hypostatizes both individual as subject and the social object that confronts it. But *mediation* by the individual is crucial here since individuals *reproduce* their alienation; the individual is not merely an empty conduit in a systemic functionality, but a thinking, feeling, sensuous, suffering, active thing. The critique of the individual expresses the critique of social relations, and vice versa. "Knowledge [*Erkenntnis*] has command of no other totality than that of the antagonistic whole, and it is only by virtue of contradiction that knowledge of this totality can be attained at all" (Adorno, 1972d: 51). What this calls into question—and this is the crucial point—is the whole sociological/philosophical distinction between genesis and production on the one hand, and the social/natural object that is produced or conceived, on the other. Dialectical thinking cannot admit of objectivism any more than it can of subjectivism. But it is also why Habermasian objections to Adorno that hold him to a standard of theory that requires strict consistency or clear formulation miss the point. They beg the questions of history and contradiction themselves.

Thus what is *true*, in the sense of being at peace, unagitated, able to be known without contradiction and therefore self-identical, without movement and change, solid and sure, perfectly present, is only the consciousness that such knowledge is beyond our reach in contemporary society and in all past societies. "Philosophy is not expoundable," Adorno writes, "Truth is undecided and fragile by dint of its transitory substance" (*ND*: 44–45/33–4). The becoming of things occurs only by virtue of society, but knowledge of *this* society cannot yield a positive reconciliation of the becoming for subjective reason. The 'aporia' for a critical practice is said to lie in the conception of negative dialectic as "the ontology of the false condition" (*ND*: 22/11). This conception however, brings forth not an ontology at all but an ethical mode of relating to others dependent on the consciousness of non-identity.

The notion of aporia here is important for Adorno and for Habermas's criticism of the former. From the ancient Greek, *aporia* means difficulty or perplexity, coming from *aporos*, which means impassable or difficult—literally no path. For Adorno, an aporia must be pursued dialectically—not necessarily in order to resolve it, but to bring forth an awareness of *why* it presents its difficulty, perplexity, or impassability. This perspective escapes Habermas who regards as aporetic Adorno's own awareness of such contradictions, and then locates the source of these aporias in the inadequacies and limits of the latter's very thought. For Habermas, an aporia is something that always can and *should* be avoided or resolved.

All that is permitted in the practice of negative dialectic is the "cognition of the process stored in the object" (*ND*: 165–66/163). That which Adorno conceives by the name "constellation" or "model" is the attempt to highlight the aspects of the object suppressed, neglected, or discarded by the concept through the continual construction of relations between identifying cognition and its object. No concept is completely adequate and the quest for a complete system of knowledge self-defeating. But constellations of concepts that reveal relations and processes keep thought alive by showing what is false in its own cognition (and in the world that is cognized). This allows the critic to become aware of what is actually true in the thought—that negation must continue to negate the unmediated appearance of conceptual thought for the sake of its concept. Constellations thus provide "order without system" (Phelan, 1993: 604).

But the idea of truth, for Adorno, "cannot be split off from that of a true society. Only such a society would be free from contradiction and lack of contradiction" (1976: 27). Adorno thus remains committed to a notion of the rational society that might be realized in the future. To hold out hope for truth is to hold out hope for a genuinely new society without (unnecessary) domination and hence contradiction (which can still be distinguished from non-dominating conflict, competition, or struggle). Just how this new society might be achieved, Adorno does not say, but in the next chapter I will suggest a promising avenue that can be pursued by following Adorno's approach to the aesthetic. But the philosophical point of truth (in the senses of an important idea as well as that of direction) remains valid for Adorno in the same way in which the 'philosophy' at the opening of *Negative Dialectics* lives on because its moment of realization was missed (15/3). Adorno still struggled with the apparently incompatible commitment to non-domination in thought, a mindfulness of the incompleteness, partiality, inadequacy, and dangers of the concept, as well as the hope for a future rational society. Such a society would be "free from contradiction" in the sense that social power would no longer exclude and dominate in private or behind people's backs while publicly celebrating freedom. But it would also be "free" from "lack of contradiction" at the level of cognitive and practical activity. This would allow a consciousness of the contingency and ambiguity of being while eliciting an engagement with the other and with otherness that does not seek to assimilate or suppress.

The "determinate negation of each immediacy" (*DA:* 33/27), the genuine task of cognition, is non-identical thinking—dialectical thinking that remains negative because, for Adorno, there can never be a cognitive adequacy of concept and thing. The negation of identity is more than a critique of knowledge, it is a critique of the psychic and social relations of domination that produce this kind of knowledge, which are intertwined with the class divisions and dominating antagonisms in modern society. (All members of society experience and participate in these relations of domination, but, of course, the forms and actuality of domination differ significantly, as do the capacities of ameliorating and compensating for their effects.) Hence, although truth itself must be freed from its expression as identification, it is not thereby given up but transformed. Adorno's notion of the true society finds its truth in the conflict and tragedy of nonidentity, a truth that can and must be respected by something that resembles an ethics. This is what is to be 'found' in the negative. The problem is that such truth almost always appears today as though it was in league with the undisciplined, chaotic other of reason and hence is feared and misunderstood, raising the specters of relativism, violence, or totalitarianism.

Negative thinking is immanently opposed to the coercive power that must accompany identity thinking because it seeks an awareness and understanding of that which is heteronomous to it. It does not suppress the heteronomous by claiming identity with its object, that is, as a self-identical thing just like oneself. The idea of this awareness is what is so irksome to the Habermasian position: the negative dialectic claims a sympathy with the objective element that is suppressed in conceptual thinking, but it must be prohibited from the attempt to 'conceptualize' it for fear of repeating the 'dominating principle' of equating concept and thing. From Habermas's perspective, Adorno is merely creating a new myth in such a formulation—the myth that a suppressed nature can return with a consciousness that negates its own dominating subjectivity consistently enough.

But the non-conceptual awareness of what is suppressed is not to be construed *merely* as some kind of anti-representation, a taboo, as with the religious *Bilderverbot*. Rather, it follows from the dialectical principle of non-identity (which is the truth of the taboo). The awareness that there is always something else, something not captured and represented by the concept or in the conceptual, something that is denied by the identifying action of the concept, is also an awareness of the *social* as well as the 'uncanny' (*unheimlich*) in the concept. This socialness is not just content to be unmasked, but process; it refers to whole sets of historical relations that literally cannot be conceived in a completely systematic way. Domination is also bound up with these relations.

However, Adorno did think that what is beyond the concept can be approached indirectly, and this is what he meant to achieve with the use of constellations. He hoped this would lead to a non-dominating experience of subjective and objective nature. Adorno's aspiration "to get beyond the concept" "by way of the concept" (*ND*: 28/15)—his performative contradiction—is a call for reason to loosen its hold on the object and its need for identity. What must be realized is that the resources of the concept can be exhausted *without* the expectation of achieving identity and that it is this that should underlie our relations with others.

This reflective effort is allied with the kind of perception involved in the aesthetic experience of the reception of art. Hence Adorno's appeal to aesthetic mimesis is an appeal to a form of judgment that cognizes without concepts but aims at that which concepts would like to achieve. As Bernstein (1989: 55) has argued, at the core of Adorno's aesthetics is a conception of art's form of cognition and praxis: "Art seeks cognition: to be really true and really purposive, but it is only semblance. Art's semblance is a semblance of the overcoming of the differentiation of reason into the isolated spheres of truth, normative rightness and beauty. Art practices are a model for an alternative form of praxis, and art products are images of things as they could be for an objective reason, a historical reason." The appeal to aesthetic mimesis cannot be the appeal to a rational Enlightenment reason, but it still denotes an appeal to *sense*, to the effort of *making sense* of the human condition. Adorno is still quite arguably committed to *something like* the enlightening end of liberation, which relies on critical knowledge, but like Marx he believes that the aesthetic cannot be abstracted from the center of this process.

In stark contrast to Adorno, Habermas's reformulation of an ethics of *discourse*, in which the conceptual, as propositional knowledge, forms only an element rather than a totality, claims to make the moral present *separate from* the dominating act of cognition. If successful, this would constitute an improvement on Adorno's concept of a non-conceptual whole—the other of subjective conceptuality that is suppressed by subjective reason in the activity of its own subjective life—because communicative reason could then *explicitly* conceive of instrumentality from a perspective other than that of instrumentality itself. Thus Habermas claims to discover "that there is already a mimetic moment in everyday practices of communication, and not merely in art" (Habermas, 1986a: 156). This is the basis on which he believes he has got beyond Adorno's performative contradiction.

4.3.4. Beyond the Subject of Critique

But Habermas's move to the theory of communicative action skirts around rather than meets squarely Adorno's requirement of a non-dominating form of cognition. Since he focuses on the development of an alternative conception of truth to one acceptable to Adorno, Habermas sets aside the most powerful of Adorno's insights into the problem of truth and seeks again to find a grounding of sorts for reason. Habermas's approach is more subtle than many neo-Kantian attempts, however, since he does not make a strong transcendental argument. Yet he does claim that the presuppositions of speech action imply a 'quasi-transcendental' necessity. This claim is central to any sense of the performative contradiction.

A further reason for Habermas not claiming a strong transcendental status for the discourse ethic nor for the theory of communicative action is that it would contradict the very theory of discourse he puts forward that relies on *claims* to truth and validity. In Habermas's words, philosophy should take the role of "stand-in and interpreter" on behalf of the lifeworld and not that imperialistic enlightenment role of an "arbiter" of culture (see *MCCA*: 1–20). Habermas regards the theory of communicative action as itself a kind of giant set of truth claims to be established through the rational discursive method at its core; the theory must ultimately find its truth in a free and open discourse that aims at consensus through testing truth-claims. This is the social-scientific research program of the self-reflexive theory of communicative action and a creditable achievement of a critical theory. But Habermas is pragmatic and non-transcendental when he needs to be and transcendental likewise when he needs to be.

For if the question is asked, why, then, should we engage in this discourse with proponents of the theory of communicative action, the Habermasian answer is that one must share a commitment to enlightening, truth-pursuing critique. This is a principle of *argument* itself. For the Habermasian, one cannot *argue* unless one is willing to argue *sincerely*; willingness to be truthful and the pursuit of truth presuppose one another.

This, however, forms its own circle around the idea of truth-content. The answer to the question why argue?, is that argument, truth, and freedom are immanently related and that especially modern life is constituted on the basis of the truth-claim. This idea of the truth-claim is itself understood to be a presupposition of language-in-use, for Habermas believes that our utterances are always oriented toward telling and seeking the truth. He wants us to be sincere and honest in public, show ourselves to others openly and without reservation.

This is because he believes that social interaction and reproduction depend on the claim to truth, the widespread pursuit of valid knowledge, for unless truth-claims are raised and truth is pursued, speech capable of possessing meaning and coordinating action would be impossible. As we saw, Habermas relies on Dummett's truth-conditional semantics here: "It is part of understanding a sentence that we are capable of recognizing grounds through which the claim that its truth conditions are satisfied could be redeemed" (*TCAI*: 317). A communicating subject cannot opt out of this process without risking mental dysfunction since one would cut oneself off from the very processes by which the self is reproduced. He or she who abandons speech abandons human society.

Habermas can only maintain his distinctions between the practical, the propositional, and the authentic, which are then united through the transcendental-pragmatic truth-claim, if the truth of the transcendental-pragmatic truth-claim cannot itself be disputed. But this truth does in fact relate to a claim, the claim to have identified the universal foundation of society in the social necessity of seeking truth (and in its corollary, the self-destructive contradiction of suppressing truth-seeking). The claim that seeking truth is socially necessary may be granted, but using it as a quasi-transcendental justification for reestablishing reason independent of its historical expression is illegitimate. Habermas is here conflating what Adorno took pains to distinguish, namely, the historical notion of rationalized society, which the latter conceived as an 'untrue' whole, and the individual who lives its (contradictory) social being as a specific rational life.

For Habermas, truth-seeking—the keystone of communicative rationality—is rational because it is social (it requires interaction) and vice versa. But, besides the problem of an unacknowledged or underemphasized circularity, this seems to invoke an overly intellectualized conception of social action as the pursuit of truth at the level of discursive interaction. The *telos* of society as an evolution of truth-claiming becomes the identity of modern society. The concept of communicative rationality entails, programmatically, that what is cognitively binding ought to be socially bonding. One of the important things Habermas's conception misses is the logic of the dialectical distinction and relation between the levels of individual communicative expression and the demands of a 'universally' coordinating social rationality, both with their claims (or demands) of truth.

In a discussion of relativism, Adorno gives us an indication of the weakness of Habermas's appeal to the performative logic of speech in order to declare the radical critique of reason contradictory: "The popular argument . . . that relativism presupposes at least one absolute—namely, its own validity—and thus contradicts itself, is paltry. It confuses the general negation of a principle with the negation's own installation as an affirmation, regardless of the specific differences in the status or role of both" (*ND*: 46/35–36). Negation cannot assert itself as a 'principle.' Philosophical critique, for Adorno, is unrelentingly negative and refuses to reconcile itself to any kind of positive, for that would merely produce a new delusion. To do so is actually to miscarry the thought-process since the dynamic aspect of thought lies in its power to explode the illusion of identity: "Non-identity is the secret *telos* of identification, that which is to be rescued in it; the mistake of traditional theory is that it holds identity as its goal" (*ND*: 152/149). Hence the misperception of the Habermasian critique that faults Adorno for a totalizing critique that nevertheless relies on the 'tools' of that same reason. Critique is purposive-rational because it uses concepts (since one cannot *think* without concepts), but it is also more than this because it is *aware* that the very instrumental nature of concepts is false and limited. Yet the critic nevertheless thinks and criticizes. Consequently, to hold out an *awareness* of non-identity as a crucial goal of critical thinking is actually to be truer to the "concept's longing to become identical with the thing" (*ND*: 152/149). Adorno's dialectical reflection is thus not a totalizing self-negation of the thinking subject because the subject becomes aware of what is 'true' in thinking (that the aim of thinking is to cultivate a care for non-identity) and what is 'false' (that one can or should remain satisfied with identity or identifying action itself). While it is still the power of conceptual thinking that opens this critical possibility, it cannot be completed by concepts alone.

To go as far as to recognize the extent of the determinations of subjectivity produced by the untrue social totality is to recognize how far all are implicated in their own domination by such determinations. "The identifying principle of the subject is itself the internalized principle of society" (*ND*: 239/241). We develop our reason in contemporary society only by virtue of our participation within the rational structure of society as a whole, and this society is constituted on an essentially contradictory principle. But neither society nor individual exist without each other: society is both non-identical to its members (a different logical type) and no more than the individuals who *make* it up (it is not an object but a set of relations actively reproduced). One must make the distinction between, on the one hand, the level of the social totality with its principle that constitutes the individual, and on the other, the level of the subjective principle of thought that expresses the social principle in particular form but which is hence still non-identical to the individual. Subjective reason is thus already intersubjective reason for Adorno. This is one reason why Habermas's attempt to prioritize the latter form constitutes no real advance over the dialectical conception of subjectivity without a parallel concern for non-identity, which is one of the crucial orientations that Adorno recognized and located at the heart of his critical theory.

In dialectical fashion, the thoughts of the individual are, and are not, his or her own. For Adorno, the totalizing capacity of late capitalist society is such that no sphere is left unaffected, and the dialectical consciousness of the individual will always be 'damaged' by this. Yet he did not give up hope, and the possibility of resistance is always preserved.[8] While Adorno may be performatively self-contradicting himself by engaging in the total critique of instrumental reason, he is also being entirely and scrupulously consistent with the dialectical principle of non-identical subjectivity.

It is this principle that Habermas must implicitly reject in order to reformulate a notion of autonomous intersubjective subjectivity that stands behind the theory of communicative rationality. In contrast to Adorno, Habermas implies a rather strong sense of subjectivity as a formal condition of communication, which undermines the transformative claims of his linguistic turn. Dallmayr's recognition of the ambivalence in Habermas's conception of communication suggests just this. On the one hand, modern communicating subjects cannot reach beyond the horizon of their lifeworld that holds all possible 'themes' for their speech-acts (communication with nature, for example, is barred as regression to the mythic), thus language presents a *boundary*; on the other hand, rational language is a *medium* of communication, *used* by subjects to attain goals and to reach understanding. Indeed, argumentation is used to create and maintain social solidarity. For Dallmayr, "(t)he stress on coordinating functions—intimately associated with rationalization processes—is bound to cast doubt on Habermas's linguistic turn, by revealing language either as a usable means or else as a property or 'competence' of individual speakers (a construal not radically at odds with the traditional philosophy of consciousness)" (1984a: 239).

For Adorno, the objectivity of subjectivity must take a certain precedence, which bars recourse to any version of constitutive subjectivity.[9] Habermas, on the other hand, requires the form of an autonomous communicative subject in order to make sense of this subject's performative contradiction. Adorno criticizes the ideology of subjectivity at great length but he did not simply wish to abandon subjectivity wholesale. The idea of a freely sociated individual does not depend for Adorno on invoking an idealized free communication community for autonomous subjects, but rather first of all on the experience of a subjectivity free from domination in an inner awareness that its own needs are not identical to the performative roles offered by society. This seems to require something like a substantive reason that might be historically expressed. "Consciousness is a function of the living subject, and no exorcism will expel this from the concept's meaning" (*ND*: 186/185). But Adorno was notoriously reluctant to go further in fleshing out the dimensions of what this might mean politically.

The Habermasian fetish of critical reason as a tool indicates that Habermas does not make the distinction in logical types of thought made by Adorno. This is no mere intellectualism we are attributing to Adorno but rather Adorno's interpretation of Marx: the social relations of the production of needs (reason at the level of society) must be reconciled with the subjective expression of needs (rationality at the level of the subject). But needs are not merely articulated, they are *felt*. What Adorno's critical reason aims at—what would be the source of a critical praxis— is a dialectic of society and its other, which is most often referred to under the sign of nature. This would be a dialectic that is beyond the self-identical subject and in pursuit of a reason that could reconcile the substance that is sacrificed for subjectivity with a non-dominating sociation of individuals free from the exigencies of self-preserving subjective reason. Indeed, Adorno's early concept of *Naturgeschichte*, an idea that can be used to interpret the idea of the dialectic of enlightenment and one to which Adorno himself returns explicitly at the end of *Negative Dialectics*, is exemplary of this kind of dialectical effort.[10]

In the next chapter I turn explicitly to an extended discussion of Adorno's alternative notion of non-dominating sociation.

4.4. A Concluding Note on Contradiction and Dialectic

The Habermasian schema clearly presents an *alternative* theory of the subject compared to Adorno's. The former also invokes a quite traditional notion of performative contradiction in order to reject the radical critique of reason. Thus it does not achieve its ostensible *Aufhebung* of Adorno's philosophy. It is also an alternative that fails, however, to furnish a useful transcendence of the philosophy of consciousness and subjectivity because it effectively abstracts so completely from the 'other' of subjectivity in order to establish the intersubjectivity of communicative action. There needs to be more than just an orientation to abstract validity for an articulation of inner need and an uncompromising yet meaningful democratic sense of the social bond. Communicative action cannot remain so independent of the sensuous individuality of human bodily and erotic need that seem to express themselves so forcefully and persistently through human sociality. What we are left with in Habermas's theory, finally, is a view of communication and communicative performative consistency that is actually more aporetic and contradictory than that expressed in Adorno's radical critique of subjective reason. For Habermasian theory does not recognize how his performative consistency closes on the non-identical of the utterance, even while it offers various concessions such as its fallibilistic assumption.

To reject the principle of non-identity (which is different from a commitment to fallibilism) is to go against the mindfulness of otherness to which one is called by the critique of identity thinking. It is to introduce a new and rather different but unacknowledged performative contradiction and disallows and denies more than it opens up and permits. What is given up in such a move is any graspable relation to the resources of non-identity that are suppressed or sacrificed for the sake of society. What I have been suggesting is that this existential relation and its suppressed object do not simply vanish with the theoretical switch to the level of *discursive* communication. The blindness of Habermas's theory causes a quite traditional recourse to such notions as performative contradiction in order to paper over the instability of his ambiguous quasi-transcendentalism. Habermas ends up begging the question with respect to one of the most central critical orientations of Frankfurt critical theory. By contrast, Adorno's negative dialectical position attempts to remain consistent with its insights into the self-contradictoriness of subjectivity and the principle of non-identity.

In the dialectical tradition, social contradiction indicates above all *movement*, that, for example, unreason appears where once was reason but also that reason can appear where once was unreason. This concept of contradiction provides one of the deepest senses of (tragic) *history* in this tradition, as well as one of its best resources of *hope*. Habermas is correct in emphatically affirming that no one can step outside the social whole, but he denies the dialectical rejoinder that no one—and no human system such as language or speech—can be fully free of the contradictions reason and domination produce in the whole. Marx and Adorno are for this reason much more willing to tolerate performative contradiction than Habermas is. Consequently, the former figures could look forward to a liberated future yet to be defined—continually *to be* defined—rather than trying to resolve (and repress) their performative contradictions through a rigorous performative logic.

5

RECOVERING THE ETHICAL AND POLITICAL FORCE OF ADORNO'S AESTHETIC-CRITICAL THEORY

It is one of the great advantages claimed for the theory of communicative action that an appeal to reconciliation with a mysterious Other within or beyond the self is no longer necessary in order to glimpse an intersubjectivity free from the domination of subjective reason. The paradigm shift to communication is to achieve this. The Habermasian other is not a radical other, unknowable or unspeakable, which is to be brought into a relationship with the self and experienced somehow only at a different, deeper level to language and subjective reason—as, for example, through aesthetic appreciation, intuition, or through love, ecstasy, religious inspiration, and other similar experiences. Rather, the other is always already an *other subject* with whom one aims at reaching understanding and agreement whenever communicative utterances occur.[1] The communicative intersubjectivities in which all competent speakers find themselves entwined reach all the way down.

If for Habermas, in his most quasi-transcendental moments, the presuppositions of language provide the ground for the happy coincidence of the universal and the particular free from the dialectic of subjectification and reification, and if indeed the primacy of intersubjective relations thereby highlights the mimetic moment already present in everyday communication between subjects (Habermas, 1986a: 156), what then becomes of the *object* (*das Objektive*), which Adorno regarded as so fundamental to the subject's power of critical reflection? The sublation of the subject/object model in the negative dialectic is, on my reading, intended to recover the notion of a free intersubjectivity by virtue of a new awareness of its social objectivity and the recognition of non-identity attendant to this. Indeed, the means by which such awareness is to be achieved can be described in a communicative way, a way in which the object can be brought to speak without the pressures, force, or repressions that attend the requirements of identification. This evokes a significant ethical relation to the other and the otherness of the objective that opens up possibilities for non-instrumental relations to subjects and to non-human nature alike (see also section 2.2.3).

Habermas wishes to retain the effort of envisioning a free intersubjectivity that is central to critical theory, but the communicative ethical force that is carried by Adorno's awareness of the object is translated in the Habermasian paradigm shift into an awareness of the communicative ethical force that accompanies the responsibility for utterances and reaching agreement in speech. This intersubjectivity is predicated on recognizing the process that stabilizes the communicative subject in oneself and enjoins it with others and thus gets at the bonding essence of society itself. This is a translation that quite explicitly exchanges the dialectic of subject and object for quite a different struggle for recognition between subject and subject. Turning now to Adorno's notion of the primacy of the object, I want to explore his understanding of social objectivity and to consider the success of the Habermasian translation of Adorno's communicative freedom into the theory of communicative action. To complete my reading of Adorno's alternative point of departure for critical theory, I will in the final sections conclude with a detailed presentation of his aesthetic-critical theory as a radical democratic political theory.

5.1. THE PRIORITY OF THE OBJECT AND THE PASSION FOR CRITIQUE

Traditional epistemology since Descartes refers fundamentally to some form of relation between a knowing subject and an object that is known, in whatever way these two entities are to be understood. Indeed, conceptual thinking itself—defining, abstraction, naming—would not be possible without necessarily assuming the entities to which the words *subject* and *object* refer. The problem faced by epistemology, then, is how it is possible to reflect upon the meaning of these entities that are apparently already needed or posited before anything like the act of reflection itself can occur. This basic problem of self-reflection is dealt with in various ways in the idealist tradition from Kant to Hegel, yet it has resisted a satisfactory or genuine resolution (in the sense of an adequate explanation). The problem has not, of course, disappeared or been rendered irrelevant by the dominant reaction to this philosophical problematic by the various brands of epistemological positivism or realism that instead simply ignore it. Indeed, Habermas contended in *Knowledge and Human Interests* that after the demise of Hegel's system, philosophical reflection on the conditions of knowledge declined into a mere naïve methodology under positivism, which lacked any equivalent to the crucial social-theoretic dimension of Hegel's critique. On the other hand, alternative philosophies such as pragmatism (for example, Peirce, Dewey) and phenomenology (for example, Husserl, Heidegger, Merleau-Ponty) reject the metaphysical priority of subject and object entirely and instead rely on other approaches, concepts, and categories without invoking the idea of an origin or foundation.

For Adorno, we are not still waiting for the brilliant philosophical solution to the question of epistemology because the problem of epistemology reflects a historical condition that testifies simultaneously to the truth and falsity of the separation of subject and object. This insight is developed famously by Lukács (1971, especially 110ff) in his critique of the antinomies of modern (bourgeois) philosophy, including the analysis of cognition, which he saw as expressions of the social relations of control and domination of a historical class. Adorno's approach, while significantly influenced by his appropriation of Hegelian phenomenology, is also thoroughly associated with Marx and the critical, dialectical tradition of Western Marxism.

Adorno sees the dichotomy of subject and object as a coercive fact of human cognitive life, an unavoidable fact with which we must live, but not one that implies a First or origin from which its Hegelian bifurcation (*Entzweiung*) springs and to which philosophy must ultimately indicate some kind of return. Just as there is no transcendental subject that constitutes empirical subjects, neither is a transsubjective identity of subject and object to be posited, found, needed, or desired.

But while the concept of the transcendental subject "presupposes what it promises to establish: actual, living individuals" (Adorno, 1969: 154), a fact the idealists themselves continually struggled with, Adorno argues that the actual experience of subjectivity *is* in fact constituted in a transcendental manner by the transcendental rationality of exchange society. In an ironic subversion of idealism that follows Marx's and Lukács' lead, Adorno points to the truth of the transcendental subject as the projection of society, and not the other way round. It is an unconscious philosophical reflection or reproduction of real and actual social relations under capitalism. These relations have priority for Adorno, such that the abstract and instrumental rationality of exchange operates as the model for the abstract rationality of the transcendental subject. Adorno's critique of the idealists flips them right way up and thereby affirms the kernel of truth in their transcendental claim. But by doing this he convicts them of their falsity by acknowledging the truth of their claims.

The empirical subject, which caused so much grief for idealism by its givenness, is actually the one that is far less actual than the alleged transcendental. In capitalist society it is a fetish. "The fetish character, a socially necessary semblance, has become historically the *prius* of that which according to its concept would be the *posterius*. The philosophical problem of constitution has turned into its mirror image; however, in its reversal, it expresses the truth about the historical stage reached; a truth, to be sure, which would be theoretically negated by a second Copernican turn" (Adorno, 1969: 155). Adorno's critique of traditional idealist epistemology thus operates as a double-edged sword that points beyond the current state of affairs: epistemology is criticized not merely as a philosophical falsity but also as an ideological symptom of the historical development of capitalist society that pushes beyond it. Kant's Copernican turn, in which the world becomes a product of subjectivity, can be negated theoretically (at first) by dialectical thought that displays the subject as a product of social relations, as a social text to be read off the cultural products or objects that arise with it. Hence Adorno's critique of epistemology is also a social critique from which it cannot be separated.

Central to this critique of epistemology and social philosophy and indeed to Adorno's critical theory as a whole is thus what he calls the "priority" or "preponderance" of the object (*Vorrang des Objekts*). Adorno expresses his materialism with this phrase, but he is subverting the traditional subject/object model rather than simply shifting its emphasis or pushing some kind of naïve realism:

> Rather, priority of the object means that the subject—for its part an object in a qualitatively different, more radical sense because it is known in no other way than through consciousness—is, as an object, also a subject. That which is known through consciousness must be a something—mediation is aimed at the mediated. But the subject, the epitome of mediation, is the How and never, in contrast to the object, the What that is postulated by any comprehensible idea of the subject's concept. Potentially, if not actually, objectivity can be imagined apart from a subject; not so

subjectivity apart from an object. No matter how the subject is defined, an entity cannot be conjured out of it. If the subject is not something—and "something" indicates an irreducible objective moment—then it is nothing at all; as *actus purus* it still needs to refer to an active thing (Adorno, 1969: 156–57).

In this intriguing passage, Adorno explores the apparent paradox of reflection upon the subject and tries to indicate why the conception of the dialectical relation of subject and object must be the result of such reflection. The concept of the priority of the object is an attempt to capture dialectically the objectivity of subjective actions. All that defines what is meant by the constituting subject—the subject conscious of itself as a subject and, as such, as a knower and a doer—all this is understood by Adorno as also of the object. The subject does not simply constitute *itself*—for this is contradictory, paradoxical, infinitely regressive; nevertheless, the subject *is* constituted in its own objectivity: "If the subject does have an objective core, then the subjective qualities in the object are all the more an element of the objective." There are essential subjective determinations in the object of cognition that cannot be eliminated (as positivism tries to do); the object of cognition is not equivalent to an object *an sich*. But the *Objektive* is prior even to these determinations, since the very "categorical equipment" from which the "subjective preparation" of the object is supposed to occur is itself determined and conditioned (Adorno, 1969: 157, 158).

Adorno thus argues that the very formal capacities that enable us to "hold" beliefs, "have" needs, "act" practically, and so on, are *themselves* historically and socially determined, specifically by class society. This is a historicizing thesis that reaches back through Nietzsche to Hegel and Marx, and its initial aim is to challenge any (conventional) claim to a foundation for the modern subject's judgment and freedom that is somehow unsullied by historically mediated reason. But a consistent pursuit of this philosophical position yields a radical critique of all ahistorical thinking. The Habermasian concern, as we have already seen, is that such a historicizing position, once the presuppositions of the philosophy of the subject have been abandoned, inevitably risks capitulation to the nihilism that continually haunts modernity.

Habermas's preference is in fact for a strongly conceived theory of the historical conditioning of human capacities, aspects of which are to be found in his recent use of Parsons's theory of learning processes, Piaget's developmental psychology, and Mead's symbolic interactionism.[2] The formation of the "deep structures" of the ego and the competencies and know-how of the practical self depend on successful learning in an intersubjective environment that changes over time. However, Habermas's universalism of rational structure is not supposed to refer finally to *competencies* of the subject, but rather lies in his concept of *communicative rationality*, whose grounding is found in the conditions for intersubjective linguistic communication itself. While Habermas parallels Adorno's move away from the philosophy of the subject, he does not then (as the latter did) affirm the inescapable particularity of reason and draw conclusions from this. Rather, as we saw, Habermas finds the universal in an intersubjectivity modeled on the pragmatics of speech, a universal need for reaching agreement that is inescapable for all speaking subjects in human society.

But Adorno did not take Habermas's preferred route out of the philosophy of the subject via a pragmatic philosophy of language. While the Habermasian contention that Adorno remained trapped by the presuppositions of subject philosophy even as he rejected its substance can be made only on this side of the paradigm shift, the latter was quite unwilling to abandon the dialectic of the subject. Adorno was always suspicious of the universal claim of intersubjectivity as presented in some brands of phenomenology (it has "the oily tone of a theology in which one has lost faith," *ND*: 273/277). But his rejection of the kind of route Habermas would develop also indicates an unwillingness to give up on the potential for a very differently motivated action that can only be discovered if one maintains a hold on the preponderance of the object in our identifications. The radical critique of reason is crucial here, for it is reason, in the form of identity thinking, in the form of the exchange principle and all its sacrificial equivalents, that dominates the individual as a social force on virtually all levels of linguistically mediated conscious life. Freedom, for Adorno, could not be a matter for the individual without free, non-dominative sociation; but this would require an end to domination, especially *class* domination.

The fact that this critique could be extended to the very grounds of ethics itself in existing society meant, for Adorno, that even the most basic elements of human experience, such as the experience of need— from the deepest to those said to be merely on the surface—cannot be understood as natural or instinctual but are thoroughly social and historical. Under the conditions of contemporary capitalism, "need" and its corollary "lack" are defined by the imperatives and values of a now mighty and extensive totalizing production process.

The thought that perhaps the cinema necessarily exists alongside shelter and nourishment for the reproduction of the capacity to work is "true" only in a world that injures people in the reproduction of this capacity and forces their needs into harmony with the employer's interests of profit and domination. . . . The question of what constitutes the essential satisfaction of needs is not to be placed under the aspects social or natural, primary or secondary, true or false; it goes together with the question of the *suffering* of the dominated majority of all people in the world. If that which *all* people right now need most urgently is produced, then one has been relieved of the all-too-great social-psychological concerns about the legitimacy of their needs (Adorno, 1972b: 394–95).

The critical distinction between false needs and what may be understood as true needs was thus maintained by Adorno, but he believed that anything resembling true needs could not be concretely determined under the conditions of contemporary capitalism precisely because of the extent of the systemic conditioning of people, the violence enacted by the system upon its subjects. Adorno tended toward a negation of false needs-claims in capitalist society since needs in themselves could be rational only beyond systems that guarantee unnecessary domination and false scarcity. Democracy, for Adorno, could never mean simply the power to satisfy needs irrespective of how those needs arise (there is no basic set of needs that exist naturally). If acceptable democratic self-reflective processes through which the legitimacy of needs can be substantively established do not order society, then democracy is to that extent absent. In the passage previously quoted, the question of "the essential satisfaction of needs" is bound up with that of present suffering because the process that produces suffering is the same one that satisfies needs. The *interpretation* of needs (their "legitimacy") hence cannot be neatly abstracted either from domination in general or, more specifically and directly, from the capitalist production process because these levels reciprocally determine each other. As we saw in Chapter 2, the culture industry, as well as enlightenment conceived as the progressive technical domination of nature, for Adorno impede "the development of autonomous, independent individuals who judge and decide consciously for themselves. These, however, would be the precondition for a democratic society which needs adults who have come of age in order to sustain itself and develop" (1989b: 135). Until the precondition of such autonomous, independent individuals has been established, the needs of individuals cannot yet be democratic needs. One of the fundamental differences between Adorno and Habermas concerns precisely just how such autonomous, independent individuals are to be conceived in their philosophical, ethical, and political senses.

But then how is this issue to be resolved, for it appears hopelessly vague to appeal to a rationality beyond current society (and, indeed, all past societies) in order to establish a critique from which, among other things, the distinction between true and false needs can be articulated. How can anything like true needs ever be discovered, given the inextricable entwinement of rationality and repression?

As we have seen in earlier chapters, Adorno regarded this condition of the thorough mediation of individual and society as utterly problematizing conventional social scientific approaches and even threatening the materialist form of critique that eschews the absolute. The popularized alternatives of behaviorism and ego psychology, for example, which, on the one hand, make for positivist control and, on the other, amount to false models of reconciliation, are of little use in completing a critical social theory: "For the specific social phenomena have emancipated themselves through the interpolation of abstract determinations between persons, especially the exchange of equivalents, and through the domination by psychology of a refined organ, the *ratio*, which is modeled after such determinations detached from human beings" (Adorno, 1972d: 50). Variants of such psychology have nevertheless been used precisely for this reason—with explicit ideological implications for social and political theory—from Hobbes, through Locke, all the way to revisionist ego psychology and B. F. Skinner. For Adorno, domination was to be understood not only as a suffering from exclusion, from a lack of satisfaction, for that would entail a capitulation to the instrumental demands of the current system; suffering from domination must also be understood in terms of the operation of the total system and, as such, primarily as an *objective* rather than a *subjective* condition (even though suffering is an intimately individual experience). In this sense, Adorno's concept of suffering is akin to Marx's concept of alienation. To find Marx, not just Hegel, in Adorno's call for the priority of the object is thus to connect the "suffering physical" (*ND*: 202/202), not only with the body, inner nature, and the object, but with objective intersubjective relations, the principles of identity and exchange, and social domination.[3] It is here that we find the *interest* in critique and in social change.

But before we examine Adorno's complex response to the difficult question of the freedom of needs interpretation, let us review Habermas's version of the theory of needs and his sense of the passion of critique, which he first programmatically presented in *Knowledge and Human Interests*. Habermas's alternative is instructive insofar as its aporias can turn us toward Adorno.

The psychoanalytic model of critical analysis in the background of Adorno's theory is in fact taken up explicitly by Habermas at the outset of his shift to the communication model. Habermas believes that the dilemma of critique can be resolved only through the necessary *articulation* of needs in the critical process of self-reflective recovery. The repression necessitated by civilization, which produces culture (collective illusion) as well as delusion (individual and social pathologies), must be understood as a linguistic process, as a model of *excommunication*: "The ego's flight from itself is *an operation that is carried out in and with language*. Otherwise it would not be possible *to reverse the defensive process hermeneutically, via the analysis of language*" (*KHI*: 241). The interpretation of needs is not to have as a (final) social-theoretic referent any conception of the natural basis of historical development, which would fall behind the stage of reflection attained by Marx, since "at the human level we never encounter any needs that are not already interpreted linguistically and symbolically affixed to potential actions." (*KHI*: 285). Knowledge of a "nature in itself" beyond its human mediation through work, language, and power is impossible; indeed, knowledge of *this* fact is itself needed to attain the further stage of *emancipatory* self-reflection that Habermas hopes to inaugurate. For once the distortions of private and public communication found in the systematic suppression of needs interpretations are understood to occur *solely* at the level of linguistic communication, then the removal of psychological "resistances" and blocks must be oriented toward freeing up the communicative process itself. This is why Habermas finds useful the *method* of a Freudian "depth hermeneutics" that seeks to identify the lost "grammatical connection" between the split-off symbol and the symptom. However, he rejects what he sees as the Freudian "biologism" or "objectivism" of an instinctual drive or instinctual rationality that is supposed to give rise to symbolic representation. Critical reflection uncovers the causality of split-off symbols and repressed motives—the Hegelian "causality of fate"—as the operation of systematic distortions to public communication itself (*KHI*: 257, 271).[4]

This is not to say that systematic distortions are caused solely *by* language (for this would implicate reason too intimately), but rather that substitute symbols affect what can be grasped only in linguistic form. Language, hence, after the linguistic turn, must be understood as the only medium of the dialogic relation in which all identities are formed. The intersubjectivities in which we are entwined have primacy for Habermas. The core of the self is intersubjective because the individual only recognizes him-/herself through a *practical* relation to others:

the achievement of individuality requires not mere knowledge or description but the *ethical self-reassurance* (*Selbstvergewisserung*) of "one who in the face of other dialogue participants presents and, if necessary, justifies himself [or herself] as an irreplaceable and distinctive person" (*PT*: 168; and see 177ff; this position is also present in Habermas's discussion of Fichte in *KHI*: 191–213). It is this notion of individualization that implicates the "higher-level intersubjectivities" and the health of their processes of communicative reproduction in the very core life of the individual. Since the mode in which concrete forms of life are reproduced is communicative action, the *unavoidable communality* evoked by the "causality of fate" is to be found in the binding and bonding of the communication community, which, when disruptions occur, cannot escape some sense of a consequent "communal responsibility" (*PDM*: 316).

Like Adorno, the Habermas of *Knowledge and Human Interests* wants to retain the utopian hope of a rational society freed from unnecessary domination that is, in the spirit of Marx, *interested* in such a rational resolution: "Just as in the clinical situation, so in society, pathological compulsion itself is accompanied by the interest in its abolition . . . for the social system too, the interest inherent in the pressure of suffering is also immediately an interest in enlightenment" (*KHI*: 288). While this formulation may be too close to the "species subject" model of society avoided by the later Habermas, it is necessary for a critical theory to link pathology at the individual level with that at the level of society. His conclusion in this text is remarkable for the reason that he has remained faithful to it throughout his subsequent work, even if he has substantially modified other major positions. In a passage that is explicitly inspired by a Freudian formulation, Habermas states the essential principle of the linguistic turn: "The goal is 'providing a rational basis for the precepts of civilization': in other words, an organization of social relations according to the principle that the validity of every norm of political consequence be made dependent on a consensus arrived at in communication free from domination" (*KHI*: 284).

As we saw in Chapter 4, the goal of or need for consensus is at times more than just a cognitive or pragmatic principle; it is also the principle of successful human sociation itself. This is why Habermas makes quasi-transcendental claims for the presuppositions of *speech*: he believes that the basis of human sociation is to be found in the unavoidable activity of linguistically mediated truth-seeking. Human sociation would not be possible without this activity; conversely, society and its members suffer when communicative action is repressed or distorted.

The process of identity formation in communicative action is the ideal mode by which disrupted consensuses are restored or founded anew. This is a need that expresses human social life in general, but it is also one that has become far more demanding in modern society under the general decline in or absence of received or mystical authority. The static stability of religious or metaphysical worldviews is no longer widely available within the fluidity and flux of meaning and the conflict over identity found in modernity.[5] Traditional authority is replaced by institutionalized processes of consensus formation whose inherent instability (*because* of their communicatively rational basis) is compensated for, on the one hand, by the reproduction of stocks of knowledge and acquired communicative skills and, on the other, by the autonomy of the de-linguistified systems media of money and power that coordinate action without the need for communicative agreement. Reification thus plays a socially useful role here for Habermas (see sections 3.1 and 3.2). The main problem from Habermas's perspective, as we saw, is that capitalism and technological administration suppress the rational potentials of modernity and produce pathological side effects as a result of the over-extension of mediatization into colonization. Identities and meanings become ossified and conflict and crisis erupt in intersubjective relations.

Hence, for Habermas, the problems of individual and social pathology are not indicative of *too much* rationality—the repression or domination of reason itself—but rather of a *deficiency* of (the right kind of) reason. The true and "natural" basis of human sociation that Habermas believes he has discovered in the need for mutual understanding and consensus is the need for a reconciled totality—which in Habermasian social-theoretic terms is equivalent to stable, undisrupted social integration. Coles (1995; 1997) has shown that this central Hegelian orientation, which produces such a relative absence of tension and paradox in Habermas's description of universality and difference, is related to the latter's communicative paradigm. Communicative rationality and the process of reaching understanding reproduce the everyday pressures toward agreement. This "pressure to decide," which is analyzed in the illocutionary force of the speech act and the unforced force of the better argument, are the constraints of socially useful coordination; they are the very constraints of Habermas's concept of *language-use*. Habermas over-emphasizes the idealized identical ascriptions of meaning and consensuality at the expense of the many alternative forms of communication that might have ethical and political bearing. "This pressure holding us together for useful coordination demands that our statements (and those we accept) be direct, defined, totally reproducible, without hesitations and ambiguities: It demands the silencing, the cessation of so much communication" (Coles, 1995: 35).

The tendency that occurs in Habermas's theory and to which it is predisposed by the way that the linguistic turn is made is an *instrumentalization of the social bond*. The discourse ethic, according to Bernstein (1995: 189–90), "transforms *forms* of mutual recognition into *abstract rules* for the coordination of action," since, in the final analysis, Habermas's definition of morality is *functional*: "In anthropological terms, morality is a safety device compensating for a vulnerability built into the sociocultural form of life" (*MCCA*: 199). What must be reappropriated from Habermas's theory is a deeper concept of mutual recognition that is not limited to the communicative rationality of merely successful self-formation, social interaction, and coordination, or the mere agreement on identical meanings. Mutual recognition must just as much express and promote an awareness of the entwinement of linguistic sociation with the suppression or at least the neglect of other forms of expression and communication, especially the radically other form of communication invoked in the negative dialectic. This is to pay attention to just what can be communicated by and through the vulnerability of the sociocultural form of life Habermas mentions, the suffering of those non-identical with the dominant and privileged forms of identity that points toward a freedom and autonomy for individuals beyond their social functions and beyond the requirements of identity formation itself.

At issue is just what Adorno refers to with the priority of the object, a position oriented toward the importance of that which cannot be fully assimilated to the concept or to language without remainder; that which is ineliminable in the object yet cannot be made fully present in its re-presentation. This recognizes a need for a special awareness that goes beyond merely acknowledging that the thing does not fit into the concept without a residue, and one that goes beyond the capacity to follow abstract rules reflectively. It is precisely the entwinement of non-identity with identity that constitutes society, for Adorno, via the dialectic of subjective reason, and it must be acknowledged for any conception of sociation that would aspire to adequacy. In Freudian terminology, this 'beyond' has its equivalent at the level of the unconscious, which lacks the possibility of linguistic expression except, for example, via the indirect image and narrative manifestations of the dream-work or the symptom, themselves manifestations of the dialectical relation between conscious and unconscious life. Habermas, as we have seen, does not recognize the relevance of conceiving non-identity or the unconscious in such ways because *all* subjectivity, no matter how intimate or primary, is due to "the unrelenting individuating force possessed by the linguistic medium of formative processes," which never lets up within communicative action (*PT*: 25–26). He therefore has no need to try to incorporate theoretically the prelinguistic sources of the self or social life in order to understand difference.

> The intersubjectivity of linguistically achieved understanding is by nature porous, and linguistically attained consensus does not eradicate from the accord the differences in speaker perspectives but rather presupposes them as ineliminable. . . . The grammatical role of personal pronouns forces the speaker and the hearer to adopt a performative attitude in which one confronts the other as *alter ego*: only with a consciousness of their absolute difference and irreplaceability can the one recognize himself in the other. Thus although the nonidentical is vulnerable, has been repeatedly distorted through objectification, and has therefore always slipped through the net of basic metaphysical concepts, it remains accessible in a trivial way in everyday communicative practice (*PT*: 48).

The nonidentical is thus translated into the dynamics of intersubjectivity and serves as an essential element of identity in Habermas's model. While this is an ingenious move on his part, it nevertheless begs the question of non-identity's entwinement with identity because non-identity is also entwined, so to speak, with *difference*. Habermas argues that we are able to *identify* only by virtue of a radical difference built into the relations of intersubjective recognition themselves and that recognition of this difference is crucial for successful consensus. Yet there is a radical non-identity not only between the representation and the thing represented but also between the recognition of difference and the identity of difference itself. It is not enough hence to recognize an "absolute difference" between and "irreplaceability" of self and other; what must also be recognized is the radical non-identity between otherness and its very identification as such. For the abstract concept of non-identity, in Adorno's usage, is a (negative) dialectical concept whose content marks an absence not a presence. Its concept reaches beyond itself without ever being able to grasp its subject matter. Adorno makes this point: "Certainly what is nonidentical and unknown becomes identical as well as being known" (that is, when the concept of nonidentity is found);

and in being comprehended, the nonconceptual becomes the concept of the nonidentical. But the nonidentical itself does not merely become a concept by virtue of such reflection; it remains the content of the concept, distinct from the concept. One cannot move from the logical movement of concepts to existence. According to Hegel there is a constitutive need for the nonidentical in order for concepts, identity, to come into being; just as conversely there is a need for the concept in order to become aware of the nonconceptual, the nonidentical (*HTS*: 147).

Habermas is, arguably, aware of this distinction and its dialectical import but suppresses it, as he suppresses the dialectic itself, with the communications-theoretic paradigm shift because

the phenomena that . . . lead to acknowledged and unacknowledged paradoxes of a nonidentical or nonreflexive consciousness can be captured in language-analytic terms only if one draws upon the *three-term model* of sign use that . . . from the very start relates the analysis of linguistic meaning to the idea of participants in communication coming to an understanding about something in the world (*TCAI*: 397).

The very notion that these phenomena can be "captured" or "caught up to" (*einholen*) shows that Habermas admits only part of the question of non-identity, an exclusion grounded in his stipulation that limits are imposed on thinking not by the paradoxes of *representation*—for these have been "caught up to" and superseded by the paradigm shift—but rather by the necessarily *performative* attitude of speakers and hearers that *permits* representation to take place.

In a statement whose context is the criticism of Kantian ethics, Adorno writes: "The question of freedom does not call for a Yes or No but rather for theory to rise above existing society just as above existing individuality. . . . The subject would be freed first as an I reconciled with the not-I, and with that it would also be above freedom insofar as freedom conspires with its counterpart repression" (*ND*: 279/283). Here, it is not another I that is most important with respect to communicative interaction but the other as not-I, as that sensuous being that must be repressed for the sake of the I (which another I-as-subject, insofar as it is also a sensuous being with reason, is also). Adorno, ever suspicious of the false universal as of false particularity, refuses to grant authenticity to a subject whose very self-reflection derives from the false universal.

Habermas is implicated here in Adorno's critique of Kant to the extent that the quasi-transcendental constraints and necessities of socially useful communication take the place of the transcendental conditions of monologic thought and action that in Kant constrain moral consciousness to the willing of and respect for universal moral norms. It is not enough merely to bring in, via the discourse ethic, the perspective of the particular—the "concrete other"—in order to fulfill the potential of moral universalism. The point is rather to challenge the very requirement (or possibility) of any moral universalism abstracted from the particular at all. To reject the false mediation of individual and society is to imply a truer basis for comprehending it; and for this, one needs to take the problem of repression seriously. Habermas's "linguistification of the unconscious" can be seen from this point of view as a result of his failure to grant any real independence to forces working behind language (Whitebook, 1995: 210).

The freedom above freedom to which Adorno refers is a freedom from the need for repression, which, as a utopian image, is paradoxical in his formulation. But it is an image that somehow cannot be avoided or abandoned if the (ir)rationality of domination is to be confronted successfully. It is this freedom that we may understand as Adorno's version of a "communicative freedom" drawn from Hegel's philosophy, that is, the freedom to approach the object without feeling the need to grasp it wholly and exhaustively by its representation in the concept. Indeed, Cornell (1992: 16) understands Adorno's idea of "reconciliation" to be a "redefinition of the Hegelian communicative freedom as the state beyond the heterogeneous as absolute otherness and beyond that which is captured by the Hegelian Concept."[6] From an Adornian perspective, it is precisely the demand for identity that is imposed on us by domination and that has achieved such extensive development under capitalist society. Once the bonds of identity thinking have been cast off, it is possible to imagine a radically different set of social relations that would be engendered by such altered thinking—and, conversely, that would be the necessary conditions for such thinking.

Hence Adorno's ideas of reconciliation and freedom are inextricably tied to a fundamental change in subjective relations to internal and external nature, which would also require equally fundamental social change (the abolition of classes, but also more than this). Yet with this Adorno does not call for the institution of a specific content for freedom or reconciliation; he does not invoke an authentic being to give meaning to the changed experience he hopes for. Rather, it is the *movement* of thought itself that needs to be rediscovered and encouraged, an attentiveness to the self and its language arising from an openness and "lasting nearness" to the other in its considered "distance and difference." There is always content to this thought but, as we will see in the following section, it is always in motion, never satisfied with its conscious inadequacy and always sensitive to the possibilites of violence inherent in thought. It is just this prospect of such fundamental individual transformation and social change for freedom that Habermasian theory abandons as unnecessary by virtue of the assimilation of linguistic meaning achieved in intersubjective agreement and communicative rationality's *class-unspecific* force. Habermas's instrumentalization of the social bond serves to suppress alternative ways of conceiving sociality for the sake of the functional need to maintain a certain kind of social integration. Even at best this risks capitulation to the legalism of status quo liberalism. At worst, it tends to reflect the interest of the capitalist system in maintaining the reliability of exchangeable identities for the sake of stable circulation, social integration, and political domination. Either way, I would contend, what Adorno had in mind with the utopian notion of reconciliation is not finally reproduced in Habermas's theory. Hence to suggest, as he does, that communicative rationality represents what Adorno sought is to significantly distort the latter's aims. Also, as Whitebook (1988: 82) has pointed out, it is bad conscience to argue with the language of reconciliation for a deradicalized critical theory that is simply no longer utopian.

5.2. LANGUAGE AND THE SUBJECT: ADORNO

How, then, does Adorno articulate the alternative toward which he pointed (paradoxically)? How can an Adornian position be recovered from the Habermasian critique, yet one that will not lead to a freezing of the sociality it wants to redeem and foster?

The paradox with which Adorno concerned himself is that while the subject "is as an object," without the subject objectivity would be "nonsensical." The subject both "is" and "is not," and subjective experience—which for Adorno, as we know, is also a deeply objective experience—needs its illusion of the subject for thought. What is unnecessary is the hypostatization of that subjectivity and the enthrallment to the concept that 'normal' thinking produces. Nevertheless, for Adorno, subjectivity cannot help but build around itself a "box" or "prison," the active construction of which is celebrated in idealism as "creativity," but which is in fact the "irresistible blinding context" of subjectivity (Adorno, 1969: 166, 159). Before any genuine reflection upon the meaning of the subject "in and for itself" can occur—for example, asking what might constitute human needs beyond those demanded through domination—subjective consciousness must free itself from the prison-house of identity thinking. This is by no means an easy task, not least because of the bewildering paradoxes and constrictions in which the subject is apparently left.

Given that the subject is an ineradicable element (but not a "bad" element in itself that ought to be eradicated, were it even possible), subjective consciousness has the potential to realize itself only when it gives itself over to the object such that its subjective reason is substantially mitigated under a new set of interobject and intersubject political conditions. "The subject is the more the less it is, and it is the less the more it believes in its own objective being [*ein für sich Objektives zu sein*]" (Adorno, 1969: 165–66). In other words, subjectivity can recognize itself better and become aware of what a true freedom ought to mean the less it asserts itself as *subject*. Conversely, subjectivity becomes less the more it hypostatizes itself as a *thing* independent of historical relations to others. This calls for a substantial weakening of the rationality of self-preservation, the assertion of self required in the face of an antagonistic, hostile, unforgiving, inhospitable world, which is only possible if this world of interobject and intersubject political relations has been radically transformed according to its own potentials. As long as capitalist productive relations produce social contradictions, antagonism, environmental destruction and waste, consumer comfort for some and rank deprivation for others, all of which extend to the global level, then freedom for all will always be denied. Freedom for all must be a radical demand that inheres in critical theory, for without it freedom will remain a merely formal or empty concept. It is a demand generated by the utopian possibility of a universality that is substantive because it cannot be abstracted from other political goods such as happiness.

The priority of the object thus refers not only to a mode of analyzing subjective reason and late capitalist society, but also projects an image of social relations that would be free from their respective dominations. The way out for critical knowledge is indicated in the first instance in the direction away from the hypostatizing equation of concept and thing and toward an awareness of what is assimilated or repressed in such dominating thought and action: the *political* interconnectedness of any identity with that which it is not. The dependence of self on other is always mediated by a set of power relations that are revealed only in the constant negation of all monadic identities. That this also expresses a radical political critique of current conditions cannot be doubted. But while a final, successful practical way out for critical political action remains a historical question that theory cannot quite predict, one may continue to track progressive resistance to the 'new world order' in many fields and regions (see, for example, Matustík, 1998; Jameson and Miyoshi, 1998).

The priority of the object turns us toward the cognitive value of aesthetic experience and representation because the aesthetic dimension, unlike the natural tendency of the conceptual, is inherently partial, enigmatic, contemplative. It operates without the expectation that a final identity can be generated. In short, it combines subjective and objective experience most clearly in a open *communicative way*. As such, however, (great) art is alienated in society and Adorno sees a critical promise that arises from its marginalization, a critical truth-content that he regards as crucial. Adorno valued the aesthetic for a variety of reasons, and we will turn to those relevant to my political argument in the next section. Before that, I want to touch upon some relevant aspects of the deradicalization of critical theory that are central to my critique of the Habermasian appropriation of Adorno's utopian image. Habermas has modified his position on art's "truth-content" (*Wahrheitsgehalt*)—or what is less contentious and more discursively oriented, its "truth-potential" (*Wahrheitspotential*)—which refers to an artwork's capacity to *disclose* something about the world. He now accepts that "the prescriptive validity of a norm and the normative validity claims raised in regulative speech acts is not a proper model for the relation between the potential for truth of works of art, and the transformed relations between self and world stimulated by aesthetic experience" (Habermas, 1985c: 203). But this appears to be a greater admission than Habermas may be willing to grant, for it is just this possibility of transforming the relations between self and world represented by the truth-content of art that implies a radical critique of the same overly regulative and linguistically mediated model of social interaction Habermas defends.

As a strategy to avoid this threat that the aesthetic presents to the Habermasian position, one response is to deradicalize the very experience of art itself, to eliminate the gap between historical society and the utopian vision Adorno finds in art. This is just what Wellmer attempts in his critique and reconstruction of Adorno's aesthetic theory and his substitution of truth-potential for truth-content in art. Wellmer believes that because art does not merely disclose reality but also opens our eyes (and ears) to new perceptions and experiences of reality, the reality manifested in art does in fact embody a relationship to *truth*. This truth, however, can only be *metaphorical* for Wellmer, for neither art nor the artist *speaks* in a literal sense, and truth, after the communicative paradigm shift, can only be properly ascribed to linguistic validity claims. But this does not mean that the truth of art is to be abandoned, since, according to Wellmer, the metaphorical truth in the work of art is "something which we can only explain by the fact that the work of art, as a symbolical construct that carries an *aesthetic* validity claim, is at the same time the object of an *aesthetic experience* that refers back to our ordinary experience in which the three dimensions of truth are interwoven in a *non-metaphorical* sense." Hence to foster the innovative and communicative potential of art is useful for democratic praxis, "for without aesthetic experience and the subversive potential it contains, our moral discourse would necessarily become blind and our interpretations of the world empty" (Wellmer, 1991: 28, 31, 34).

But Wellmer's central claim that truth in art can only be metaphorical (which he then uses to justify his discourse-theory interpretation of art's truth-potential) fails in the end to make its case. It fails in one way because a philosophical claim about the truth of art (whether its truth is metaphorical or not) and a claim about the truth-content of art ("*Antigone* reveals the truth about law and authority") are made at different levels; hence the truth or falsity of one does not necessarily decide the truth or falsity of the other.[7] In other words, Wellmer's claim is a non-metaphorical truth-claim, not one of those claims whose supposedly metaphorical status is in dispute. Hence it cannot purport to give an account of the truth of art as such, for both kinds of claims can be included in the constellation of meanings to which the concept of truth belongs. Wellmer's claim also fails because it does not demonstrate that truth cannot be non-discursive (as in, for example, the truth often ascribed to insights without their needing to be spelled out linguistically).

Moreover, as Zuidervaart has suggested, due to Wellmer's emphasis on truth-potential, communication, and the interplay of plural rationalities, his Habermasian "domestication" of artistic truth effectively slights the "languages of suffering" to which Adorno's aesthetic theory in particular and his critical theory in general attest: "Adorno's metaphilosophical claims are not simply claims about the connections of history, art and truth. They are part of an attempt to lend voice to unmet needs and unfulfilled desires" (Zuidervaart, 1991: 304). This concern with the emphatic language of suffering is at best marginalized by—at worst lost subsequent to—the new concerns accompanying the communicative paradigm. This is a need for acknowledgment within critical theory of the drive toward liberation from suffering, the Freudian "passion for critique" that Habermas still recognized in *Knowledge and Human Interests*, but which even then was being de-radicalized as the paradigm shift emerged. This would constitute a rather different *force* of the lifeworld than Habermas's, and a different ethical call arising from the tensions, contradictions, and interests of the objectivity of life itself. But it is a force that gets replaced by the tamed force of productive communication in Habermas's theory that has, finally, no non-violent or ethical justification beyond its gesture toward functionality as I argued above. This ethical compulsion is precisely what is supposed to be identified by the Hegelian causality of fate (as Bernstein, 1995: 179, has argued— the force found in popular religion that Hegel thematized in terms of recognition, love, and life).

The incompatibility that some allege between Adorno's simultaneous appeals to philosophical truth and aesthetic truth is false if one accepts Adorno's fundamental position that the languages of philosophy and art, while different and distinct, constitute similar relationships to the non-identical social product.[8] For this one needs a theory of language that takes the non-identical seriously in both conceptually mediated and mimetically mediated communication. It is easy to see the importance, indeed definitively so, of the non-identical for art and its language, but an essential relationship to the non-identical is less straightforward when it comes to philosophical language, which is mediated precisely by the rationality of identity in *concepts*. Hence Peter Hohendahl argues that Adorno's attempt to integrate philosophy and art is bound to fail because it must conflate two incompatible notions of language: "Whereas conceptual language cannot escape the moment of identification in the process of making judgments [*Urteile*], the logic of the artwork is exclusively based on the configuration of its material. The more Adorno underscores [the artwork's] 'lack of conceptuality' [*Begriffslosigkeit*], the more he widens the gap. . . . Therefore, *Aesthetic Theory* must attempt to resolve this dilemma and undermine its solution at the same time" (Hohendahl, 1995: 239).

However, once one recognizes the non-identical ground of conceptually mediated communication, then this accusation of "incompatibility" does not seem as serious. For where does the "concept" end (if I may be permitted some rhetorical play), that is, where is its boundary? At the edges of the conceptual image held in the mind? Similarly, where does the word or sentence end? In the "white space" after its inscription on the page? In the silence after its sonorous utterance? If a move is made beyond a reified conception of language, then it becomes clear that the accepted "need for concepts and categories as modes of conveying thought" (Hohendahl, 1995: 240) does not commit one to the need for concepts, categories, or linguistic utterances *exclusively* in order to express truth. Nor does the "need for concepts and categories as modes of conveying thought" mean that cognitive thought itself can *only* be "conveyed" in these forms. Indeed, Hohendahl's recognition that concepts and categories are needed as modes of conveying thought already implies that concepts are not *equivalent* to thought. To accept this need as somehow definitive for any coherent notion of truth (as Hohendahl seems to do, and as Wellmer's Habermasian position seems to indicate) is to conflate conceptually mediated communication with linguistically mediated communication—and, more important, to exclude the relevance of "prelinguistic" or non-identical elements for thought itself. Adorno did not aim to *identify* philosophical language with the language of art or assimilate one to the other, but rather, like Hegel, by holding both forms in radical tension, he meant to point to their crucial, common dialectical relationships to non-identity and (as we have seen) to the social basis of these relations:

> As an expression of the thing itself, language is not fully reducible to communication with others. Nor, however . . . is it simply independent of communication. . . . Language as expression of the thing itself and language as communication are interwoven. The ability to name the matter at hand is developed under the compulsion to communicate it, and that element of coercion is preserved in it; conversely, it could not communicate anything that it did not have as its own intention, undistracted by other considerations (*HTS*: 105).

One may contrast rather starkly the Habermasian pressure to reach consensual *understanding* with Adorno's insistence on the need for *intelligibility*, which, following the Hegelian program of "pure onlooking [*reines Zusehen*]," demands a "spontaneous receptivity" of the object, not an "intellectual forced march." In this philosophical association with aesthetic experience, the ideal is "nonargumentative thought," in which thought, like the objects it analyzes, remains "inherently in motion" (*HTS*: 140–41). This is why Adorno could find Proust or Kafka valuable: the recognition is *involuntary* and *defamiliarizing*, which opens up a very different communicative relation and experience to those favored by Habermas. "Contemplation without violence, from which arises all the joy of truth," Adorno writes, "requires that the contemplator not annex the object: nearness by distance" (*MM*: 112/89–90). We are thus ever turned back toward the understanding of and care for the non-identical.

The subject, for Adorno, exists only by virtue of its *relations* to other subjects and objects that are non-identical. Subjectivity and objectivity are separate and distinct, but they are thoroughly mediated in the conceptual process as a *necessity* of subjective self-consciousness. When Adorno says, "To be an object is also part of the meaning of subjectivity; but it is not equally part of the meaning of objectivity to be a subject," he is making explicit the distinction between subjective and objective existence. But he is also implying the difference between intersubjective relations and subject/object relations. Yet because the cognitive relation requires conceptual mediation, subject/subject relations and subject/object relations cannot be completely and unequivocally distinguished. Subject/subject relations are nevertheless inherently different from subject/object relations *because* the subject is confronted by its non-identity in another subject: "Subjectivity changes its quality in a context it is unable to develop out of itself" (*ND*: 184/183). Nondominating interaction in the intersubjective realm demands more from the subject than perhaps does nondominating relations to nature (although the two are necessarily related). This *qualitative* difference has to do with the need for the social solidarity that is the human social other of subjective reason.

Materialist dialectical thought conceives of this distinction between subject/subject and subject/object relations as partly comprising the conditions of real, existing subjectivity, as I have been arguing throughout. As such, Adorno's dialectic criticizes the (un)conscious denial or suppression of the distinction by subjective reason, either as a matter of course in everyday thinking or on the grander scale in idealist philosophy or ideological political theory:

> Only insofar as it is for its part also not-I does the I relate to the not-I and "do" something. Only then would this act itself be thinking. By means of a double reflection thought overcomes its supremacy over its Other because thought is already penetrated with otherness in itself. . . . No ontological abyss yawns between the moment of reality in [the transcendental function] and the activity of the real subject, and neither, therefore, does one yawn between the intellect [*Geist*] and labor (*ND*: 201/201).

Here Adorno again states the impossibility of completely abstracting thought from action—hence of finding reason purified of the (historical) practice that establishes it—*because* the I is immanently related to its own non-identity. The I cannot find itself securely through language alone, even though it is only through reason that it becomes an I at all, because it is reason's own non-identity with itself that grounds the rational use of language.

Non-identity is constituted by the tension between concept and object, but in the cognitive sphere of theory and epistemology it can easily be suppressed, just as the non-identical human labor in the commodity is so well suppressed in capitalist society. The otherness of the subject is found in the object also—for a subject, an object should never be merely objective, however much it may be "objectified." Subjects and objects have a similar cognitive existence for the subject since their presence is mediated through *concepts*; therefore, neither subject nor object can be truly *present*. But because objectivity is in subjectivity *unlike* the way subjectivity is in objectivity, the intersubjective relation demands a qualitatively different *thinking and acting* on the part of subjects if these subjects are to be true to their concept. (No 'return to nature' or simple mimesis of the natural world is implied here, for that would entail dangerous regression.) Intersubjectivity entails a respect of difference and a hermeneutic of non-identity that can be developed to a full extent only in freedom, freedom from the domination of subject/object by the subject, which is ultimately a freedom from the compulsion of subjective reason that happens to have been developed to such a refined extent in late capitalism.

But such freedom, as Adorno tirelessly pointed out, "would arise only with the establishment of a free society" (*ND*: 272/276). This freedom is therefore neither asocial (the alleged "non-reason" of art) nor antisocial (nihilistic) because it projects a transfigured reason that makes possible a reconciliation of individual and society. What occurs in existing society is the denial of the importance of the non-identical and the assimilation of subjects to their concept. Alternatives to non-dominating subjectivity and intersubjectivity are denied under current conditions, which enact a primal history while at the same time expressing this history as developed to the extreme in late capitalism. Yet Adorno's theory clearly points in the direction of a new set of social relations that are not inconceivable nor completely unclarifiable. Of course, Adorno's suggestion of what would constitute a free society resists any positive, programmatic formulation that would merely turn it into a 'bad' utopia: "The idea of reconciliation bars its positive positing in the concept" (*ND*: 148–49/145). Thus one is prevented from following Habermas in developing a full-fledged political theory of the state, a taboo that has led so many to frustration with Adorno's basic position. But other expressions of the ethical or political meaning of the negative dialectic are possible that attain a definite shape and point toward a free(er) society, such as Coles's (1995: 38) conclusion that the aim of production and government should be to encourage and make possible social practices that "pursue the contours of an ethics of receptive generosity."

Adorno's hope for the reconciliation of individual and society does not entail effacing the difference between universal and particular either. His notion of freedom in a reconciled state demands that the tension between individual and society be maintained, not reified or abolished. For liberation necessitates a recognition of just this tension— this coercive, dominating ground of subjectivity itself—to which one of the most important ethical responses is a compassion for the unavoidable suffering entailed. Cornell suggests that a "self-transparent solidarity would allow for much greater fluidity in relations between subjects, but it would not totally end the experience of the divide between the internal and external." Against Habermas, the ethical relations of intersubjective recognition that are free from the domination of the concept and of class depend on establishing a non-dominating relation to objectivity and otherness as a condition for their own existence rather than vice versa. It is not the level of intersubjective recognition via linguistically mediated interaction that establishes the possibility of such freedom, but rather recognition of the sensual basis of subjectivity itself—"the recognition of the shared human plight which comes from the subject's reflection on his 'natural side'" (Cornell, 1992: 33–34). Adorno arrived at such a position not because he neglected intersubjectivity but because he pursued the intersubjective mediation of subjectivity so consistently and extensively.

Let us conclude this section with a final look at Adorno's concept of subjectivity. The "How" to which he refers in the passage quoted earlier (pages 146–147) cannot be a thing (the "What"), yet it must have existence, for otherwise "it is nothing." The objectivity of that which is referred to as "subject," the "active thing," is rather a *relation*. It is a social relation *because* it is subjectivity; yet, as subject, it is always secondary to its "socialness"—never the sole "constitutive thing." As such, the true existence of any particular subjectivity (the "empirical subject" of epistemology) is always the social objectivity, the intersubjective relations of a conflictual, antagonistic totality. The most basic subjective, immediate experience cannot be what it appears—immediate, positive, perfectly present—because "consciousness is at the same time the universal medium and cannot jump across its shadow, even in these, its own *données immédiates*" (*ND*: 50/39–40). Consciousness exists by virtue of an objectivity on a logically different, *collective* level. This is a circle—there being no origin—but it is not the vicious circle of infinite regress faced by Fichte and others within the monadically focused philosophy of the subject. For Adorno, "society is immanent in experience," and what must be grasped philosophically is the dialectical relation of subjectivity and objectivity that allows the priority of the object to come "shimmering through" the veil of reified subjectivity woven around it by the subject (Adorno, 1969: 157, 162). In turn, we get at subjectivity—for subjectivity is essential—only through the object, through objectivity. But this means that what we need for dialectical thinking is "not less subjectivity, but more" (*ND*: 50/40).

The "not less subjectivity, but more" here suggests that the "reason" of liberation is nevertheless to be found within the subject, the individual—that is, a reason that can find expression through individual motivation or intention—even though such intention can never be thought of as entirely or essentially originary or willed. Subjectivity itself is a product, and it is "objectivity," but it is not merely a *blind* product or object, despite the astonishing blindness to which the history of subjectivity attests. New and better ways of thinking and acting can result if an aesthetic-critical theory is pursued consistently. Yet how this might motivate or help organize transfigurative political action remains a crucial question (but see Coles, 1997: 180–220, for an excellent pursuit of negative dialectical implications drawn from Adorno's thought for contemporary coalition politics). For Adorno, this motivation for reason must be rooted in the object, in the objective existence and social experience of subjectivity, which is by necessity repressive, painful, alienating, conflictual. By virtue of an awareness of subjectivity's own entwinement in and responsibility for this suffering—the social "objectivity" of subjectivity—a recognition of common cause becomes possible. This might be something like a substantive solidarity that is material to the extent that, following the ethical orientation of the tradition of critical theory, all deserve freedom from suffering. In the final section below I suggest that aesthetic experience can point in the direction of such substantive solidarity, which makes it politically crucial to critical theory.

Overcoming identity thinking could potentially release us from the incessant striving that drives late-capitalist society. But happiness is an elusive state, and no complete happiness such as that most closely experienced in ecstasy or in religious love or joy seems possible in this, the enlightened world, or in any future world that does not entirely negate secular enlightenment. Adorno's concept of reconciliation is to a certain extent his substitute for the ancient notion of the *good life*, as Dallmayr has argued, which is a notion that no longer has connotations of rule by the virtuous or of a single goodness, but rather suggests "a situation permeated by the willingness to let others be, or to respect and cherish them in their distinct being and goodness" (1981: 136). But it is also more than this, for it provokes an engagement that does not remain satisfied with a letting be but rather, as I have been arguing, elicits an ethical, communicative response to the Other and otherness, one that seems crucial for a critical theory to remain critical.

Let us turn in this final section to the political relevance that Adorno finds in art and in aesthetic mimesis. I would like to extend my reading of the democratic, egalitarian Adorno implicitly against, among other things, overdrawn interpretations of the mandarin Adorno and his elitist aesthetic, but especially against the view of his turn to art as the despairing response of an implacable, pessimistic critical theory. Drawing from his rich reflections on art and the aesthetic in the uncompleted but substantial text of *Aesthetic Theory*,[9] I highlight the potential of the mimetic shudder (*Erschütterung*), the shock occurring in aesthetic recognition. I hope that this might contribute to an understanding of the historical-practical dimension of democratic politics so often regarded as missing from Adorno's work.

5.3. ART AND THE RECOVERY OF NEGATIVITY AND NON-IDENTITY: TOWARD A POLITICS OF THE 'MIMETIC SHUDDER'

One may understand Adorno's aesthetic-critical theory as having an important critical relationship to the tradition of German Romanticism that culminates in Nietzsche. It is not at all merely an affirmative relation, however, for he was, among other things, extremely sensitive to the theoretical and historical misuse of the central Romantic position of the primacy of the aesthetic and to the abolition of art (that is, the destruction of its autonomy) through its unmediated absorption into society. Moreover, against the Romantic veneration of the premodern, Adorno's orientation is toward the future: "Rationalization is not yet rational; the universality of mediation has yet to be transformed into living life" (*AT*: 64). His critical view is utterly opposed to a political aesthetic or aestheticization of politics as in, for example, the Nazi's aestheticization of politics or the victory of spectacle over the public sphere (see Jay, 1993: 74). Adorno does not call for an artist-warrior as the savior or Legislator of a new polis. And his antagonism against a political aesthetic also extends to politically left articulations such as Brecht's, while at the same time finding value in the works themselves. But despite Adorno's emphasis on the negativity of critique, and despite his circumspect attitude toward articulating a political theory that might be developed from his insights, the aesthetic remains a deeply political category for Adorno through which we may glimpse the political possibilities of his thought. An Adornian aesthetics of democracy, as I will present it here, offers a promising contribution to rethinking the political under the conditions of late capitalist society.

Adorno's hostility toward art's politicization has more to do with his desire to preserve the specific critical value of art's distance from society than with denying a deep political importance to art and the aesthetic. This can be related to his critique of enlightenment rationality and its correlate ethical thought. Despite Adorno's attacks on modern morality following Kant, which is perhaps most scandalously presented in *Dialectic of Enlightenment*, his critique of Kantian ethics and morality is nevertheless redemptive as a whole: while a (traditional) moral philosophy is to be rejected, the truth of historically mediated moral life is to be recovered for critique and for freedom.[10] For, like all intellectual products in Adorno's view, moral philosophy is not simply abstract philosophy, nor morality merely ideology. There is always a historical content to morality and philosophy that is non-identical to their professed concerns, but that must be brought to awareness if moral or philosophical questions are to be properly understood and their deepest intentions recognized. As fateful or distorted expressions of the damaged human life under the conditions of a repressive, one-track enlightenment and more broadly the antagonistic conditions of social domination, struggle, and instrumental purposes, moral philosophy and moral critique are inadequate positions from which to develop a proper perspective on their objects. The subject of morality cannot be stabilized for critical purposes. In this sense, the human subject or rational intellect is, for Adorno, both real and illusory: it exists because virtually nothing escapes its domination, a condition capitalism has historically developed to the extreme; but it is illusory due to its necessary entwinement with domination, which entails that it is not what it passes itself off to be. The crisis of modernity is a crisis of enlightenment and its self-understanding whose social dimension requires an analysis of social domination (see Chapter 2). Adorno's relationship to Nietzsche the anti-moralist and the aesthetic is thus mediated by the materialism of Marx: "Anti-morality, in rejecting what is immoral in morality, repression, adopts morality's deepest concern: that with all restrictions all violence (*Gewalt*) too should be abolished. This is why the motives of intransigent bourgeois self-criticism coincide in fact with those of materialism, through which the former attain awareness" (*MM*: 95/119).

Adorno does not quite seek to *replace* morality with some form of aesthetic praxis, behavior, or style. What is important is, in the first instance, the possibility of cultivating a new way of thinking to which new forms of practice and intersubjective relations can correspond and from which they can evolve. His aesthetic-critical theory is, in this sense, committed to developing an alternative to the traditional notion of critical enlightenment inherited from Kant that is to be achieved through special attention to the possibilities presented by art and aesthetic recognition.

The failure of morality (and, more broadly, of Reason and culture), for Adorno, is rooted in the operations of all that falls under the spell of identity thinking. Adorno's sensitivity to the damage done by this violence solicits his wish to encourage an attentiveness to the limited, damaging nature of thought that remains satisfied with the closure and commensurability of the concept as well as to the dominating subject such thought fosters. Since *incomplete* comprehension is all we can hope for, the unrepresentability of the social totality ought not necessarily result in its dismissal as a concept but rather should bring forth the dialectic.[11]

The philosophical alternative Adorno favors, the negative dialectic, is, as we have seen, an attempt to bring the difference between the concept and its subject matter to the fore, to hold their difference in view and thereby foster an awareness of that which is beyond capture by the concept. Given Adorno's conviction that the critique of false thought is also immanently the critique of the wrong condition of society, his implacable resistance to the domination of identifying thought must also be understood as a practical-political act of resistance against the domination of capitalist society. It is important for Adorno, in this sense, to anticipate or perceive the essence of the changed society in that of a changed thought. While Adorno does not offer a positive alternative or program of transformation that would constitute a political theory in the traditional sense, he intimates his politics in his mode of philosophizing. By preserving dialectical thought not as doctrine or method but as the *expression* of the "things one cannot speak about . . . the nonidentical," even though "expressing it identifies it at the same time" (*HTS*: 101–2), he practices a subversion of the status quo that offers itself as an ally to contemporary radical social movements.[12] His thought thus qualifies as utopian even though his critical vision remains relentlessly negative— but it must remain so in order to keep faith with its reason, which elicits a solidarity with the subjected, the repressed, the vanquished and disfigured that arises from an appreciation of what thought actually is and what it does. While he can go as far as to refer to the "reconciled" condition in contrast to the antagonistic whole of class society, this vision suggests only the *potential* of what would be a genuinely free life in which unnecessary domination and antagonism toward the other is absent. "The goal of the revolution is the abolition of fear" (Adorno, 1977a: 125). This concept of reconciliation, it hardly needs repeating, does not at all project some Hegelian final identity of subject and object.

The problem that such thought faces, Adorno emphasizes tirelessly, is first and foremost its own self-conscious limit, since that which would escape the deadly enchantments of the concept cannot be theorized. This is forever the stigma attached to philosophy because philosophical language can never finally fulfill its fundamental urge to know anything completely. Yet this problem is not as serious as it first appears, for philosophy, once chastened by this knowledge, can turn it to its advantage by allying itself with that which does claim to speak the language of non-identity, namely, art. In contrast to philosophy, art's mode of communication is non-conceptual, which, as an *experience*, is central to what philosophy would hope to achieve *with concepts* but cannot quite. But philosophy cannot *become* art, that is, retain its claim to identity (knowledge) at the same time as claiming to communicate the non-identical, the non-conceptual, without betraying its very meaning *as* philosophy. Philosophy and art are similar not in form but in their "behavior" or "mode of conduct" (*Verhaltensweise*) toward their respective opposites, whereby art obstinately pits itself against meaning while philosophy refuses to cling to any immediate thing (*ND*: 26–27/15).

Philosophical language, like all language, has a double character that forever reproduces a tension in the linguistic subject: "As a system of signs, language is required to resign itself to calculation in order to know nature and thus gives up the claim to be like nature. As representation, it is required to resign itself to the image in order to be nature whole and gives up the claim to know nature" (*DA*: 24/17–18). The mimetic powers of aesthetic representation and experience can complement Adorno's critical theory, but the critical theory does not then find itself theoretically completed. On the contrary, it is able instead to articulate the lack and absences with far more effect and power. Non-identity is forever beyond *discourse*, but not beyond awareness and insight evoked by language. "The utopia of cognition would be to open up the non-conceptual with concepts, without making it their equal" (*ND*: 21/10). What I wish to stress here is the potential productiveness of this tension that draws its power from a thinking-action that takes the aesthetic aspect of its cognition and the cognitive aspect of the aesthetic seriously.

Thus neither is art merely or solely art or beautiful appearance because it continues to point or bear witness to human beings' continued but repressed need for something like the irretrievably exiled primal happiness of wholeness. Yet this *promesse du bonheur* can never be redeemed in a 'fallen' world. "The dread of losing the self and along with the self canceling the border between itself and other life, the fear of death and destruction, is intimately associated with a promise of happiness that has threatened civilization at every moment. Its path was that of obedience and labor, over which fulfillment shines perpetually as mere semblance [*Schein*], as beauty deprived of power" (*DA*: 40/33). Nevertheless, in art's concept and experience lies the frustrated desire for absolutely and finally overcoming domination and the suffering of labor. This (im)possibility, this necessary illusion, is at art's core. "Art's *promesse du bonheur* means not only that hitherto praxis has blocked happiness but that happiness is beyond praxis" (*AT*: 12). This denial is indeed emphatic and grim. "The secret of aesthetic sublimation is its representation of fulfillment as a broken promise" (*DA*: 148/140).[13] Art bears witness to the hope of fulfillment but its form nevertheless confirms the unrealizable, impossible potential for a final reconciliation of social reason with its other.

Hence art does not simply offer a representation of a better world, even while it represents unmet needs and unfulfilled desires, for art's broken promise and its non-conceptuality are opposed to this. "Art is no more able than theory to concretize utopia, not even negatively" (*AT*: 32). The subversiveness of Adorno's view of art lies elsewhere than in any specific political *content* vouchsafed to art. But this raises an important difficulty in clarifying what exactly art offers, which has to do with the incomprehensibility of art itself and of what art actually represents. For Adorno, this refusal of its own meaning is one of art's most important aspects and cannot be simply analyzed away without destroying what he regards as art's truth content.

Adorno's thoroughgoing focus on the non-identical character of art has recently led Schoolman (1997) to derive a non-liberal defense of the liberal principle of "non-interference" from Adorno's aesthetic theory. Schoolman argues that "art must become blind and admit the opacity of difference. For it is only by admitting the darkness of being that art can be free of the illusion that the difference between 'subject' and 'object' can be overcome." For Schoolman, art "represents" an "unknown and impenetrably mysterious nature," it expresses the impossibility of knowing difference in itself, and it embodies the utter indeterminacy and contingency of our being. Art can thus teach reason that it must turn away from what it thought of as its ground—nature, the objects that service its projects—and ought instead to become creative of ever new forms (of life), productive of its own authenticity (1997: 85, 65, 70). By letting an unfathomable nature "be," reason turns toward itself and its own impossible ground and encourages a sensitivity to the differences beyond its own identifications. Such sensitivity is essential for the non-violent relations of identity and difference desired by critical theory. Yet no final reconciliation is possible: for Adorno, *every* identity depends on a violent constitutive representation of difference. Hence Schoolman advocates a quasi-liberal politics of "letting be" in which difference is recognized through an aesthetics of "darkness" and protected from the violence of all identifying thought. This releases a politics of darkness from a traditional liberal "passive tolerance" and from a simple notion of the unproblematic way in which differences may co-exist together without requiring a final identity (that is, as a simple plural diversity).

Yet this still does not acknowledge the conflictual and competitive nature of the political construction of identity in which the operation of hegemonic identities continually threaten the liberal ideal of letting difference be. Hence Connolly (1993) argues that any such politics must reach deeper to a politics of "agonistic respect" in which genealogical practices continually display the relational and contingent identity of the self and thereby undermine such hegemonic projects. Schoolman is sympathetic to this yet contends that genealogy must turn its tools of inquiry upon itself and recognize that *all* identities are only milder versions of hegemonic counterparts. Thus genealogy cannot itself hope to allow a reconciliation with the inaccessible difference. This returns Schoolman to the aspiration of what he understands as Adorno's aesthetics of darkness. By allying an Adornian "politics of darkness" with a post-Nietzschean "politics of agonistic respect" of difference, Schoolman hopes to mutually enhance each position and establish more securely the complementary ethical sensibilities nurtured by those such as Adorno and Connolly (Schoolman, 1997: 88–89).

What concerns me here is not the admirable ethic and form of politics Schoolman hopes to foster but rather his apparent neglect of the cognitive value that art offers and how this could affect politics. It seems that Schoolman overemphasizes the unknowability of the radical difference displayed in art and thereby risks, despite his best intentions, delivering Adorno over to the very Habermasian critique he wants to rescue him from.[14] Adorno's move is not simply based on a denial of possible positive knowledge of that "excess of life" beyond the concept, which gives rise to an affirmation of the need to respect that nonidentity and difference. For this would, in a way, confine Adorno's philosophy to a wholly negative orientation, even perhaps a negative ontology, which, admittedly, might make it more attractive to a thoroughgoing contemporary post-Nietzschean position. This would in any case sacrifice the dynamic of his dialectical thinking. But what Adorno was instead trying to offer us by enlisting art and the aesthetic through his meta-critique of knowledge and cognition is the possibility of a truly new way of thinking, a new cognition that is also most centrally concerned with truth and genuine understanding, even if 'truth' can only be conceived today as contradiction and if understanding requires utmost effort coupled with potentially very disturbing and confusing experiences. What's more, the motivation for this effort originates from a desire to reach out to that that is dominated *through* knowledge and cognition, a knowledge and cognition without violence that is not to be satisfied with letting things be. Only after such a general condition was achieved in actuality, that is, in society, could the frustrated drives of knowledge and cognition themselves finally be redeemed on an ongoing basis and a condition approaching happiness, among other things, would then be a real possibility.

Indeed, as Horkheimer and Adorno themselves argue, it is the fear of the objectivity of truth that petrifies the thrust of enlightenment as an overwhelming need to know absolutely, the fear that keeps it bound to the "false clarity" imposed by dominant thought. By "making taboo as vague and dubious long-windedness all thinking attached to the negative, or at best alienating it, this notion holds the spirit bewitched in an ever deeper blindness" (*DA*: 4/xiv). Darkness, obscurity, and blindness are all dialectical products of this enlightenment, not its counterpoint or corrective; they require the remedy of a negativity able to employ an alternative dialectic of seeing and illumination. "In the unreconciled condition, nonidentity is experienced as negativity" (*DA*: xiv/4; *ND*: 41/31). Hence, I would contend, a letting be of nature and a respect for difference are ethical options not finally because of the categorical imperative imposed by the unknowable, utterly mysterious, unfathomable absence expressed by art or the incomprehensible, unrepresentable, ineffable otherness registered in art. For while art represents the unrepresentability of the unrepresentable, or as Schoolman says, "expresses the inexpressibility of the inexpressible" (1997: 67), what must in turn also be acknowledged is that art is thereby most eloquent in speaking to us of this darkness it alone is privy to. Thus there must be more to be expected from the appeal to the aesthetic for Adorno than a contemplative letting be, or simply a liberal respect of difference.

Schoolman emphasizes that art presents us with a model for coming to terms with the unknown, and indeed it is the unknown that provides him with the central trope of the "politics of darkness." This interpretation of Adorno's aesthetic theory[15] needs to do more justice to art's utopian dimension, for what is "draped in black" is, for art (and Adorno), *utopia*, and not merely a shrouded nature. Because it is the yet-to-exist that is "draped in black," utopia remains a "recollection of the possible in relation to the actual that suppresses it; it is the imaginary reparation of the catastrophe of world history; it is freedom, which under the spell of necessity did not—and may not ever—come to pass" (*AT*: 135). This recollection, which Adorno then projects as the hope for a future state of reconciliation between self and its other, is a potential that is, except perhaps in the nightmare vision of total administration and reification, always reproduced along with every turn of the dialectic of enlightenment. Neither does the fact that it may not ever come to pass imply a pessimistic or fatalistic position but reflects instead the caution that whenever we believe we are beyond the dialectic of enlightenment we most certainly are not. I will return to this recollection of art in a moment.

This utopian dimension is related to the central paradox of the aesthetic as a whole (but does not find its limit in the unknown): "How can making bring into appearance what is not the result of making; how can what according to its own concept is not true nevertheless be true?" (*AT*: 107). This is the paradoxical task of a redemption of illusion, of trying to discern how something that has been consciously constructed as a depiction of something else, and therefore is historically and aesthetically bound, can also illuminate something that was not culturally constructed in such fashion. Adorno's specific answer parallels the extremely difficult solution he gives to the question of representation itself, that what is represented must be understood as *both* true and false, *both* present and absent at the same time. The aesthetic is brought forth in this paradoxical way by Adorno to complete the ethical dimension of critical theory and to retain the claim to truth in dialectical fashion.

Rather than mitigate his philosophical claims in the face of the mysteries and indeterminacies of aesthetic meaning, Adorno looks beyond the incomprehensibility of art to its enigmaticalness (*Rätselcharakter*), which is what is actually to be comprehended. But again, following from the enigma, philosophy cannot hope to comprehend the artwork as a strict hermeneutic object—that is, it cannot explain the substantive meaning of the work without becoming a science of art criticism. Without its enigmatic character, art becomes just another object of study for the classifying intellect and would lose its ability to function critically and even to be experienced as art. Its enigmaticalness is to be preserved, but somehow made relevant. In order to suggest that there could be a meaning to this enigmaticalness, Adorno makes reference to his contemporaries' use of *écriture* in this context and describes all artworks as writing, or more precisely as "hieroglyphs for which the code has been lost, a loss that plays into their content" (*AT*: 124). Certainly this insistence on enigmaticalness has drawn criticisms and dismissals of Adorno's position for invoking a mythic or mysterious reconciliation with nature that, in principle, is unable to be clarified or understood. But, as I have already suggested, such criticisms are more appropriately directed at an aesthetic theory that insists simply on the utter unknowability of art's object.[16] For Adorno explicitly states (in this case, against phenomenology) that aesthetics "is not involved with its object as with a primordial phenomenon." The language of art is already developed; the subject inheres within the works already such that it is precisely by way of this subjectivity that the work itself becomes something objective, that is, other (*AT*: 351, 353, 355–56). Thus the enigmaticalness of art is to be understood with specific reference to the historically acting and speaking subject, which is how Adorno can claim that art needs philosophy, needs the production of its truth content, but, conversely, why the reified language of concepts needs to be mitigated by its consciousness and mimesis of art's language.

Yet, as Adorno stresses time and again, the language of art is mute, or rather, non-conceptual; it is gestural, visage, expressive, and comportment; and this speechless communication takes priority over its signification. Art's unique "eloquence" (*Sprachcharakter*) suggests that we must look beyond the artwork itself, beyond the semblance character, in order to approach art's truth content (*Wahrheitsgehalt*). This is a unique knowledge of history that evokes a profound experience of the entwinement of the natural and the historical: "Artworks bear expression not where they communicate the subject, but rather where they reverberate with the protohistory of subjectivity, of ensoulment. . . . This is the affinity of the artwork to the subject and it endures because this protohistory survives in the subject and recommences in every moment in history" (*AT*: 112–13). The knowledge one approaches through the experience of art is found in an awareness of the sacrifice made necessary by the very success of the reason of society, of the history of class domination, and of the reification that has admittedly also made such experience and awareness themselves possible. Social reason and art stand opposed, alienated from one another, yet they are intimately entwined as well.

But the way in which one reaches this knowledge or truth content cannot imitate the way in which science arrives at its truth content. The truth content of artworks cannot be immediately identified because such content emerges only through the utter particularity of the artwork itself and cannot thus be generalized. The *difference* of the particular artwork is key and directly participates in the expression of its truth content. The mediatedness of thought is qualitatively different from that of artworks: what is mediated in art must be mediated through a 'second reflection' in order to produce a properly comprehensible aesthetic experience (*Erfahrung*). "However," Adorno writes,

> it is no guarantee of their truth that artworks transcend themselves through their realization. Many works of the highest quality are true as the expression of a consciousness that is false in itself. This is recognized only by transcendent criticism, such as Nietzsche's critique of Wagner. The failing of that kind of critique, however, is not only that it judges the matter from on high rather than measuring itself by it. This criticism is also impeded by a narrow-minded notion of truth content, usually a cultural/ philosophical notion that neglects the immanently historical element of aesthetic truth. The separation of what is true in itself from the merely adequate expression of false consciousness is not to be maintained, for correct consciousness has not existed to this day, and no consciousness has the lofty vantage point from which this separation would be self-evident. The complete presentation of false consciousness is what names it and is itself truth content. It is for this reason that the works unfold not only through interpretation and critique but also through their rescue, which aims at the truth of false consciousness in the aesthetic appearance. Great artworks are unable to lie. Even when their content is semblance, insofar as this content is necessary semblance the content has truth, to which the artworks testify; only failed artworks are untrue (*AT*: 129–30).

One of the greatest problems that might then be discerned—especially after the modern emancipation of autonomous art—is that reified social reason cannot approach the meaning of art as anything but apparently incomprehensible, potentially dangerous, and, as a consequence, the stuff perhaps to be assimilated into the art market, or suppressed in censorship. If it is safely pleasurable, it is domesticated in the frivolous, 'happy' art of the culture industries. Here it is turned into a diversion from the numbing world of work that, under Adorno's dialectical reversal, succeeds in such pleasurable diversion only by repeating in leisure activities the same kinds of standardized routines that consumers believe they are in fact escaping. But if the critical value of art can be destroyed by society, transformed repressively in an aestheticized politics, or made docile—the aesthetic corollary of disenchantment: 'de-artment' (*Entkunstung*)—then the reverse is not true. Art can never excise its essential social element: "Figuration, which articulates the wordless and mute contradictions, thereby has the lineaments of a praxis that is not simply a flight from real praxis; figuration fulfills the concept of art itself as a comportment... The immanence of society in the artwork is the essential social relation of art, not the immanence of art in society" (*AT*: 232).

For Adorno, genuinely important art can never abstract itself from society, from its social content, nor from its critical stance toward what is non-art. Yet if art cannot concretize utopia, it does have the *appearance* of a negative utopia. Art suggests a realm of happiness that is denied under the conditions of society, but it does not—cannot—seek to act on this, to bring some idyllic state of affairs into being. This denial, far from being an admission of pointlessness or even political quietism exactly, uncovers a crucial insight into the potentially explosive character of art: "The immanence of artworks, their apparently a priori distance from the empirical, would not exist without the prospect of a world transformed by self-conscious praxis... Praxis is not the effect of works; rather, it is encapsulated in their truth content. This is why commitment is able to become an aesthetic force of production" (*AT*: 247).

This could be read as a denial of the enlightening effects of art (and, by extension, the texts of an aesthetic-critical theory themselves), if by effects we mean the kind of inspiration or spur to direct action for which political art is mobilized. Adorno was never very sympathetic to this kind of link between theory and practice. Yet there is a deeper sense here in which Adorno is in fact reconceptualizing the theory/practice question by emphasizing the *performative* actualization of what he understands as worthy of the name *enlightenment:* praxis is "encapsulated" in the artwork's "truth content." The insight Adorno draws upon here, which runs through all his philosophical work, is that "theory and mental experience need to interact" through a "nimbleness" or "mobility" of mind that involves "a double mode of conduct" (*ND*: 41/3). This double mode of thinking-action reflects the double character of language itself introduced earlier.

What now becomes clearer is the association of philosophically informed thought with aesthetic experience that Adorno wishes to promote. The trembling tension in language requires that thought, like the objects it analyzes, remains "inherently in motion," which constantly challenges linear thinking with a more appropriate ideal, suggested by Hegel's work, of "nonargumentative thought." Just as dialectical thought rejects the Cartesian *res extensa*—matter extended in space—on account of the nonidentical constitution of the object, neither can the subject be static "like a camera on a tripod; rather, the subject itself also moves, by virtue of its relationship to the object that is inherently in motion" (*HTS*: 140–41, 98). The Hegelian identity of identity and nonidentity, which is called Becoming, "trembles within itself. . . . The unfolding of the concept is also a reaching back, and synthesis is the determination of difference which is submerged, 'vanished' in the concept; almost, as in Hölderlin, like the anamnesis of the natural that must reach downwards" (*ND*: 160/ 157). The obvious image here is a circling of thought, or "curvilinear" thinking, that attempts a mimesis of the object, of nature, or of the other, by performing its cognitive achievements like the way artworks are brought into being. The ethical import of this mimetic action is that the thinker not identify the other, that is, perceive him or her according to an existing classificatory scheme, but identify *with* the other by suspending his or her subjectification in a difficult act of open receptivity of otherness. "You will find love only where you may show yourself weak without provoking strength" (*MM*: 255/192). Self and other are brought into a non-violent relationship by mimetic communication that is at the root of human learning (and freedom).

5.3.1. *The Politics of Mimetic Shudder*

Dialectical thought can thus bring into being a new political culture to assist the social subject in its least violent and most productive relationships to the other, to its own non-identical past, and to all that is different and alien. But if this utopian image of what dialectical thought can do is attractive ethically and politically, it remains to be seen just what could constitute the motivation for individuals to embark on such a difficult journey. For all the immediate interests of the self lie in maintaining its identity, in not giving it up or weakening it in the face of an other, which harks back to the primal fear behind the urges of self-preservation. Moreover, there is a 'natural' tendency of language toward reification. It is here that the *force* of the mimetic shudder presents its greatest political potential.

Art is social because its alienated existence is entwined with the very process of enlightened liberation from nature (disenchantment): art's very actuality is derived from domination and mastery. Furthermore, art itself, in its technique, does violence to its object. This makes artworks socially culpable; yet each, Adorno argues, seeks to expiate this guilt through its synthetic expression, to rescue over into form something of the amorphous to which they ineluctably do violence (*AT*: 234, 50). The wordless gesture of art turns out to be in fact its most powerful and important aspect for it opens up to the subject a consciousness, an experience, of what is repressed for the sake of its own being, and therefore what is also still a part of it. This is the anamnestic possibility of aesthetic experience, a remembrance or recollection of reality that is non-existing or not-yet-existing, a reality nonetheless experienced by the subject beyond the world of real things. "Art has truth as the semblance of the illusionless . . . (H)istory alone frees the work from being merely something posited or manufactured: truth content is not external to history but rather its crystallization in the works" (*AT*: 132–33). This notion of the recovery of the objectivity of subjectivity must be stressed for its crucial ethical and political import. Through this experience an underlying social solidarity shimmers in the distance before the alienated/alienating subject. But again, the political content of art is not its message:

> The language of artworks is, like every language, constituted by a collective undercurrent, . . . the eloquence of their collective substance originates in their image character and not in the 'testimony'—as the cliché goes—that they supposedly wish to express to the collective. The specifically artistic achievement is an overarching binding character to be ensnared not thematically or by the manipulation of effects but rather by presenting what is beyond the monad through immersion in the experiences that are fundamental to this bindingness (*AT*: 86).

To the social(ized), rational being who actually approaches art with the openness necessary, such an experience is a shock. It is a shock that arises not from art's stimulus of some primal impulse or repressed emotion but from the recipient's disappearance into the work, the moment of being shaken for which nevertheless the whole of consciousness is required. This experience Adorno calls the "shudder" (*Erschütterung*) (*AT*: 244), an aesthetic experience whose cognitive value is akin to the shock of recognition. It is a subjective response to the objective truth of art, colored by fear of the overwhelming.

This is a far greater disturbance to the stability and reassurance of the self than, for example, the non-aesthetic mere realization of one's own mortality. Reaction to human finitude has a long history of giving rise to irrational counterdesires for personal legacies, for immortality, or the mystical fantasies of an immortal soul. Alternatively, finitude can evoke counterdesires for nirvana, as I mentioned—the complete escape from self into undifferentiated existence. (In Freudian terminology, the drives associated with Eros and Thanatos.) Indeed, the twin responses to death anxiety and death denial that accompany increasingly individuated forms of consciousness and whose contrasting political forms of progressive social versus reactionary fascist revolution are sometimes understood to coordinate with the two most popular forms of denying death: self-assertion and self-effacement (Zimmerman 1994: 54–55). Adorno's reference is to a more reflective and profound experience of human finitude without such dangerous production of delusions. Yet it maintains its orientation to a possible future that has broken with the dialectic of enlightenment. The shudder is more akin to a consciousness of the transience of the self, to seeing one's own significance erased in the face of an overwhelming force, admittedly, but which turns out to be the power of the non-identical, the profound experience of the historical itself. It is thus not an *utter* self-effacement that occurs; the shudder describes rather the shattering of a certain *kind* of semblance that hides a true consciousness of historical semblancing itself:

> Shudder, radically opposed to the conventional idea of experi-ence [*Erlebnis*], provides no particular satisfaction for the I; it bears no similarity to desire. Rather, it is a memento of the liq-uidation of the I, which, shaken, perceives its own limitedness and finitude. To catch even the slightest glimpse beyond the prison that itself is, the I requires not distraction but rather the utmost tension. . . . For a few moments the I becomes aware, in real terms, of the possibility of letting self-preservation fall away, though it does not actually succeed in realizing this possibility. The I is seized by the unmetaphorical, semblance-shattering conscious-ness: that it itself is not ultimate, but semblance (*AT*: 245–46).

This describes a momentous, if fleeting experience that has ex-tremely suggestive possibilities. But its deconstructive thrust ought not point to nihilism for nihilism is rather the result of an unmitigated will to power, a response to the utter positivity of mere facticity. Indeed, Adorno's theory is to be viewed as an antidote to the nihilism that con-tinually haunts modernity as well as a critique of the domination that is at the root of existent suffering.[17]

Neither is the shudder equivalent to the awe-inspiring dread and terror evoked by images of irrational nature, of the mysterious and exalted authority of Being, nor the similarly overwhelming fear of an omnipotent God whose works in the world are immeasurable to those of human beings. All such phenomena and experiences are finally unknow-able by human *reason* in the conservative idiom, which is, of course, also the point: providence can be observed but not questioned. Such sublime images are, however, intended thereby to command the reverence and respect of inherited practices, traditions, and of the will of God, which reinforce socially binding feelings and promote virtues such as moderation in the populace.

Edmund Burke's (1958; 1968) central consideration of the sublime in this respect is worth mentioning.[18] Burke sought to ground hierarchical society in the aestheticized political truth deriving from natural passions. The positive social passions underlying sympathy, imitation, love, and ambition (toward improvement) must be united with the virile energy and awe-inspiring respect awakened by the delightful terror of the sublime if the polity is to avoid either narcissistic decline or violent destruction. The sublime, for Burke, refers not to our direct experience of the most powerful feelings of pain, danger, and terror, but rather to such experience at a safe distance, removed from direct threat but still evocative of the terrible sources of such feelings. Thus when we contemplate images and ideas "conversant with terrible objects" we derive a delight quite different to simple positive pleasure, or the love we feel in the face of beauty. The sublime crushes and forces an awesome admiration and respect, which, according to Burke, should be attached to the personages of political authority.

Later, in response to the French Revolution, Burke came to distinguish more clearly between this good sublime, which was best invoked through the distancing medium of poetic words, from the bad sublime of the idea image—the sublime "ideologie" of rational revolution. This latter cold and theoretic passion could excite a destructive fanaticism that brought down governments and erased the necessary social mediations of tradition, manners, and customary belief under the brute force of naked power. Burke thus emphasized an aesthetic of submission and awful, mystical reverence because he regarded these passions as most important for social bonding—quite in contrast to the passions of freedom that he associated with destruction. This is an older, simpler anti-bourgeois critique, which is clear from its aesthetic invocations for the sake of a naturally unequal social order and a political rule that cannot and should not be transparent to reason.

Although Adorno might agree with Burke that social power cannot be made *completely* transparent, he would deny that the relations of social power cannot be altered in such a way as to undermine the violent force of reason *as* social power, that is, as myth. This is one of the decisive differences between the conservative and the critical theorist. And rather than seek to confirm or uncover any natural order of (traditional) being, the consciousness evoked in the mimetic shudder points toward the contingency or complete historicity of being. Faced with this, the self is required to take responsibility for the illusions of social life, which I believe points in the direction of a liberatory democratic politics.

The political call is for an art that can deliver such mimetic shock. But again, this is an art that is not at all *simply* shocking, and not simply offensive (though such art might have a useful effect on the remnants of neo-Victorian prudishness). However, the shock of manufactured and standardized excitement or terror has been a staple of culture industry products systematically since at least the 1970s. Hollywood continues to exploit such shock and sublime excitement in suspense, adventure, and horror film genres, while apocalyptic and millenialist themes abound. The safe experience of the wrath of God, nature/cosmos, or the threat of evil is encouraged, but poses no real danger because the standard resolution of Hollywood narratives always completes and concludes it (despite intermediate destruction, the hero(ine)/city/human race/world is saved in the end). North American mainstream mass media news reporting, especially in television, might also be cited for its sensational moral or moral-political concerns as an imitative form, which dominates to the extent of the virtual exclusion of that for which it substitutes: the reporting of political events and the provision of relevant political information.

The vast (male-consumed) shooter or adventure computer game market, in which terrible first-person violence, destruction, and death can be experienced safely by the player, provides another related example. The moralist's reaction to such unhealthy consumption usually focuses on the desensitization to violence and the erosion of the ethical response to the suffering of others that such activity is supposed to promote. But more dangerous is the subjectification process embodied in the action. No matter how life-like, real, or 3-D the game's architecture, it reinforces standardized patterns of behavior and expectation that instead imitate the reified, dead world of capitalist production. No matter how adventurous, wild, shocking, and exciting the games are, they still require and reproduce an instrumentalized subjectivity and experience whose attendant satisfaction lasts only as long as the game is in operation. Thus the games have that addictive quality reproduced by consumer culture as a whole, for they continually promise and deliver a satisfaction that, as it happens, can only be achieved under their direct influence (merely thinking about the game is no equivalent). But the culture industry reproduces pathological addiction because it only *simulates* integral gratification—it constantly promises a *real* satisfaction that it cannot actually deliver, but the substitute gratification it does deliver constantly draws the consumer back for more precisely because it is hollow.

The culture industry sublime can thus be seen to function in parallel but perverted ways to aspects of Burke's good sublime, only this time it elicits a respect for postmodern charismatic (substitute) leadership, American (or American-way) hegemony, and, most abstractly, the hierarchy of market-oriented values. This sublime functions instead in the interests of maintaining capitalist consumption by reproducing a depoliticized, unmotivated, and non-participatory public formed by and through the public morality of mass consumption. The essentially monadic, aggregated good that is institutionalized is radically at odds with the achievement of a collective, public good.

The shock of recognition in the mimetic shudder, by contrast, "bears no similarity to desire" (*AT*: 245) and so cannot deliver satisfaction at all. The democratically important mimetic shock in art is instead a shock associated with *recognition*. It is a shock that can be induced by representational art, such as that experienced by nineteenth century audiences in the critical effects produced by the caricatures of Honoré Daumier and Picasso in the early twentieth. This specific critical distancing (and there are multiple claims to a critical-democratic aesthetic) is incorporated into twentieth-century modern art and reproduced in the experiences of such diverse work as Expressionism, photomontage, twelve-tone music, or absurdist theatre.

But can such shock of critical distancing be reproduced today under conditions in which the modern experiences of space and time have been substantially disrupted by postmodern consumerism, global pluralism (or relativism), and multinational globalized production? The critical distance elicited by the enigmaticalness of art is apparently erased in the fusion of commercial and fine art associated with Fluxus, Dadaism, or Warhol (whose precursors, it should be noted, are found in the art into life efforts of pre-Stalin Soviet artists such as Rodchenko and Popova in the 1920s). If art can continue to shock in valuable ways, it must be shocking not just in the offensiveness of controversial works such as Andres Serrano's *Piss Christ* (a crucifix submerged in a yellowish liquid) or Karen Finley's *We Keep Our Victims Ready* (a performance piece featuring the artist's nude body smeared in a brown substance). Some political science fiction, which can tend toward the utopian (Ursula K. LeGuin) or dystopian (William Gibson), or deploys both in ambiguous combinations (Marge Piercy, the films of David Cronenberg), thematizes historical semblancing (recently through sophisticated cyborg themes) that explicitly presents the entwinement of technology and the production of the self (see also Haraway, 1985). The photography of Cindy Sherman can produce the shock of mimetic recognition if properly understood not as portrait photography (which still implies an original subject who is represented) but as a graphic depiction of the self as a social text without a real substrate. The disappearance of the historical referent clearly manifests itself in the aesthetic dilemma of the contemporary historical novel, which can itself stage this problem—as Jameson observes in the novels of E. L. Doctorow—and at least offer a real insight into the new stage of representation that is to be derived from the shock of grasping this new limitation (Jameson, 1991: 21–25). Finally, the shudder itself can be represented, as in the momentous shuddering experiences often featured in the novels of Robert Stone that seem to want to remind us of the sublime experience of the shock itself (for example, the diving sequence in Stone 1992: 225–28).

It is no doubt premature to ascribe historical significance to postmodern art since it has not yet produced a properly postmodern political culture articulated directly in an enduring political movement. Although certainly one should mention the substantial political campaigns of groups such as the poststructuralist-influenced ACT UP insurgency in the 1980s (for a discussion, see Reinhardt, 1997: 142–78) or the more recent, entirely mass media based resistance movement called "culture jamming," which combats the commodified image fetish using the tools of the postmodern advertising image themselves (see the journal of the movement: *Adbusters*). I would suggest that the success of any such movement that opposes postmodern capitalism and attendant domination will continue to depend on the shudder in some way as part of its critical operation. This would be, of course, always in conjunction with other clear cognitive and political requirements appropriate to an effective political movement. These include the important effort to map the cognitive space of the new world order in relation to the matching historical consciousness of class domination, which Jameson (1991) has advocated under the name "cognitive mapping," and the coordination of such efforts with new forms of organization that correspond to the new configuration of social forces under multi-national capitalism.

Returning to the specific contribution Adorno's concept of mimetic shudder: the mimetic shudder opens out upon the possibility of a moment of peace, of reconciliation understood as freedom from the need to maintain self-striving—the striving of the self's preservation and the self that can but strive—which in turn allows the repressed mimetic self to flourish. A peace of the soul, so to speak, relieved of its consuming burden of self-preservation but conscious of the domination necessary for its existence. This is the utopian moment of desire to which art bears witness. The beautiful in art survives, Adorno writes, "because as the forming force it recognizes the violence of that by which it measures itself. It is through this idea that art is related to peace. Without perspective on peace, art would be as untrue as when it anticipates reconciliation. Beauty in art is the semblance of the truly peaceful. It is this toward which even the repressive violence of form tends in its unification of hostile and divergent elements" (*AT*: 258).

Thus art experience contains an enormously hopeful phenomenon that Adorno believes critical theory can redeem for the current alienated social and political context. The hope is not for communion with one's Creator or with the souls of eternity, and nor is it for final rest in some idealist post-political, post-historical space of the identity of subject and object. That would in fact be death. Instead, the hope is for a free association of aesthetically aware individuals who recognize their thorough interdependence and responsibility in domination, an interdependence and domination that is a condition of their reason and their existence as free and independent selves. The semblance of one's self depends on a relation to the social objectivity that is itself beyond each individual self yet dependent on the active-passive self-fashioning and intersubjective engagement that responds to the reflective consciousness. The only philosophically defensible concept of reason as freedom is one that recalls its incompleteness and pauses in its purposes in order to cultivate its awareness of the other's suffering as well as its own.

The mimetic shudder is thus revealed finally not as an end but as an initial moment on the way to a deep and profound opening up to the possibilities of a spontaneous, creative, and empathetic life. That this life is overwhelmingly denied under late capitalism might provoke a political gesture from those who are able to experience this lack, but it is the shaking and shuddering that becomes possible in the encounter with great art that precedes and prepares such a possibility in a valuable way. The mimetic shudder is thus a deconstructive force that points toward a profound political reconstruction. It is a force—for force will always be necessary in all political resistance that has any chance of being successful—that works through great art and seeks to ally itself with the practical-political force of resistance movements.

5.3.2. Aesthetics and Democracy: Some Conclusions

A non-dominating mimesis does not seek to capture its objects wholly in its representations, its subject would not experience the *need* to exclude what cannot be grasped in its concept. But it does not thereby *forget* or abandon that which it cannot incorporate. It is thus a resolute consciousness of the utter limits of reason and language, and of the pain, negativity, and wish brought forth by this permanent lack and absence of the full object (and of the primal happiness promised by its complete possession). But it also brings forth the need to face this condition, to acknowledge and respond to it without succumbing to despair or repression. A non-dominating mimesis indeed has overcome the primal fear of the uncomprehended and hostile and finds room for these absences in the space occupied by its representations. Adorno presents this attentiveness in his mode of writing, in the form of the essay, in parataxis and chorismos—the *performance* of the negative dialectic—which helps him and the reader of his texts resist the spell of conceptual thinking. Even under the social conditions of rational domination it is possible to preserve a pre-dominative representation of the world free from fear and the requirements of repression that preserves likewise the desire to actually bring about such a condition. It is this utopian vision that drives the liberatory spirit toward a break with the dialectic of enlightenment and its endless sacrificial logic, which has found its greatest political ally in capitalism.

Art and aesthetic mimesis become so important, cognitively, politically, and ethically, for the way in which they not only permit imagination of the new but release the mimetic force of recognition. Permanently in tension with its own drive, non-dominative mimesis elicits the awareness and receptivity of difference, and a respect and responsibility for difference emerges. It is *because* art cannot "cast off the cloak of semblance," cannot "act as if it is what it appears to be," that it knows its truth content and becomes important for a liberated politics. It is a content that is not thereby known like one 'knows' objects but it can be *perceived*, brought to awareness, by an appreciation of the way the character of artworks operate as semblance. While Adorno always emphasized the comprehended experience (*Erfahrung*) of art over its mere 'felt' experience (*Erlebnis*), it is clear from my discussion that, with respect to the mimetic shudder, the force of aesthetic experience must be intimately entwined with such proper comprehension. Yet "redemption through semblance is itself illusory, and the artwork accepts this powerlessness" (*AT*: 107): *mere* art will not bring about redemption of its content or reconciliation of the antagonistic reality from which it springs and to which it opposes itself. Nevertheless, art becomes a spur, an inspiration that must finally connect with an historical social movement that shares its underlying interests in non-dominative mimesis. But if artworks must be maintained in their precarious tension *in order to* preserve their cognitive and ethical value for Adorno, then it is only

by the strength of its deadliness do artworks participate in reconciliation. But in this they at the same time remain obedient to
myth. This is what is Egyptian in each. By wanting to give per-
manence to the transitory—to life—by wanting to save it from
death, the works kill it. With good reason the power of artworks
to reconcile is sought in their unity, in the fact that, in accord
with the ancient topos, they heal the wound with the spear that
inflicted it (*AT*: 134).

Adorno's radical critique of reason is entirely consistent with his
dialectical vision that reason can be made reasonable only under the
right social conditions. The politics of critical theory, then, is very centrally and concretely concerned with the politics of *sensibility*, the thinking of the conditions of possibility of a new political being. This orientation
is important in the long tradition of utopian thinking, which has taken
the theme of *envisioning* a new constitution for political life (see Wolin,
1960). It is also why aesthetic comportment is integral to transformative
or transmogrified political practice at the individual or intersubjective
levels.

Since art cannot *replace* authority or the political, a democratic
society composed of competing, conflictual interests and diverse identities can best be governed in association with an institutional recognition
of what is required for an undamaged selfhood that respects its aesthetic
and non-identical elements and thus group identity. For Adorno, this
undamaged identity would not "annex the alien," for it would remain
"distant and different in its lasting nearness" (*ND*: 191–92/191). The
mimetic receptivity of an undamaged identity is the presupposition of
the fellow feeling, compassion, sympathy, and love toward other people
as they are and remain other and different.[19] There is no doubt that this
entails an extraordinary challenge, for it requires individual moral, ethical, and aesthetic self-formation (autonomy) and self-actualization (freedom) as well as requiring non-repressive collective identities that
encapsulate intersubjective/subject-object relations of engagement (political life). It raises a (Hegelian) question of the proper *mediation* of individual and the polity. This mediation should help establish a mimetic
receptivity of the other and a mimetic receptivity to otherness.

What does it mean to say that our communication is at root
aesthetic, that our representations of reality, the fundaments and touch-
stones of truth, are, as Rorty (1979) has contended, cultural artifacts?
Avoiding either Rorty's postmodern pragmatism or Habermas's pragmatics of language, Adorno shows us that the underlying medium of

communication is an aesthetic comportment that is repressed by the reification of language and social domination but need not be for an authentic communication and interaction. With respect to our relations to art, this is to acknowledge that thinking—conceptually mediated consciousness—arises from the body and from historical existence in the world and cannot be abstracted away from its corporeal, historically marked origins without further violence and damage. In Adorno's language it is also to say that suffering begets speech—"*Weh spricht: vergeh!*" (*ND*: 203/203). Any notion of communicative rationality adequate to its concept must be a rationality that acknowledges its aesthetic dimension, its corporeal medium and reference. This acknowledgment by no means invalidates or undermines its self-understanding as *reasoning* but rather confirms it by opening a precise path to the political, to the possibility of taking responsibility for and being responsive to this suffering and desire. This, I hope to have gone some ways toward showing, does not require a philosophy of the subject for its completion, but neither does it require abandoning the concept of the social totality.

Reconcilement is thus like democracy: it is always to come and must always be striven toward in the mindfulness of the radical contingency and indeterminacy of our experience and despite our knowledge that we can never possess or capture it once and for all. Such a state of affairs would not thereby be, of course, beyond justice, law or agonistic politics of conflict, struggle and competition. It might, however, be understood as the (post)modern equivalent of the activity and participation associated with the ancient notion of an ethical politics (but without implying the rule of a specific class)—the ancient recognition that the good life is itself an aesthetic part of the political.[20]

The recognition of the violence of identity and the subject's entwinement with it, which calls for responsibility, can bring us into a non-violent relationship with others that is predicated on a receptivity of non-identity. This is a political insight that pushes law and administration not necessarily in the direction of ever higher levels of formal abstraction—the extension of rights and duties to more groups, activities and aims, the attempt to incorporate excess difference within higher level identities, and so forth. Rather, it should impel law toward a letting be of difference and otherness *as* difference and otherness (and here one may cite the sympathetic work of Derrida and Cornell in the legal sphere). That is, *as* the presentation of difference and otherness, communication is possible *of* difference and otherness only if the non-identity of identity—what I have been emphasizing as the socially repressed, historical content of identity—is permitted to enter political discourse. My use of the artwork as the prime example of how this occurs in the aesthetic domain is transposed into the political domain via the experience of the mimetic shudder that confronts the monad with an aesthetic shock that threatens its self-possessed and illusory integrity.

Only with such openness can we expect individuals to be encouraged to speak in their (aesthetic) language that expresses a material, historical experience of particularity to which others may then be expected to respond with a similar open communicativity. Language is never completely or utterly alien to the self or to the other, for all language is "constituted by a collective undercurrent" (*AT*: 86). Yet this collective undercurrent can only become visible to thought through the tension and contradiction also inherent in the operation of language, which means that it can never really be revealed outside this process. The assimilation to the *subject* of language that is risked by reified abstraction—abstraction that is nevertheless necessary for all such intersubjective communication—can be countered and minimized by a mimetic assimilation to the *object* that is offered by the model of the artwork. Once such conducive conditions of communication are achieved in a more general way, the struggle for recognition of *difference* becomes an *enjoining* process of education and cultural development oriented to and facilitated by an aesthetic sensibility. This aesthetic sensibility is attuned to the importance of the gap between the representations we deal with on a daily basis and the non-identical, historical contents that cause a trembling in our consciousness.

But this aesthetic sense itself is ungrounded, ungroundable, because there is no final way to decide where unknowable nature and eminently representable human history separate. Life itself is incontestable, even if historical and contingent, and even if, as damaged and mutilated by instrumental purposes, it does not 'live' as life should. That life is worth living, while being a value judgement, is nevertheless an assumption without which social philosophy itself and indeed all intellectual activity would be pointless. An openness to and compassion for the suffering of the other brought forth by a mitigation of one's *own* self-striving—a discovery of the contingent conditions of one's own self—paradoxically grounds the self more securely not only because it thereby becomes conscious of its own illusion of presence but because through this openness or opening it receives itself from the other and gives that of itself to the other.

Not only does mimetic shuddering evoke a trembling of the self, of the things existing for the self, which causes an opening through which the non-identity of the object may shimmer through, but it shutters the stark light cast by identifying perception in order to allow an aesthetically informed, reflective contemplation to occur. (The image of shutter here plays on the English appearance of the German for the shudder: *Erschütterung*.) It works against the unyielding 'gaze' which has been the dominant trope of enlightenment by calling it to shut its eyes from time to time in order to allow other sense-making and new perceptions to enter thought. It thereby prevents a dogmatic appropriation of its ethic as a *morality*, a command code conceived for a self-identical subject, without denying the need for morality, law, and a certain social order.[21] A politics that appreciates the mimetic shudder is fundamentally a democratic politics. It reminds those engaged in politics, in struggles against domination and oppression (as well as those seeking to preserve their power), that the stakes are not only about whose justice or which rationality (which inevitably risks a decline into relativism, for that is the ironic consequence of all myopic ethics), but about fighting and resisting dogmatism and the violent complacence of remaining satisfied with any identity.

6

CONCLUSION

My criticism of Habermas's social and political thought and my desire to recover the relevant meaning and value of the alternative Adorno offers have been clearly intertwined in this book. The sacrifices and drawbacks of Habermas's work, I argue, can be clarified for critical theory especially with reference to Adorno's thought. A quite different notion of communicative freedom as a utopian project without a foundational subject can then be reconstructed within the tradition of critical theory. The following concluding remarks are intended to throw into relief the contrasts I have drawn between Adorno and Habermas and the reconstructed debate between their positions, and to underscore my Adornoesque alternative to Habermasian critical theory.

I have throughout stressed that the most promising articulation of critical theory requires a grasp of the import of the negative and the constitutive nature of non-identity. To articulate such a commitment is just what Adorno thought was required in the face of the history of civilization, its discontents, and especially the politicized culture and social conditions of late capitalism. But, as I have repeatedly emphasized, such a project that takes non-identity seriously is permanently in tension with its own critical, liberatory efforts. Attention to this tension via the very presentation or present-ing of communicative ideas entails great care and sensitivity to the operation of language, the social basis of language and the dynamics of communication, which Adorno performed with masterful skill. It should be clear that this tension and its attendant care and sensitivity should not therefore be regarded as logically contra-

193

dictory, incoherent, or merely a matter of style. Rather, it testifies to the ethic elicited by the call of critical thought to freedom. The spirit of the negative dialectic constantly pushes theory beyond itself (in this respect "negative dialectic" is something of a misnomer because Adorno does not quite offer a new *dialectic* at all). The negative dialectic, as I stated at the outset, is constantly drawing our attention to the obscurity, indeterminacy, and radical contingency of being; to our present time opening onto the future at the same time as recalling the past; to the emergence, perception, and articulation of new needs and unfulfilled desires. It is radically non-dogmatic, but also the opposite of complacent intellectualism, constantly wishing to gauge the historical spirit against the possibilities for democratic advance offered by the times.

Critical theory must maintain an orientation to *truth*—but a truth whose only verity might be that the whole, once identified, is then also the untrue. What Adorno made clear was that the dialectic cannot be presented in terms of a strict logic—as the kind of philosophy that his critical theory opposed so passionately and that has since been so effectively criticized again by poststructuralism and deconstruction. He sought to show that thought could not be understood adequately in metaphysical, ontological, or epistemological terms but rather ought to be located in close constellatory proximity to the *aesthetic* whose non-identical form should inspire thought to remain in motion. The aesthetic in this sense opens a unique window onto the histories of suffering and domination that comprise the reified formations of subjectification.

Adorno's vision is quite clearly distinct to and incommensurate with the central thrust of Habermas's theory, despite superficial similarities and continuities such as their concern with the ethics of communication. In particular, Adorno's 'justice of cognition' cannot suggest a precursor to Habermas's discourse ethic. Despite the latter's explicit conception of a *cognitive ethic*, his sacrifices for the sake of reaching agreement and expanding consensuses marginalize or silence the ethical and cognitive importance of much that Adorno valued most highly. For Adorno, the importance of disruptive, dissensual, contradictory, paradoxical, uncanny communication lies not only in its destabilizing effect upon positivity and reified identities.[1] Identity thinking reinforces the modern desire for a sovereign subject that legislates its own being and becoming by constantly resolving its objective life as self-identical. I have suggested that Habermas's theory is hence in some respects a non-critical, 'traditional' theory insofar as certain pivotal aspects support the interests of subjects shaped for and by the identifying, reified, exchanging interactions of capitalist society.[2] It is rare for Habermas to contest the formation of such subjects seriously.

But to destabilize such identities should not eliminate subjectivity entirely; for the subject is not *simply* fiction—it is always more than this on account of it being a something. There is an objectivity to subjectivity whose recognition is reflectively possible only through a recollection of its constitutive non-identity. For Adorno, this means there is an ineliminable aesthetic component to our communications whose reverberations need to be recognized and not suppressed or ignored. Such a shuddering of our identifying thought is, I argue, crucial not only in order to shake free and preserve the diversity of communication so necessary to democracy, but also to allow and foster alternative modes of relating to each other and to the non-human that might be established against reified forms. Capitalism, the most advanced and powerful form of the identity principle, can be challenged only by recourse to the power of the non-identical, which is hidden from view under the great mass of reifications weighing down our normal discourses. Conceived critically, attention to the aesthetic undercurrent of our communications can make a substantial contribution to loosening the grip maintained by the constraints of the everyday and the compulsions to identify.

For Adorno, the absence of compassion for the dominated life under existing conditions expresses itself in the suffering of all, for which there can only be compensations (necessary illusions, the consolation of art, the false happiness provided by the culture industry, consumerism, etc.), but to which all manner of pathological gratifications are also related (cosmetic manipulation and self-discipline, iconolatry, cathartic revenge, the liberation of gratuitous violence, *Schadenfreude*, etc.). Alternatively, compassion itself is exploited by the culture industry or sublimated harmlessly into good works—or, more ambiguously, into the operation of the welfare-state. For human beings to *feel* differently toward one another a *cognitive* liberation is also necessary, which is why in the history of critical theory liberation has meant something like an aesthetic education (see, for example, Weber, 1977).

In this sense it should be clear that Adorno's stress on the *social* conditions of becoming aware of the falsity and sacrifices of identification cannot be equated with Habermas's linguistically mediated truth-seeking activity. For the *telos* of satisfactory—or at least meaningful—intersubjective relations should not be abstracted from the potential messiness, jarring contradictions, inherent tensions, and delightful complexity that can arise from the openness elicited by constant attention to the non-identical. Put most simply, the basic aspiration underlying Habermas's social and political thinking is that *what is cognitively binding ought to be socially bonding*. The rejection of such a preoccupation does not necessarily lead to anti-democratic, skeptical, or despairing positions that pay no attention to the need for some kind of solidarity or ethical relations. Moreover, it is clear from my discussion that Adorno could not accept the force of cognitive agreement as an adequate model for social solidarity. But nor could he think that an alternative, more adequate, solely *theoretical* formulation of the social bond is possible or more important even desirable, for the truly rational society would not *require* such theory or philosophy. The truth of the *Bilderverbot* warns that the absolute cannot be reached at all.

The need to facilitate alternative modes of being and communication to those forced upon us by the reified world leads me to affirm that a utopian projection is decisive for any continuation of the project of critical theory, despite the unease or downright hostility that the notion of utopia generates for many contemporary thinkers.[3] This utopian spirit orients critical theory toward a new historical epoch, the liberated society, and all such equivalents. But for Adorno, again, this does not of course mean that he believes he could or that we can some day theorize just what that liberated society would look like or how it would be constituted positively. Adorno's approach was not to theorize the social bond—to say what it *is*—but constantly to point out what it is *not*. The negativity of thought must be stressed at the same time that one acknowledges thought's drive toward truth and freedom. The poststructuralist critique of critical theory often misses this crucial aspect of Adorno's approach to truth and the importance of his utopian view of freedom.

Thus again there remains an unavoidable tension in the negative dialectic. It lies in the awareness that as soon as we think we are beyond the dialectic of enlightenment (in theory or in practice), we most certainly are not; as soon as we think the liberated society might be upon us, we become blind to the dominations and sacrifices that establish it. This might be the key insight that all concrete, historical revolutions of liberation have failed to acknowledge or institutionalize. Adorno's critical theory teaches us that the utopian hope for final liberation cannot be positively actualized—but that its continued projection must remain vital in order to preserve the non-identical tension that can control domination. Hence I think the problem of the incapacity or political weakness of sheer negativity is largely a false one once the immanent political nature and operation of the negative dialectic are recognized.

But there is a deeper related worry that needs to be kept in mind. Intentionally weak institutions that could facilitate the kind of communicative awareness and sensibility I have been advocating will always face the danger of being overrun by constitutively strong institutions and mimetically insulated, highly subjectified beings. Perhaps there is no way to completely remove this kind of danger short of capitulating to a kind of force antithetical to genuine freedom. The venerable doctrine of eternal vigilance (interpreted as an eternal care for negativity and non-identity) may be one of the most important practical tenets of democracy. But observations concerning the entropy of the human constitution motivated thinkers as diverse as Plato, Machiavelli, and Tocqueville to regard the decline of politically constituted societies as inevitable, which consequently led them to assert the need for a periodic return to founding principles. With Adorno there are no founding principles and no ethical whole to which one may return; negation is a practice that continually looks forward, back, behind, below, always as a response to its awareness of the exclusions of non-identity. Negation cannot itself be a positive principle, which problematizes anything resembling its institutionalization. The astonishing complexity of political thinking and acting that this represents should be a source of wonder and inspiration rather than discouragement or despondency.

The paradoxical situation Adorno's thought ushers in might seem to utterly dash the hopes of philosophy, expressed over two millennia, for a redemption of the promise inherent in the sheer existence of reason and its capacity to produce knowledge. This has indeed provided a strong and persistent motivation for much philosophical and scientific inquiry, though in fact, as Marcuse pointed out, such hopes reach their limit in the concept of reason as freedom. Thus the materialist views reason as insufficient for liberation and inevitably attracts condemnation for dangerous irrationalism, secular messianism or eschatology, and so forth.

Yet to accept, as Adorno and postmodern philosophy do, that no final referent exists that can be somehow true beyond the eternal play of signifiers, is not at all to affirm the irrelevance of ethics or the utter folly of the hopes of philosophy in the face of foundationless political (power) struggles. Accepting that there can only be endless critique and negation, endless dynamics of power and resistance, endless suffering and guilt born of the unavoidable and inevitable violence done in all civilized action only points toward a kind of nihilism or a Nietzschean aesthetic politics if one *also* gives up on a political option that could minimize domination and guilt without the expectation that this will usher in a completely transparent world.

But does this answer the important question of politics that the Habermasian position finds so wanting in Adorno's critical theory? The crucial issue here is whether Adorno's critique of society can in fact have a political theory abstracted from the ethical orientation of its critique. My account affirms that it cannot in the way Habermas retains the differentiation of autonomous spheres of the political, the economic, and the aesthetic. But my reading of Adorno has also sought to move the inquiry forward from the question of whether a critical political theory could amount to more than simply advocating a pragmatic respect for democracy and a democratic ethos in the face of far worse alternatives. In a post-traditional, postmetaphysical age whose political talk is constantly being challenged by the reactionary forces of lost or disappearing traditions, fundamentalist theocratic groups and regimes, homegrown hate, backlash racism, backlash sexism (or heterosexism), and state violence or state indifference, (and these are just the worst), there certainly seems to be a pragmatic need for such respect. Democracy at a certain level needs toleration of difference, pluralism, efforts of impartiality, the recognition of guidelines for reasonable discussion, debate, decision-making, and so forth. An openness to differing ways of life has been a hallmark of the liberal society, despite the limitations of the liberal concept of toleration itself (see Brown, 2000, for a contemporary critique of toleration). The pragmatism of liberal democracy is to be respected as far as it goes, which is not, after all, very far (and that is the problem). In short, if all Habermas is saying politically is that talking about things and reaching agreements are better than solving conflicts through violence, then few would disagree with this.[4] But this, of course, is not *all* Habermas is saying, for he believes that the freedom promised by his concept of communicative rationality meets the requirements of a *critical* theory. The course I have navigated in the preceding chapters aims to show why a far deeper and more open approach to non-identity and otherness is required in order to redeem the promise of a critical theory.

The important question does not really concern choosing a liberal or a non-liberal state, society, or way of life at all. It consists in responding to the aesthetic sense that stands behind, works through, and in most cases is repressed or distorted in our communications with each other. It consists in recognizing that as communicating and sociated beings we are subject to forces and formations beyond our control and beyond direct consciousness that must in many cases be fought if freedom is to have meaning.

Likewise, the force of the better argument is a *progressive force* to which Habermas appeals because he recognizes, like a critical theorist, that the existential, empirical, social forces that coerce human beings in society must be resisted by some kind of counterforce. He believes that if the counterforce of reasonable discourse were institutionalized, then the distorting and subjugating forces prevailing in capitalism and administration would be at least held in check if not pacified to a large degree.

Marx had a parallel if far more dramatic idea that the collective consciousness and solidarity of the working class *as a class* would constitute
a progressive historical force that could successfully confront the violent
forces of capitalism, thereby once and for all destroying such class-based
force in history.

Adorno, as I have tried to show (especially in section 5.3), appeals to a different force again. This is the force associated with the
aesthetic experience of dramatic insight, perceptiveness, and intelligibility that is invoked to combat the distortions, falsity, and suffering caused
by un/necessary domination and by the resilience of reification. I have
posited the acute concentration and penetration of this force in the moment of the mimetic shudder. One of the most succinct criticisms that can
consequently be made against Habermas's appeal to the force of the
better argument is that it simply will not be *enough* of a force to seriously
challenge the domination of capitalism and instrumental reason. This is
partly because it cannot distinguish itself from them well enough and
partly because it cannot recognize the depth and extent of reification and
domination in contemporary society. The route Habermas has chosen for
critical theory thus has its own set of aporias that are, arguably, far more
serious than the ones faced by Adorno in the absence of an historical
addressee or revolutionary subject.

By contrast, for Adorno and critical theory, the social force with
which one keeps faith is a shuddering collective undercurrent that can
never find explicit expression but whose mimetic perception could, under the right conditions, inspire the common cause of disparate progressive social movements dedicated to radically reducing extant suffering in
the world. Adorno reaches for or gestures toward what Marcuse wanted
to foster with the "new sensibility" not by explicitly developing a new
science or new set of values consistent with a new socialist society but by
theorizing the role of art as a *negative* force, a jolting, shaking, shuddering force that will free the monadic consciousness from its self-imposed,
society-induced subjectificiation. What is uncovered is not raw energy or
undisciplined erotic or destructive drives (and so should not lead to a
repressive desublimation) but the presenting of underlying historical
processes of subjectification themselves. The hope is that this experience
will elicit in the subject the collective undercurrent of language as a
social force, a non-identical force of solidarity that will bring people together to resist their disfigurement and to work for liberation. This potential of radical resistance is carried by all human subjects because they
are always both less and more than what they think themselves to be and
less and more than what contemporary society holds them to be.

NOTES

CHAPTER ONE. INTRODUCTION

1. There were many other figures who, being scholars and writers in their own right, can also be described as fellow travelers of the central figures of the Frankfurt school. Among these may be included Ernst Bloch, Siegfried Kracauer, Alfred Schmidt, Alfred Sohn-Rethel, and in the United States, Barrington Moore. Held (1980) presents a general introduction to the Frankfurt school that points in the direction of Habermas's later work. Dubiel's (1985) account is also quite sympathetic to Habermas's position. Jay's (1973) pioneering early history of the Frankfurt school is certainly still worthwhile, even though it concludes its chronicle in 1950. A comprehensive history of the Frankfurt critical theory (but one that will seem rather unsympathetic in its representation of Adorno) is found in Wiggershaus (1994). Finally, Kellner (1989) provides a broad account that focuses on the contemporary relevance of critical theory.

2. Beech and Roberts (1996: 106). The principal texts Beech and Roberts recognize in what they call the 1990s "new aestheticism" on the Left are Bowie (1990), Eagleton (1990), Jameson (1990), Bernstein (1992).

3. Habermas has described his relationship with Adorno and other core members of the Frankfurt school in a number of interviews that provide glimpses of his admiration for his mentor as well as the clear differences between them. Adorno was a strong supporter of Habermas in Frankfurt (for example, he defended the latter against Horkheimer, who was not favorable to Habermas's presence at the Institute—and after Adorno's death he did leave to take up the directorship of the Max Planck Institute in Starnberg). But at the same time Habermas believes that Adorno never fully recognized the fundamental differences between their positions (see Habermas, 1986a; 1992a). See also Wiggershaus (1994), who has clearly been influenced by Habermas in his descriptions of their relationship.

4. Indeed, Marcuse's (1958) book on Soviet Marxism was one of the first systematic critiques of actually existing European socialism by an avowed critical theorist in the West.

5. For an introductory overview of this shift, otherwise known as the linguistic turn, see Rorty (1967). A more recent general survey that heralds a further refinement of this general philosophical and theoretical turn to language is found in Sills (1992). Another survey that focuses on questions of language in relation to political philosophy is Dallmayr (1984b).

6. I occasionally leave the word *paradigm* in scare quotes to register the problematization this term introduces. It is not that I necessarily reject the notion of paradigm itself or its meaning following Kuhn's (1970) radicalization of it. Indeed, to some extent, a Kuhnian interpretation of it might be appropriate to the shift under examination. However, Habermas does not really use the term in a Kuhnian manner for he believes that there are no significant problems left over from the superceded paradigm that have not been answered, at least tentatively, by the new theory. Since it is just this that I dispute, I occasionally introduce the scare quotes.

7. The adequacy of Habermas's understanding of those he regards as irrationalists—such as Foucault and Derrida—is of course open to question and critique, notably on the very point of their alleged irrationalism.

8. An interesting error in Habermas's systematic misreading of Horkheimer and Adorno occurs as he is concluding one of his central points against the latter. Habermas contends that "The 'dialectic of enlightenment' is an ironic affair: It shows the self-critique of reason the way to truth, and at the same time contests (*bestreitet*) the possibility 'that at this stage of complete alienation the idea of truth is still accessible'" (*TCAI*: 383). Habermas quotes from the German translation of Horkheimer's *Eclipse of Reason* (1947) (written in English), which is included as Part 1 of the German edition of Horkheimer's *Zur Kritik der instrumentellen Vernunft*. In the passage from which Habermas quotes (I refer to the original English edition), Horkheimer does *not* in fact "contest the possibility of truth" as Habermas represents with his paraphrase. Instead, Horkheimer is suggesting the exact *opposite*. The full passage reads: "The possibility of a self-critique of reason presupposes, first, that the antagonism of reason and nature is in an acute and catastrophic phase, and second, that at this stage of complete alienation the idea of truth is still accessible" (1947: 177). The passage in the German translation Habermas uses contains no errors, and McCarthy's translation is true to Habermas's original. Perhaps this curious mistake is an example of the wish being the father of the thought.

CHAPTER TWO. CRITICAL THEORY AND THE ECLIPSE OF IDEOLOGY: THE EARLY FRANKFURT VISION AND ITS TRANSFORMATION

1. Louis Althusser's (1971) reformulation of the concept of ideology deserves note as a major spur to Marxist social and political debates in the 1970s. Although a key moment in the (Marxist and post-Marxist) discourse over ideology, a consideration of the Althusserian view is clearly beyond the scope of the present work.

2. Thus Fukuyama's (1992) well-known thesis on thesis end of history is really thirty years late.

3. New translations of Horkheimer's early work have been accompanied recently by renewed discussion of the early program of critical theory. See Benhabib, Bonß, and McCole (1993) and Horkheimer (1993a).

4. When Horkheimer and other Frankfurt theorists speak of bourgeois philosophy, which is also equivalent in most respects to what Horkheimer calls traditional theory, they are speaking as materialists and mean forms of thought that in general express an unreflective correspondence to the material social and economic conditions of capitalist society that function to legitimate that society. That is, bourgeois thought is thought that cannot adopt a *critical* attitude to the contradictory conditions of capitalist society because, as an expression of and having an interest in those very conditions, it is *structurally* unable. However, as will be discussed below, bourgeois philosophy is not ideology understood as *merely* false or functional consciousness, for it contains a kernel of truth in which critical theory is also interested.

5. For a discussion of the excesses of scientistic and positivist approaches to the objects of the "human sciences" in the nineteenth and twentieth centuries, see Gould (1981).

6. The publication of Marx's early philosophical work, which revealed an important new dimension to his *oeuvre* and established him without doubt as a philosopher, occurred only in the latter 1930s.

7. Critical theory thus distinguishes itself from both liberal critique, which is made in the name of freedom from illegitimate constraint or subjection, and conservative critique, which is made for the sake of lost traditions and practices. The concept of freedom associated with a life free from domination is, in the Frankfurt tradition, also associated with a vision of a radically new society as well as the idea of a new kind of individual or subject of such a society. While freedom does not *necessarily* imply such a transfigured life, for Habermas and critical theory it implies a genuine *autonomy* for human beings, a freedom not merely from the constraints others may place on one's action, but from illusions and self-deceptions imposed unconsciously and heteronomously by the objective 'society.' One's very life experience and perception of needs must be clarified if an authentic and rational life is to be possible. This is why social critique is *necessary*.

There is thus said to be a link between critical theoretical insight into the nonimmediately apparent structure and content of society (critique of ideology and fetish) and the clarification of historical struggles in terms of actual human needs and experience which contains an orientation to an emancipated future. Following Habermas in many respects, Benhabib refers in this context to two moments of critique, the "explanatory-diagnostic" and the "anticipatory-utopian." "The explanatory-diagnostic function of critical theory," she writes,

> corresponds to the epistemic viewpoint of the observer.... Here the social system is viewed as having internal contradictions, limitations, and crises. The anticipatory-utopian dimension of critique addresses the

lived needs and experiences of social agents in order to interpret them and render them meaningful in light of a future normative ideal. Without an explanatory dimension, critical theory dissolves into mere normative philosophy; if it excludes the dimension of anticipatory-utopian critique, however, it cannot be distinguished from other mainstream social theories that attempt to gain value-free knowledge of the social world (1986: 142).

But Benhabib betrays a slip into a non-dialectical notion of critical theory here in the way these so-called moments of critique are conceived. A dialectical notion of critical theory—which I take Marx's to exemplify—would not link two moments in Benhabib's fashion. This kind of link suggests an external kind like that which exists between a car and a trailer. Instead, theoretical critique ought to be conceived *simultaneously* as transformative critique: the knowledge produced by the *theory* is simultaneously *critical, transfigurative*. *Kritische Theorie* is also *theoretische Kritik*. Dialectical critique hence has affinities with the dialogical critique of the psychoanalytical tradition. (For brief discussions, see sections 3.3 and 5.1. For a recent treatment that explicitly looks to the psychoanalytic tradition for resources to renew critical theory under contemporary conditions as an alternative to Habermasian theory, see Whitebook, 1995. I have many objections to Whitebook's understanding of Adorno, however.) The question that Benhabib raises—of having one aspect of critique without the other—simply cannot arise in *dialectical* critique since this misconstrues its mode of thinking. One does not get critical theory by coordinating epistemology (social theory) with normative philosophy; one gets mainstream social theories that moralize.

Moreover, in another clear contrast to dialectical critique, Benhabib's notion of the critique of "lived needs and experiences" that are rendered "meaningful in light of a future normative ideal" sounds very much like 'traditional' critique to which critical theory is usually contrasted. That this future normative ideal, conceived in Habermasian fashion, is yet to be determined through unconstrained, discursively achieved agreement does not really change the fact that it is a new set of norms that is to be introduced. Marx, it will be recalled, criticized utopian socialists for their unhistorical and moralistic critiques that "deaden the class struggle." (1978: 499); he maintained instead that the working class "have no ready-made utopias to introduce *par décret du peuple.* . . . They have no ideals to realize, but to set free the elements of the new society with which old collapsing bourgeois society itself is pregnant." (1974a: 213). While Marx was of course aware that there may be a pragmatic need for ideals in the struggle to get to the future classless society, in an important sense, if not one of its most important senses, the idea of freedom in critical theory means freedom from the need to determine and then realize such norms—ideally freedom from the need for the institution of social justice as a response to a determinant unjust state of affairs. The progressive nature of the struggle was to be found instead in the attempts to isolate and bring forth the emergent forms of incipient social relations perceived in the capitalism of the day.

8. On this point see also the critique of Laclau and Mouffe offered by Coles (1997: 186–91) who draws attention to the absence of an ethical call in their work.

9. Against Lyotard's premature abandonment of large historical narrative and against general postmodernist conclusions that, following the utter illegitimacy of foundationalism, social criticism must consequently be local, *ad hoc*, and untheoretical, Fraser and Nicholson (1990: 25–26) argue that many of the genres rejected by postmodernists such as large historical narrative and social-theoretical analyses of domination and subordination are in fact necessary for effective social critique, especially for feminist critique of the subordination of women. Moreover, in the context of cultural theory, where postmodernist critical theories have found their most ready adherents, Jameson (1981: 59) has gone a step further by contending that "no working model of the functioning of language, the nature of communication or of the speech act, and the dynamics of formal and stylistic change is conceivable which does not imply a whole philosophy of history."

10. Lyotard's (1984) well-known text heralds the coming of the new age in which the modes of political legitimacy characteristic of modernity no longer maintain validity. For an impressive effort to write a systematic cultural history of the epoch named the postmodern that does not, however, lose sight of the (late capitalist) social totality in which postmodernism operates as a "cultural logic," see Jameson (1991). In political-economic terms, a structural adjustment and transformation in the global order of world capitalist production has been in progress since around the end of the 1960s (see, for example, Cox, 1987). We might note an approximate correspondence between the development of this transformation of global political economy and the arrival of the postmodern.

11. For an inspired analysis of nineteenth-century culture featuring discussions of Marx and Baudelaire and their interpretations of the modern experience, and for a general discussion of the transformation of urban space as part of the transformation of social life, see Berman (1982).

12. "Technology and Science as 'Ideology'" (Habermas, 1971b). The scare quotes around the word 'Ideology' in the title already give us warning that the term is suspect.

13. The 1947 version is revised from a shorter 1944 mimeograph. I will on occasion attribute aspects of this text to Adorno alone, but I do not intend with this to raise questions of authorship of specific passages or chapters (such philology is not really possible here since the text is a result of collaborative dictation and extensive conversation). My reason for this is more that, between the authors of *Dialectic of Enlightenment*, Adorno did far more to develop and to take heed of the text's insights centrally in his subsequent work.

14. Documenting the moments of this crisis of modernity or reason as what it is, the radical undermining of the philosophical, social, and political claims of the Enlightenment, was and remains scandalous to contemporary official academic thought. On the other hand, the wholesale critique of the Enlightenment philosophical and political project from neoconservative positions has gained substantial momentum in recent decades in the United States and Europe, undermining

the dominance of liberal-democratic thought. For example, the political theory of Leo Strauss has had substantial influence on the political right in the United States recently (see Drury, 1997), and scholars influenced by Strauss have crafted rejections of contemporary critical political thought from anti-democratic, anti-egalitarian positions on the postmodern right (see, for example, Rosen, 1987; Zuckert, 1996).

15. For a critique of Sloterdijk's conception of ideology and its cynical end, see Žižek (1989: 28–33). A recent definitive capitalist triumphalist text is Fukuyama (1992). For a useful discussion of the contemporary situation of democracy in and against capitalism, see Dryzek (1996).

16. For a fine presentation of these kinds of problems in negotiating alliances at the level of theory, see Albert, et al. (1986).

17. I allude to Adorno's famous opening line of *Negative Dialectics*. For recent survey collections on the state of philosophy, see Baynes, Bohman, and McCarthy (1987) and Niznik and Sanders (1996).

18. Besides recent volumes concerning the text itself and its contemporaneity (Kunnemann and de Vries, 1989; Rudolph, 1992; van Reijen and Noerr, 1987; Wilson and Holub, 1993), a substantial number of studies, conferences, symposia, and dedicated journal issues have emerged over the past decade following a growing interest in Adorno's work in general (which have often included specific examinations of this text). At the beginning of the 1990s, Jameson (1990) explicitly offered an interpretation of Adorno as ahead of his time, as a—perhaps the—thinker for the 1990s, which has been followed by an increasing number of studies dedicated to Adorno's relevance in the postmodern era. See, for example, the essays in Pensky (1997), Huhn and Zuidervaart (1997), as well as Jarvis's (1998) fine introduction to Adorno.

19. Unfortunately, a number of these commentators characterize this kinship by describing the theses and positions expressed in *Dialectic of Enlightenment* and by Adorno as anticipations or precursors of postmodern and poststructuralist concerns and positions (for example, Hoy, 1994: 119–39; Rocco, 1994; 1995; Ryan, 1982). Nägele (1986), Shapiro (1989), and Cornell (1992) present appreciative readings that generally avoid this forecast of later positions. A useful comparison between German critical traditions and French poststructuralism is found in Dews (1987). Despite the sympathy expressed for critical theory, such a characterization as anticipation suggests that critical theory only went some of the way toward addressing these concerns or articulating full-fledged postmodern positions. In any case it implicitly or explicitly declares that critical theory had an inadequate or only partial grasp of essentially postmodern insights. What is objectionable is that such a portrayal implies that critical theory is in fact a forerunner to or even inchoate subgenus of theoretical postmodernism proper. My position, by contrast, is that critical theory offers an autonomous alternative to postmodern and poststructuralist theory that shares some intellectual inspirations and traditions (for example, in Kant, Hegel, Nietzsche, and for some postmoderns, Marx and Freud) but which is in fact more of a direct theoretical *competitor* for the contem-

porary ground on which, for example, current concerns for the other and otherness are articulated rather than merely anticipating or approximating this ground.
20. See also note 16, Chapter 5.

21. In the French philosophical thought of the late twentieth century, a parallel
question is also raised by Derrida who (without a theory of the culture industry)
seeks to reach a non-violent relation to the other even though "the phenomenon
presupposes its original contamination through the sign" (1978: 129).

22. "The first, objective abstraction takes place," Adorno argues,

> not so much in scientific thought, as in the universal development of the
> exchange system itself; which happens independently of the qualitative
> attitudes of producer and consumer, of the mode of production, even of
> need, which the social mechanism tends to satisfy as a kind of second-
> ary by-product. Profit comes first. . . . Above and beyond all specific
> forms of social differentiation, the abstraction implicit in the market
> system represents the domination of the general over the particular, of
> society over its captive membership . . . Behind the reduction of men to
> agents and bearers of exchange value lies the domination of men over
> men. . . . The form of the total system requires everyone to respect the
> law of exchange if he does not wish to be destroyed, irrespective of
> whether profit is his subjective motivation or not (1969/1970: 144–53,
> 148–49).

23. Habermas claims that Horkheimer and Adorno "anchor the mechanism
that produces the reification of consciousness in the anthropological foundations
of the history of the species, in the form of existence of a species that has to
reproduce itself through labor" (*TCAI*: 379). See also my discussion of this in
section 4.3.3.

24. Adorno opposed overtly political or committed art (he lacked enthusi-
asm even for Brecht at times) because he believed its intention interfered with
art's critical potential, and in any case rarely produced very good art. Hence this
kind of charge accepts at face value Adorno's insistence on the importance of
art's autonomy from society, yet it neglects the great power and practical-political
potential Adorno nevertheless saw in art. For selections on the aesthetics and
politics debate in the twentieth-century German critical tradition, see Adorno, et
al. (1977). For an exploration of the aesthetic resources of Adorno's theory in the
context of the present work, see Chapter 5, especially section 5.3; extended discussions of Adorno's aesthetic theory are provided by Zuidervaart (1991) and
Nicholsen (1997).

25. My extended discussion of Habermas's charge of performative contradiction with respect to Adorno occurs in sections 4.3 and 4.4. For a further critique
of Habermas's and Apel's deployment of the performative contradiction argument that is articulated from a position sympathetic to poststructuralist and
deconstructionist philosophy, see Hernnstein Smith (1997). Jay (1992) addresses

performative contradiction in relation to a clarification of specific poststructuralist positions, and Knodt (1994) with respect to the systems theory of Luhmann.

26. It should be pointed out that the context for the positions Hoy expresses in the cited text are part of a principal debate format with Habermasian critical theory that is defended by Thomas McCarthy (1994) in the other half of the book. Hoy's critique of Horkheimer and Adorno is part of his more general debate with critical theory and its legacy.

27. Rocco (1994) similarly suggests that we read *Dialectic of Enlightenment* "against the grain" in the direction of a Foucaultian approach.

28. Hoy's objections focus extensively on the dialectic and how it generates pointless utopian and dubious philosophy of history. Hoy regards utopian visions as products more of fantasy than theory (126), and of little use to the pragmatically oriented critical history he promotes. Indeed, utopianism seems to be erroneously equated with totalizing thought and universalism (107–8) and the mere presence of a utopian element, even the 'negative' one he sees in Adorno's later thought, seems a black mark against it (note 30, 140–41). Yet he neglects to consider how aesthetic visions—the objective illusions produced by phantasy—bear upon theory production itself, how they are indeed necessary elements to any adequate notion of theorizing. This, of course, was one of the central questions pursued by Frankfurt theorists such as Adorno and Marcuse.

29. This is Habermas's programmatic position: "What raises us out of nature is the only thing whose nature we can know: *language*. Through its structure, autonomy and responsibility are posited for us. Our first sentence expresses unequivocally the intention of universal and unconstrained consensus" (1971a: 314).

30. Adorno later famously formulated the negative dialectic as anti-ontology: "the ontology of the false condition" (*ND*: 22/11). He was a life long critic of Heidegger and also wrote an extended critique of Husserl, yet there are notable affinities between certain interpretations of Heidegger and Adorno which some have attempted to draw out (for example, Dallmayr, 1991).

In an early essay on "The Idea of Natural History," which in many respects provides the groundwork for the approach to the entwinement of nature and history in *Dialectic of Enlightenment*, Adorno elaborates his anti-ontology. This essay questioned how it is possible to know and interpret the alienated, reified, dead world of convention, of "second nature," a world that "encounters us as ciphers" (1984: 118). The point of such knowledge, however, was not to generate a general conceptual structure to decode the origin of the "transience" [*Vergänglichkeit*] and "signification" [*Bedeutung*] of the facts of human experience, but instead to comprehend the historical facticity of consciousness in its uniqueness. Excluding the static from human intention, which is the historical dynamic, merely leads to false absolutes; and isolating intention from its unsurpassably natural elements leads to false spiritualism. "Nature itself," Adorno writes,

> is transitory. Thus it includes the element of history. Whenever an historical element appears it refers back to the natural element that passes

away within it. Likewise the reverse: whenever 'second nature' appears, when the world of convention approaches, it can be deciphered in that its meaning is shown to be precisely its transience . . . The basic quality of the transience of the earthly signifies nothing but just such a relationship between nature and history: all being or everything existing is to be grasped as the interweaving of historical and natural being. As transience all original-history [*Urgeschichte*] is absolutely present. It is present in 'signification'. 'Signification' means that the elements of nature and history are not fused with each other, rather they break apart and interweave at the same time in such a fashion that the natural appears as a sign for history and history, where it seems to be most historical, appears as a sign for nature (Adorno, 1984: 120–21).

31. This is a more active sense of perception than that expressed in Nietzsche's similar and well-known formulation that all knowledge is "perspectival." Moreover, Horkheimer and Adorno have in mind Freud's sense of projection. It bears mentioning, however, that Nietzsche's formulation is not relativist or subjectivist either but rather points out the historical nature of all expressions of knowledge that cannot help but depend on specific construction, intention, and sensory or linguistic embodiment. If all *actual* knowledge is elicited by and elicits a specific view, as this suggests, it does not follow that all knowing is of equal value or merit. It does, however, challenge the modern self-understanding of epistemology, which relies on a false abstraction from perspective to an allegedly universal Archimedian point and which cannot admit the confusion of vision and image with concept. This challenge is also contained in Horkheimer and Adorno's position.

CHAPTER THREE. HABERMAS AND THE CRITIQUE OF REIFICATION

1. The issue of the system can really only come up, from the Habermasian viewpoint, with the transition to modern society and its uncoupling from lifeworld contexts. This is not to say that systems of purposive-rational action were unimportant in premodern societies. Rather, these systems could not be accurately identified as *autonomous* subsystems separate from the dominant order and the imperatives of the cultural and political formations within which they were situated. For example, Aristotle (1976: 171–202) strictly subordinates trade and barter to the ethical goals of the polis. Other structural features of premodern societies such as institutionalized class stratification and relations are, it is clear, also determinate in the subordination of these spheres of purposive-rational action. It is not that the phenomena of social reproduction abstracted by the system did not exist before modernity, but that society was formally undifferentiated. However, even this explanation is flawed according to class analysis, which would argue that the systems spheres are only able to be abstracted out to the extent that a mercantilist followed by a capitalist class rise to power with material interests in such 'decoupling.'

2. I will not undertake an extended examination of Habermas's earlier critique of Marx. While the details of his criticisms concern a number of important theoretical and political issues which are played out in later texts such as *The Theory of Communicative Action*, I would like to address only those that bear centrally on the present topic of ideology critique and the question of reification. The elements of his earlier critique of Marx are contained in several texts, primarily Habermas (1971a; 1971b; 1974; 1976b; 1979a). For discussions see Postone (1996: 227–42) and Rockmore (1989).

3. The theoretical priority of language and communicative rationality is discussed in sections 4.1 and 4.2. For a parallel view that emphasizes the evolutionary priority of communicative structures in Habermas's theory, see (1979a; 1979b).

4. While modern differentiation can be viewed from the systems perspective as an unmitigated advance since its increased complexity leads to greatly increased steering capacities for the system as a whole, what cannot be counted as an advance in reason is systemic rationalization brought about *at the expense* of the lifeworld. This is why perhaps Habermas's most serious criticism of systems theory is its inability to conceive of increases in complexity that are achieved through the sacrifice of a rationalized lifeworld *as costs* (1987b: 186). At best, pathologies and crises related to rationalization are seen by systems theory as the 'normal disequilibria' of self-regulating systems that must constantly adapt to complex, changing environments (1987b: 292). In contrast, for Habermas, pathology and social crisis must be understood *critically*. The idea of a social *crisis* is hence central, for if systemic disequilibria are viewed as somehow necessary conditions for a system's health, then these phenomena cannot really be said to indicate crisis in an emphatic sense. In order to conceive of such a concept of crisis, Habermas believes, one must have recourse to the *lifeworld*, which represents the sphere in which critical conditions are *experienced* as disruptions, distortions, and painful disturbances. The internal relationship between system and lifeworld provides the key for comprehending rationalization crises critically.

5. See *TCAII*: 356–73. Juridification (*Verrechtlichung*) refers in general to the tendency toward an increase in positive law in modern society (*TCAII*: 357). This process is understood not only as a result of the historical cementing of bourgeois ideology in institutional form. It also represents the increasing need for capitalist social integration to be secured via lifeworld resources and hence to compensate for the inherent instability of capitalist systemic development. Juridification occurs via the functional need for systems media to be anchored in the lifeworld. The more steering functions need to be stabilized, the more demands must be placed on their institutional anchors in the lifeworld. Positive law expands further and further into new domains of the lifeworld as a correlation of the needs of system reproduction, development, and stability. Yet the more this occurs the less it is possible for consensually regulated communicative action to succeed in newly juridified contexts. Hence the negative effects of the latest wave of juridification are felt, for example, in the disempowering and commodifying form of welfare-state compensations to the clients of the state. Or they are felt in the

disaffection and cynicism of citizens unable to derive a satisfactory political identity from a suppressed and limited democratic process which the state compensates for by bolstering the citizen's role as consumer in its place.

6. Even Habermas's most sympathetic critics have expressed dissatisfaction with his abstractions of lifeworld and system by virtue of which he distinguishes mediatization from reification. McCarthy (1985) has warned of the dangers of incorporating systems theory too easily by pointing out the porousness of systems, the shifting boundaries of organizations, and the embeddedness of their regulating features as elements interpretively deployed by the acting members of even formally constituted organizations. He questions Habermas's use of systems theory concepts to mark the differences between action within and outside systems. McCarthy has further criticized Habermas's uncoupling of the political-administrative system from the lifeworld, a move that suggests too extreme a distinction between the public sphere of politics (for example, democratic forms) and the delinguistified administration of legitimized power. Closer to my present concerns, Fraser (1985) has criticized Habermas's concept of reification for its gender blindspots, arguing that central concepts in Habermas's social theory are not gender-neutral, and further that the very distinctions he maintains between lifeworld and systems concepts replicate rather than combat male dominance in the social spheres and institutions they name.

7. Both Benhabib (1986: 123–33) and Habermas (*TCAII*: 338) make use of this distinction between the two views of crisis, which is derived in this case from Lohmann (1980).

8. In this sense, Habermas sides with Hegel against Marx with respect to Hegel's (1967b) view of the necessary connection between the concepts of freedom and (bourgeois) civil society. Habermas of course recognizes that today the concept of civil society means much more than the Hegelian "system of needs" (see *BFN*: 329–87, especially 366–73).

9. Such constraints on the system by institutions of the lifeworld, which reverse the direction of Habermas's idea of systemic colonization, are only possible in this form once the lifeworld has been uncoupled from the system. Hence the kind of constraints placed upon systemic development in traditional societies—constraints that may, on Habermas's account, lead to crisis and evolutionary advance—cannot be of the same order. With respect to such evolutionary social advance, Habermas maintains that systemic steering problems are only resolved when the endogenous learning mechanism in the sphere of moral-practical consciousness decisive for structures of communicative interaction introduces a new level of social integration. This in turn makes it possible to implement available but suppressed technically useful knowledge—that is, it makes possible an increase in productive forces and system complexity that solves the existing systemic blockages (Habermas, 1979a: 147–48, 160). The development of modern social bureaucratization or the technicizing of politics are hence not progressive evolutionary developments for instead of institutionalizing the latent communicative rationality structures of modernity they rather circumvent them.

10. However, contra Habermas, there continue to emerge Marxist inspired visions of the possibility of a classless society without capitalist markets, which instead rethink distribution and consumption in democratic ways and provide alternative models to the 'coordinator' class societies of the former Soviet Union as well as to Habermas's liberal-democratic reformism. See for example, the model of "participatory economics" in Albert and Hahnel (1991).

11. Habermas's first major work in this area is (1976a); see also "Legitimation Problems in the Modern State," in (1979a). Claus Offe (1984) has pursued a Habermasian line in his studies of crisis in the state. In Habermas's (1996) more recent work, he has returned to the questions of the state and legitimate power.

12. Heller (1982: 35) has drawn attention to this and suggested that undistorted goal-rationality and undistorted communication are equally aspects of freedom, which demands socialization of inner nature without repression, both in communication and the creative activity of labor.

13. For Marx's suggestion of a life free from fetishism, see (1954: 82–84).

14. In a parallel vein that makes a similar mistake, Benhabib puts forward a Habermasian interpretation of defetishizing critique as a procedure by which "the given is shown to be not a natural fact but a socially and historically constituted, and thus changeable, reality" (Benhabib, 1986: 47). This may be what it is for Hegel, but it is *not* a full description of the critique of fetish for Marx. Marx describes the "definite social relation" between human beings that "assumes, in their eyes, the phantasmagoric [*phantastische*] form of a relation between things" (Marx, 1954: 77, translation altered). Benhabib's interpretation of this passage indicates *merely* that social relations assume the appearance of 'natural' or objectified forms. The point, however, is that they assume *phantasmagoric form* and that it is from *this form* that the product of social labor appears as a thing, reified. This is also why Marx finds an analogy to the mystifications of religious thought. The "peculiar social character" of the labor that produces commodities produces their fetishism *because* the "mutual relations of the producers . . . take the form of a social relation between the products" (Marx, 1954: 77, emphasis added). A *social relation between products*. It is this "phantasmagoric form" that assumes the social character of capitalist society—it does not thereby become reified itself, but rather mystifies through reification the real social relations of production (and hence of domination) in society. This is the sense by which Marx can say that the producers' "own social action takes the form of the action of objects, which rule the producers instead of being ruled by them" (1954: 79).

15. Assessing Habermas's theory against its intended aim to be practically enlightening, Misgeld (1985) argues that the objectivating attitude and highly general arguments required by Habermas for inquiry into systems organization cannot be meaningfully translated back into the particular participant perspectives of the lifeworld such that it could critically inform actors dealing with everyday social realities. Hence Misgeld contends that Habermas's Hegelian impulse to give primacy to a theory of the whole (via a reconstructed theory of social evolution and objectivist systems theory) does not recognize the entwinement of theorizing in actual histories and in the practical organization of society.

16. Spivak's (1988) considerations on this point are illuminating for her attempt to recover Value in the context of cultural theory, though it is important to note that she proceeds in a non-dialectical manner.

17. While never actually mentioning Marx by name, the first major interpretation of Marx via Freud is made by Marcuse (1955), who, it should be mentioned, also manages a serious critique of Marx at the same time.

18. Ollman (1993: 39–78) identifies three distinct modes of abstraction in Marx's method: the abstraction of extension, level of generality, and vantage point.

CHAPTER FOUR. FROM THE PURSUIT OF TRUTH TO THE PARADOXES OF APORIA AND CONTRADICTION: HABERMAS AND ADORNO

1. For the extended argument Habermas makes concerning this general methodological point, see his discussion of the rationality debate in English social theory in *TCAI*: 102–41.

2. Lyotard (1984: 65–66), in arguing against Habermas, contends that consensus is not the end of dialogue. Instead, Lyotard argues that the "search for dissent" coupled with the assumption of the heterogeneity of language games ("paralogy") is the end of dialogue. Lyotard only partially engages Habermas's claims regarding the goal of consensus, since what is important for the latter is not just that it is "possible for all speakers to come to agreement on which rules or metadescriptions are universally valid for language games" (65), but rather that there is a binding force contained in language games.

3. Derrida (1978) also makes a similar move to Horkheimer and Adorno in recognizing a "pre-ethical" violence that stands behind norms and authority.

4. The criticism of the total bureaucratization of society refers also to systems theory. Habermas's early engagement with Niklas Luhmann's version of systems theory led to his assimilation of certain systems-theoretic ideas into critical theory, yet at the same time he maintained that systems theory on its own could not live up to its claims to provide an adequate model of social action (see Habermas and Luhmann, 1971). Habermas continues his critique of Luhmann in 1976a: 130–42, *TCAII*, and *PDM*: 368–85. I discuss Habermas's integration of systems theory in sections 3.1 and 3.2.

5. On Habermas's problematic readings, Adorno's performative contradiction is also different from the performative contradiction of Foucault or even Derrida, who wish to drop out of the modern emancipatory-enlightenment discourse altogether. This claim is of course highly contentious, since for some avowed post-Nietzscheans or postmodernists like William Connolly and Connolly's Foucault, developing a "constructive theory" (distinguished from what is called merely a "deconstructive theory") is in fact a centrally important task (see Connolly, 1991: 57–63). Derrida, also often regarded as anti-enlightenment, constantly speaks of the need for *critical thinking*, one of the lights of enlightenment, as well as *ethics*. Derrida seems quite clearly and most centrally committed to the idea of

democracy and to preserving its present and future against the possibility of the 'worst' (see, for example, Derrida, 1992b; 1994). See also Jay (1992) for an account of the performative contradiction of poststructuralism that is rather more self-conscious than Habermas allows.

6. Habermas is here reminiscent of Buck-Morss's characterization of the anti-system paradox of Adorno's method in relation to the Marxist goal of revolution-ary transformation. Buck-Morss (1977: 187), writing before Habermas here, observes that Adorno's hope for revolutionary transformation was never given up, yet it could no longer express itself positively: "Only by keeping the argu-ment circling in perpetual motion could thought escape compromising with its revolutionary goal." The paradox was, however, that critical thought had to re-main negative to avoid the domination of instrumental reason, and so it could not *work* toward the *actual* realization of a transformed society, for that would make it 'instrumental.' It ought to be noted that Buck-Morss's sympathies lie for other reasons much more with Adorno than with Habermas regarding the con-sequences of this situation.

7. Despite this, it is a characterization that is mentioned and tacitly accepted by Jay in his essay and by others sympathetic to Habermas's critique of Adorno. For example, Jay (1992: 263), and Benhabib's (1986: 169) critique of Adorno.

8. "The process in which the individual becomes independent, the function of exchange society, terminates in the abolition of the individual through integra-tion. What produced freedom changes into unfreedom. . . . On the other hand, in the age of universal social oppression the image of freedom against society lives only in the features of the mistreated or crushed individual. . . . Freedom be-comes concrete in the changing forms of repression: in resistance to these forms" (*ND*: 259/262, 262/265).

9. Clearly, Adorno's concept of non-identical subjectivity is at odds with the Habermasian intersubjective subjectivity, despite the latter's quite explicit differ-ence to the traditional notion of constitutive subjectivity. Perhaps most important, as I have been stressing, the difference of Adorno's concept has to do with the absence of the need to refer in his theory to some equivalent to the idea of the ideal communication community. Honneth (1995a) has extended the Habermasian con-cept of intersubjectivity under the Hegelian theme of the struggle for recognition in directions that clearly delineate it from traditional notions. However, Honneth's efforts seem to remain paradigmatically dependent on the linguistically mediated claims of communicative action that still has difficulty accessing or taking account of the Adornian mindfulness of the objectivity of subjectivity.

10. See note 30, Chapter 2.

CHAPTER FIVE. RECOVERING THE ETHICAL AND POLITICAL FORCE OF ADORNO'S AESTHETIC-CRITICAL THEORY

1. While the subject is not a category rejected *tout court* by Habermas, the observation that a concept of subjectivity remains important for him is not in itself a damning criticism (just as it ought not be a criticism of Adorno, who was

also interested in thinking the subject in a more satisfactory way). Habermas has been careful to warn against an "undialectical rejection of subjectivity" (*PDM*: 337), and he believes that his concept of intersubjectivity serves as a superior option to such a rejection. Dews (1995) goes even further to contend that even those such as the late Foucault and Derrida have made tangible concessions to the correctness of Habermas's criticism, where one may perceive the emergence of a new sensibility toward (Habermasian) intersubjectivity in their most recent work. I think, however, that Dews may overestimate the significance of the concessions he identifies in those such as Foucault and Derrida for they, like Adorno, could never accept the centrality Habermas attributes to the *binding* nature of the former's concept of communicative rationality.

2. Indeed, it is through Habermas's discussion of Mead that the question of the intersubjective (social) formation of subjectivity has been most developed; see "Individuation through Socialization: On George Herbert Mead's Theory of Subjectivity" (*PT*: 149–204).

3. This is not, of course, to deny that Adorno was also a critic of Marx. It is to claim against many (such as Anderson, 1976; Connerton, 1980; Kolakowski, 1978; Mandel, 1978) that Adorno's critique is compatible with Marx's, even that Adorno's critique draws its meaning from Marx's. Likewise, Jameson's (1990) treatment of Adorno's Marxism as the most compelling form for the postmodern can draw on Adorno's uniquely non-dogmatic approach to Marx and Marxist theory in order to retain a strong critique of capitalism and class society in the face of increasingly fragmented and deceptive postmodern figurations of capital and class. Earlier Marxist complaints about Adorno, especially those concerning political practice, seem less and less appropriate for current conditions. For example, Rose's reproach that Adorno's response to the paradox of anti-humanism was a "preoccupation with style," the presentation of a "morality" or "praxis" of thinking, from which no "recipe for social and political action" could be developed (Rose, 1978: 138–39, 148) now seems rather misguided. Rose's critical reference point seems often to invoke an older, vintage Marxism, to which Adorno is often held accountable and not surprisingly fails to live up.

4. But Habermas has not finally pursued a model of practical–political enlightenment based on the psychoanalytic model, since there are difficulties with such an attempt from a Habermasian perspective; see McCarthy (1978: 205–13).

5. While the process of disenchantment and the decline of religious/metaphysical worldviews is a feature of modernity and modernization, it would appear not to be as universal or as inevitable as the nineteenth- and early twentieth-century theorists once thought. For instance, the United States, which has developed such an advanced culture industry and such ravenous consumers among industrialized nations, has nevertheless found religion to be most persistent and resilient. Indeed, while a worldwide decline in mass religion occurred during the first half of the twentieth century, the latter part of the century has witnessed its significant rebirth and invigoration. Popularized American religion in this period tends to be fundamentalist, evangelist, and millennialist (millennialism, especially, having a significant history in the United States), and is highly mediated

by mass culture and charismatic leadership. Indeed, fundamentalist Christian movements built around televisual evangelism acquired substantial social power in the 1970s and significantly influenced the Reagan administration in the 1980s. The Nation of Islam has also achieved substantial success recruiting among American Blacks. This has occurred not only in the United States, but especially in the third world where new theocratic states have been established or reestablished after the departure of colonial administrations. Hence the classic Weberian thesis would appear to be relevant for certain European countries under certain conditions rather than as a global modernization thesis.

For a figure such as Charles Taylor, on the other hand, the new scientific, unbelieving modernity and enlightenment rationalism actually remain parasitic on religious belief such that the modern self cannot be complete without some sort of religious element or its equivalent. With respect to the present point under discussion, he argues that many major *progressive* (not reactionary) social movements in the nineteenth and twentieth centuries either began as religious movements or drew heavily from religion for their staunch moral positions (which also ironically took them away from the church because of the complicity of organized religion). For Taylor, the replacement of religious/metaphysical worldviews with a new modern "ethics of belief" remains dependent on important elements of religiosity that are not, as Habermas contends, sublimated into the binding power of a *discourse* ethics. See Taylor (1989).

6. The term "communicative freedom" is not quite explicit in Adorno, but his clear concern with communication justifies such an expression in describing his approaches to the object and to freedom. Cornell's ethical reading of Adorno's 'communicative freedom' links it to the communicative freedom that Theunissen (1980: 45–46) attributes to Hegel:

> The [Hegelian] awareness that the self-conscious subject comes home in and through the relationship to otherness is what Michael Theunissen has called "communicative freedom." . . . Communicative freedom, in other words, is the coincidence of love and freedom in which "one part experiences the other not as boundary but as the condition of its own realization." Under the circumstances of communicative freedom "reality would have found its substantive 'truth' and thus become fully real . . . everything would be related to such an extent that the relata would not retain their separateness." Under Theunissen's interpretation, which is also the one I adopt, the full integration of the relata is what Hegel means by Absolute Knowledge. . . . For Adorno, communicative freedom cannot be thought of as unification of the relata into a comprehensive totality without violating the coincidence of love and freedom (Cornell, 1992: 15).

Theunissen (in the passage quoted by Cornell but left out in her ellipses) makes it clear that in Hegel this "true reality is marked by the specific New

Testament coincidence of love and freedom. . . . Whereas freedom . . . is founded on indifference to others and on the domination of them, communicative freedom is complete only as the freedom of all things possible, whose idea the world owes to Hegel's historico-philosophical view of Christianity." Adorno's negative dialectic retains a relationship to the Hegelian requirement of the coincidence of love and freedom, but rejects Hegel's invocation of the deeply intimate experience of love and religious communion derived from the early Christian ethical community in order to give full meaning to his concept of freedom.

7. I follow Zuidervaart (1991: 290–98, especially 295 and 298) on the objections to Wellmer raised in this paragraph.

8. Of course, if one does not hold that truth itself can have a substantive meaning of any kind whatsoever, then the (in)compatibility between philosophical and aesthetic truth is not an issue.

9. Adorno still intended to complete a final revision of *Aesthetic Theory* when he died. The text was published posthumously in 1970 under the editorial direction of Gretel Adorno and Rolf Tiedemann.

10. I am in accord with Coles (1997: 75–137), insofar as his reading of Adorno's *oeuvre* and *Dialectic of Enlightenment* in particular recognizes the latter's assuredly consistent concern with productive ethical questions and responses. Coles argues that Adorno can be taken in further fruitful ethical directions toward *caritas* and a politics of "receptive generosity." What I emphasize here (which Coles does not) is the importance of the aesthetic dimension to Adorno's ethics that has direct bearing upon the lessons we can learn for contemporary politics. Others such as Dallmayr (1997; 1981), Hullot-Kentor (1989), and Cornell (1992) have also read Adorno in consistently ethical ways.

11. Fredric Jameson has dedicated significant work to this general question, taking inspiration from Adorno's orientation toward culture as a figuration of material relations that are nevertheless part of the very culture under scrutiny. The unfigurable social totality can be glimpsed in partial fashion only by a materialist analysis sensitive to the depth and extent of the dialectical interpenetration of culture, politics and 'economic' relations. See for example, Jameson (1981; 1984; 1991).

12. Adorno was much maligned by the Student Movement and the New Left in the late 1960s and 1970s for failing to support their radical causes. My position, which is sympathetic to Jameson's, is that Adorno may yet have much of value to offer the forces of social change today. Jameson remarks provocatively: "Adorno was a doubtful ally when there were still powerful and oppositional currents from which his temperamental and cantankerous quietism could distract the uncommitted reader. Now that for the moment those currents are themselves quiescent, his bile is a joyous counter-poison and a corrosive solvent to apply to the surface of 'what is'" (1990: 249).

13. In this context Adorno criticizes the culture industry precisely for presenting the opposite to art's broken promise: mass culture deceives its consumers

into thinking that the gratification it offers is *equivalent* to genuine happiness, thereby promising what it cannot ever deliver. "Pain as the very truth of pleasure," as Jameson (1990: 147) observes: "with this deeply felt paradox we touch the central dialectic of Adorno's conception of experience and his notion of authenticity."

14. See note 16 below.

15. Schoolman sometimes betrays his overemphasis of the pure negativity of art in Adorno by referring to the latter's aesthetics (for example, 1997: 75) rather than his aesthetic theory. Adorno does not initiate a return to philosophical aesthetics and does not use the term "aesthetics" in reference to his *own* thought. For to present an aesthetic *theory* and not merely a theory of art is to retain the purchase on a trans-aesthetic *truth*—a central category for Adorno's reflections on art, but one rarely, if ever mentioned in Schoolman's treatment. A politics based on a conception of non-identity as the utter unknown and unfathomable more resembles a pre-Hegelian, Kantian style of philosophy of the thing-in-itself that has abandoned the insights of relationality and mediation offered by Hegel's teachings. This is just what Adorno does not want to abandon with his idea of non-identity. On this point, for example, see Dallmayr's (1997: 35–39) discussion of Adorno's exit from Hegel's system that nevertheless preserves the latter's deepest intention toward ethical life.

16. Indeed, as we saw, this is one of Habermas's central criticisms. For Habermas, Adorno has little choice when faced by the total reification that descends from the latter's alleged understanding of reason as wholly instrumental reason. Adorno can therefore *only* appeal to the guidance of a blind and uncomprehended nature, which cannot be theorized, as an alternative to the violence of (instrumental) reason. Schoolman recognizes that Adorno does not reduce reason to instrumental rationality in *Aesthetic Theory*, but erroneously thinks that this is a departure from *Negative Dialectics* and *Dialectic of Enlightenment* (Schoolman, 1997: 71). It is not, as I try to make clear here. Yet Schoolman risks unintended support for Habermas's main critique of Adorno precisely by maintaining that what is most important about art is its relationship to the utterly "unknown" and unknowable, "impenetrably mysterious nature." This is as misleading for Adorno's negative dialectic as it is for his aesthetic theory. Elsewhere I think, Schoolman's numerous insights work against this overemphasis of unknowability in favor of the tension and shuddering dynamism I foreground here.

17. Derrida (1995) has also spoken of what can be granted from the "gift" of death that has certain affinities with my reading of this existential need to reconcile with human finitude in a historically different way. But again, the negative dialectic takes the *historical* as what has to become the explicit content of reflection and not some primordial, indeconstructible substance that is revealed through a negative ontology.

18. My presentation of Burke below is indebted to the useful discussions of his thought in Eagleton (1990: 52–69) and Mitchell (1986: 116–49).

19. Adorno perhaps comes closest to a Romantic position here, but his insistence on a "nearness by distance" (*MM*: 112/89–90) decisively distinguishes him from this tradition. The English translation of this passage quoted from *Negative*

Dialectics (*ND*: 191–92/191), it should be noted, leaves out the crucial Eichendorf reference: "What consciousness experiences as an alien thing cannot be taken out of the dialectic of the extant: negatively, this is coercion and heteronomy, yet it is also the scarred figure of what would be loved and what the spell, the endogamy of consciousness, does not allow to be loved. Over and above Romanticism, which felt weltschmerz and suffering in the face of estrangement, rises Eichendorf's saying, the 'beautiful alien.' The reconciled condition would not annex the alien with philosophical imperialism, but would instead find its happiness where the alien remains distant and different in its lasting nearness, beyond the heterogeneous and beyond that which is one's own." See also Gebauer and Wulf (1995: 281–93).

20. Indeed, Josef Chtry (1989: 484–85), in his comprehensive treatment of the German quest for aesthetic political being, argues that a plausible translation in modern idiom of Aristotle's "good life" might be "aesthetic state."

21. For a recent defense of Foucault's aesthetics of existence that argues against the need for a command ethics from a poststructuralist standpoint, see Bennett (1996).

CHAPTER SIX. CONCLUSION

1. Such regard is, of course, quite dissimilar to the value accorded to doubt, testing, challenge, etc., that a critical fallibilism holds central—for example, Karl Popper's philosophy of science.

2. Given Habermas's self-conscious respect of the tradition of critical theory and his often circumspect and somewhat ambiguous formulations of certain key positions (for example, his ambivalent quasi-transcendentalism), the proximity to traditional theory is often far clearer in the less subtle and less ambiguous work of his followers.

3. However, prominent commentators today tend to agree that the outlines of a utopian project are somehow definitive for the survival of critical theory. See, for example, Axel Honneth's recent affirmation in Critchley and Honneth (1998) and Panitch and Leys (1999). But it has been Fredric Jameson (for example, 1981; 1990; 1991) who has consistently championed the need to maintain a critical utopian sense in theory and for the invigoration of progressive political movements.

4. Indeed, one might observe that such a commitment has been a central tenet of political philosophy itself in the European spirit—one need only recall Plato's privileging of talk over force in the first book of the *Republic* to get a sense of how fundamental this is to the tradition. Plato, of course, does not stop there or remain satisfied with prioritizing talk over sheer power for his political theory. Moreover, the political point of talk for many of the ancients was its *persuasive effect*, which achieves a political purpose but which does not rely on achieving the kind of conviction of free and rational agreement that Habermas holds as an ideal. This constitutes one of the most fundamental differences between ancient and modern views of political talk.

Bibliography

Adorno, Theodor, Walter Benjamin, Ernst Bloch, Bertolt Brecht, and Georg Lukacs. 1977. *Aesthetics and Politics*. London: Verso.

Adorno, Theodor W. 1938. "Über den Fetischcharakter in der Musik und die Regression des Hörens." *Zeitschrift für Sozialforschung* VII (3): 321–55.

———. 1951. *Minima Moralia: Reflexionen aus dem beschädigten Leben*. Frankfurt: Suhrkamp Verlag.

———. 1961. "'Static' and 'Dynamic' as Sociological Categories." *Diogenes* 33 (Spring): 28–49.

———. 1966. *Negative Dialectik*. stw. 113 ed. Frankfurt: Suhrkamp.

———. 1968. "Is Marx Obsolete?" *Diogenes* 64 (Winter): 1–16.

———. 1969. "Zu Subjekt und Objekt." In *Stichwörte: Kritische Modelle 2*. Frankfurt: Suhrkamp.

———. 1969/1970. "Society." *Salmugundi* 10–11 (Fall/Winter): 144–53.

———. 1970. *Äesthetische Theorie*. Ed. G. A. a. R. Tiedemann. Frankfurt: Suhrkamp.

———. 1971a. "Die Aktualität der Philosophie." In *Gesammelte Schriften*. Ed. R. Tiederman. Frankfurt: Suhrkamp.

———. 1971b. "Die Idee der Naturgeschichte." In *Gesammelte Schriften*. Ed. R. Tiederman. Frankfurt: Suhrkamp.

———. 1971–1986. *Gesammelte Schriften*. Ed. R. Tiederman. Frankfurt: Suhrkamp.

———. 1972a. "Reflexionen zur Klassentheorie." In *Gesammelte Schriften*. Ed. R. Tiederman. Frankfurt: Suhrkamp.

————. 1972b. "Thesen über Bedürfnis." In *Gesammelte Schriften*. Ed. R. Tiederman. Frankfurt: Suhrkamp.

————. 1972c. "Über Statik und Dynamik als soziologische Kategorien." In *Gesammelte Schriften*. Ed. R. Tiederman. Frankfurt: Suhrkamp.

————. 1972d. "Zum Verhältnis vom Soziologie und Psychologie." In *Gesammelte Schriften*. Ed. R. Tiederman. Frankfurt: Suhrkamp.

————. 1973 [1966]. *Negative Dialectics*. Trans. E. B. Ashton. New York: Continuum.

————. 1974 [1951]. *Minima Moralia: Reflections From a Damaged Life*. Trans. E. F. N. Jephcott. London: New Left Books.

————. 1976. "Introduction." In *The Positivist Dispute in German Sociology*. Trans. Glyn Adey and David Frisby. London: Heinemann.

————. 1977a. "Letters to Walter Benjamin." In *Aesthetics and Politics*. London: Verso.

————. 1977b. "The Actuality of Philosophy." *Telos* 31 (Spring): 120–33.

————. 1981 [1967]. *Prisms*. Trans. Samuel Weber and Shierry Weber. Cambridge, Mass.: MIT.

————. 1982. "On the Fetish-Character in Music and the Regression of Listening." In *The Essential Frankfurt School Reader*. Ed. A. Arato and E. Gebhardt. New York: Continuum.

————. 1983 [1956]. *Against Epistemology: A Metacritique. Studies in Husserl and the Phenomenological Antinomies*. Trans. Willis Domingo. Cambridge, Mass.: MIT.

————. 1984. "The Idea of Natural History." *Telos* 60 (Spring).

————. 1989a [1962]. *Kierkegaard: Construction of the Aesthetic*. Trans. Robert Hullot-Kentor. Minneapolis: University of Minnesota Press.

————. 1989b. "The Culture Industry Reconsidered." In *Critical Theory and Society: A Reader*. Ed. S. E. Bronner and D. M. Kellner. New York: Routledge.

————. 1991a. *Notes to Literature*. Ed. R. Tiedeman. Trans. Shierry Weber Nicholsen. 2 vols. Vol. 1. New York: Columbia University Press.

————. 1991b. "On Lyric Poetry and Society." In *Notes to Literature*. Ed. R. Tiedeman. Trans. Shierry Weber Nicholsen. New York: Columbia University Press.

————. 1992. *Notes to Literature*. Ed. R. Tiedeman. Trans. Shierry Weber Nicholsen. 2 vols. Vol. 2. New York: Columbia University Press.

————. 1993 [1963]. *Hegel: Three Studies*. Trans. Shierry Weber Nicholsen. Cambridge, Mass.: MIT.

———. 1997 [1970]. *Aesthetic Theory*. Trans. Robert Hullot-Kentor. Minneapolis: University of Minnesota Press.

———. 1998. *Critical Models: Interventions and Catchwords*. Trans. Henry W. Pickford. New York: Columbia University Press.

Adorno, Theodor W., Else Frenkel-Brunswik, Daniel J. Levinson, and R. Nevitte Sanford. 1950. *The Authoritarian Personality*. New York: Harper.

Agger, Ben. 1990. "The Crisis of the 'Crisis of Marxism'." *Berkeley Journal of Sociology* 33: 187–207.

Albert, Michael, Leslie Cagan, Noam Chomsky, Robin Hahnel, Mel King, Lydia Sargent, and Holly Sklar. 1986. *Liberating Theory*. Boston: South End Press.

Albert, Michael, and Robin Hahnel. 1991. *Looking Forward: Participatory Economics for the Twenty First Century*. Boston: South End Press.

Althusser, Louis. 1971. *Lenin and Philosophy and Other Essays*. Trans. Ben Brewster. New York: Monthly Review.

Anderson, Perry. 1976. *Considerations on Western Marxism*. London: New Left Books.

Anon. 1978–79. "Theory and Politics: A Discussion with Herbert Marcuse, Jürgen Habermas, Heinz Lubasz and Tilman Spengler." *Telos* 38 (Winter).

Apel, Karl-Otto. 1980. "The A Priori of the Communication Community and the Foundations of Ethics." In *Towards a Transformation of Philosophy*. London: Routledge and Kegan Paul.

———. 1987. "The Problem of Philosophical Foundations in Light of a Transcendental Pragmatics of Language." In *After Philosophy: End or Transformation?* Ed. K. Baynes, J. Bohman and T. McCarthy. Cambridge, Mass.: MIT.

———. 1990. "Is the Ethics of the Ideal Communication Community a Utopia? On the Relationship between Ethics, Utopia, and the Critique of Utopia." In *The Communicative Ethics Controversy*. Ed. S. Benhabib and F. Dallmayr. Cambridge, Mass.: MIT Press.

Arnason, Johann P. 1991. "Modernity as Project and as Field of Tensions." In *Communicative Action: Essays on Jürgen Habermas's The Theory of Communicative Action*. Ed. A. Honneth and H. Joas. Cambridge, Mass.: MIT.

Avineri, Shlomo. 1972. *Hegel's Theory of the Modern State*. Cambridge: Cambridge University Press.

Baynes, Kenneth. 1995. "Democracy and the Rechtstaat: Habermas's *Faktizität und Geltung*." In *The Cambridge Companion to Habermas*. Ed. S. K. White. Cambridge: Cambridge University Press.

Baynes, Kenneth, James Bohman, and Thomas McCarthy, eds. 1987. *After Philosophy: End or Transformation?* Cambridge, Mass.: MIT.

Beech, David, and John Roberts. 1996. "Spectres of the Aesthetic." *New Left Review* 218: 102–27.

Benhabib, Seyla. 1986. *Critique, Norm and Utopia: A Study of the Foundations of Critical Theory*. New York: Columbia University Press.

Benhabib, Seyla, Wolfgang Bonß, and John McCole, eds. 1993. *On Max Horkheimer: New Perspectives*. Cambridge, Mass.: MIT.

Bennett, Jane. 1996. "'How is it, Then, That We Still Remain Barbarians?' Foucault, Schiller, and the Aestheticization of Politics." *Political Theory* 24 (4): 653–72.

Berman, Marshall. 1982. *All that is Solid Melts into Air: The Experience of Modernity*. New York: Penguin.

Bernstein, Jay. 1989. "Art Against Enlightenment: Adorno's Critique of Habermas." In *The Problems of Modernity: Adorno and Benjamin*. Ed. A. Benjamin. London: Routledge.

Bernstein, J. M. 1992. *The Fate of Art: Alienation from Kant to Derrida and Adorno*. University Park: Pennsylvania State University Press.

———. 1995. *Recovering Ethical Life: Jürgen Habermas and the Future of Critical Theory*. London: Routledge.

Bernstein, Richard J., ed. 1985. *Habermas and Modernity*. Oxford: Basil Blackwell.

Bewes, Timothy. 1997. *Cynicism and Postmodernity*. London: Verso.

Böhme, Harmut, and Gernot Böhme. 1983. *Das Andere der Vernunft*. Frankfurt: Suhrkamp.

Bowie, Andrew. 1990. *Aesthetics and Subjectivity: from Kant to Nietzsche*. Manchester: Manchester University Press.

Brown, Wendy. 2000. "Reconsidering Tolerance in the Age of Identity." In *Toleranz: Philosophische Grundlagen und gesellschaftliche Praxis einer umstrittenen Tugend*. Ed. R. Forst. Frankfurt and New York: Campus Verlag.

Buck-Morss, Susan. 1977. *The Origin of Negative Dialectics*. Sussex: Harvester Press.

Burke, Edmund. 1958 [1757]. *A Philosophical Enquiry concerning the Origin of the Ideas of the Sublime and the Beautiful*. Ed. J. T. Boulton. New York: Columbia University Press.

Burke, Edmund. 1968 [1790]. *Reflections on the Revolution in France*. Ed. C. C. O'Brian. London: Penguin.

Cahn, Michael. 1984. "Subversive Mimesis: T. W. Adorno and the Modern Impasse of Critique." In *Mimesis in Contemporary Theory: An Interdisciplinary Approach*. Ed. M. Spariosu. Philadelphia: John Benjamins.

Chaloupka, William. 1999. *Cynicism in America*. Minneapolis: University of Minnesota.

Chytry, Josef. 1989. *The Aesthetic State: A Quest in Modern German Thought*. Berkeley: University of California Press.

Coles, Romand. 1995. "Identity and Difference in the Ethical Positions of Adorno and Habermas." In *The Cambridge Companion to Habermas*. Ed. S. K. White. Cambridge: Cambridge University Press.

————. 1997. *Rethinking Generosity: Critical Theory and the Politics of Caritas*. Ithaca: Cornell University Press.

Connerton, Paul. 1980. *The Tragedy of Enlightenment: an Essay on the Frankfurt School*. Cambridge: Cambridge University Press.

Connolly, William. 1993. *The Augustinian Imperative: A Reflection on the Politics of Morality*. Newbury Park: Sage.

Connolly, William E. 1983. *The Terms of Political Discourse*. 2nd ed. Oxford: Martin Robertson.

————. 1991. *Identity\Difference: Democratic Negotiations of Political Paradox*. Ithaca: Cornell University Press.

Cornell, Drucilla. 1992. "The Ethical Message of Negative Dialectics." In *The Philosophy of the Limit*. New York: Routledge.

Cox, Robert W. 1987. *Production, Power, and World Order: Social Forces in the Making of History*. New York: Columbia University Press.

Critchley, Simon, and Axel Honneth. 1998. "Philosophy in Germany." *Radical Philosophy* 89 (May/June): 27–39.

Dallmayr, Fred. 1997. "The Politics of Nonidentity: Adorno, Postmodernism—and Edward Said." *Political Theory* 25 (1): 33–56.

Dallmayr, Fred R. 1981. *Twilight of Subjectivity: Contributions to a Post-Individualist Theory of Politics*. Amherst: University of Massachusetts.

————. 1984a. "Appendix: Lifeworld and Communicative Action." In *Polis and Praxis: Exercises in Contemporary Political Theory*. Cambridge, Mass.: MIT.

————. 1984b. *Language and Politics*. Notre Dame, Ind.: University of Notre Dame Press.

————. 1984c. *Polis and Praxis: Exercises in Contemporary Political Theory*. Cambridge, Mass.: MIT.

————. 1991. *Between Freiburg and Frankfurt: Toward a Critical Ontology*. Amherst: University of Massachusetts Press.

Derrida, Jacques. 1978. "Violence and Metaphysics: An Essay on the Thought of Emmanuel Levinas." In *Writing and Difference*. Trans. Alan Bass. Chicago: University of Chicago Press.

———. 1992a. "The Force of Law: The 'Mystical Foundation of Authority'." In *Deconstruction and ther Possibility of Justice*. Ed. D. Cornell, M. Rosenfeld and D. G. Carlson. Trans. Mary Quaintance. New York: Routledge.

———. 1992b. *The Other Heading: Reflections on Today's Europe*. Trans. Pascale-Anne Brault and Michael B. Naas. Bloomington: Indiana University Press.

———. 1994. *Spectres of Marx: the State of the Debt, the Work of Mourning, and the New International*. Trans. Peggy Kamuf. New York: Routledge.

———. 1995. *The Gift of Death*. Trans. David Wills. Chicago: University of Chicago Press.

Dews, Peter. 1987. *Logics of Disintegration: Post-structuralist Thought and the Claims of Critical Theory*. London: Verso.

———. 1995. "The Paradigm Shift to Communication and the Question of Subjectivity: Reflections on Habermas, Lacan and Mead." *Revue internationale de philosophie* 49 (194): 483–519.

Drury, Shadia B. 1997. *Leo Strauss and the American Right*. New York: St. Martin's Press.

Dryzek, John S. 1996. *Democracy in Capitalist Times: Ideals, Limits, and Struggles*. New York: Oxford University Press.

Dubiel, Helmut. 1985. *Theory and Politics*. Cambridge, Mass.: MIT.

Eagleton, Terry. 1990. *The Ideology of the Aesthetic*. Oxford: Blackwell.

Eder, Klaus. 1982. "A New Social Movement?" *Telos* 52 (Summer): 5–20.

Foucault, Michel. 1973. *The Order of Things: An Archeology of the Human Sciences*. New York: Vintage.

———. 1980. *Power/Knowledge: Selected Interviews and Other Writings 1972–1977*. Ed. C. Gordon. Trans. Colin Gordon, Leo Marshall, John Mepham, Kate Soper. New York: Pantheon.

———. 1988. "Critical Theory/Intellectual History." In *Politics, Philosophy, Culture: Interviews and other Writings 1977–1984*. Ed. L. D. Kritzman. New York: Routledge.

———. 1991. "Adorno, Horkheimer, and Marcuse." In *Remarks on Marx: Conversations with Duccio Trombadori*. New York: Semiotext(e).

Fraser, Nancy. 1985. "What's Critical About Critical Theory? The Case of Habermas and Gender." *New German Critique* 35 (Spring/Summer): 97–131.

———. 1989. *Unruly Practices: Power, Discourse, and Gender in Contemporary Social Theory*. Minneapolis: University of Minnesota Press.

Fraser, Nancy, and Linda J. Nicholson. 1990. "Social Criticism without Philosophy: An Encounter between Feminism and Postmodernism." In *Feminism/Postmodernism*. New York: Routledge.

Freud, Sigmund. 1989. "'Wild' Psycho-analysis." In *The Freud Reader*. Ed. P. Gay. New York: W. W. Norton.

Fukuyama, Francis. 1992. *The End of History and the Last Man*. New York: Free Press.

Gebauer, Gunter, and Christoph Wulf. 1995. *Mimesis: Culture, Art, Society*. Trans. Don Reneau. Berkeley: University of California Press.

Geuss, Raymond. 1981. *The Idea of a Critical Theory: Habermas and the Frankfurt School*. Cambridge: Cambridge University Press.

Geyer, Michael. 1997. "Germany, or, the Twentieth Century as History." *South Atlantic Quarterly* 96 (4).

Gould, Stephen Jay. 1981. *The Mismeasure of Man*. New York: W. W. Norton.

Grenz, Friedemann. 1974. *Adornos Philosophie in Grundbegriffen: Auflösung einiger Deutungsprobleme*. Frankfurt: Suhrkamp.

Gill, Stephen, and David Law. 1988. *The Global Political Economy: Perspectives, Problems, and Policies*. Baltimore: Johns Hopkins University Press.

Habermas, Jürgen. 1971a [1968]. *Knowledge and Human Interests*. Trans. Jeremy J. Shapiro. Boston: Beacon Press.

———. 1971b. "Technology and Science as 'Ideology'." In *Toward a Rational Society*. Trans. Jeremy J. Shapiro. London: Heinemann.

———. 1974. *Theory and Practice*. Trans. John Viertel. London: Heinemann.

———. 1976a. *Legitimation Crisis*. Trans. Thomas McCarthy. London: Heinemann.

———. 1976b. *Zur Rekonstruktion des Historischen Materialismus*. Frankfurt: Suhrkamp Verlag.

———. 1979a. *Communication and the Evolution of Society*. Trans. Thomas McCarthy. Boston: Beacon Press.

———. 1979b. "History and Evolution." *Telos* 39.

———. 1982. "A Reply to My Critics." In *Habermas: Critical Debates*. Ed. J. B. Thompson and D. Held. London: Macmillan.

———. 1983a. "Does Philosophy Still Have a Purpose?" In *Philosophical-Political Profiles*. Trans. Frederick G. Lawrence. Cambridge, Mass.: MIT Press.

————. 1983b. "Modernity—An Incomplete Project." In *The Anti-Aesthetic*. Ed. H. Foster. Washington, D.C.: Bay Press.

————. 1983c. *Philosophical-Political Profiles*. Trans. Frederick G. Lawrence. Cambridge, Mass.: MIT Press.

————. 1983d. "Theodor Adorno: The Primal History of Subjectivity—Self-Affirmation Gone Wild." In *Philosophical-Political Profiles*. Trans. Frederick G. Lawrence. Cambridge, Mass.: MIT Press.

————. 1984. *The Theory of Communicative Action: Reason and the Rationalization of Society*. Trans. Thomas McCarthy. 2 vols. Vol. 1. Boston: Beacon Press.

————. 1985a. "Civil Disobedience: Litmus Test for the Democratic Constitutional State." *Berkeley Journal of Sociology* 30.

————. 1985b. "Psychic Thermidor and the Rebirth of Rebellious Subjectivity." In *Habermas and Modernity*. Ed. R. J. Bernstein. Oxford: Basil Blackwell.

————. 1985c. "Questions and Counterquestions." In *Habermas and Modernity*. Ed. R. J. Bernstein. Oxford: Basil Blackwell.

————. 1986a. *Autonomy and Solidarity: Interviews with Jürgen Habermas*. Ed. P. Dews. London: Verso.

————. 1986b. "Nachwort von Jürgen Habermas." In *Dialektik der Aufklärung*. M. Horkheimer and T. W. Adorno, Frankfurt: Fischer.

————. 1986c. "The New Obscurity: the Crisis of the Welfare State and the Exhaustion of Utopian Energies." *Philosophy and Social Criticism* 11 (2): 1–18.

————. 1987. *The Philosophical Discourse of Modernity: Twelve Lectures*. Trans. Frederic G. Lawrence. Cambridge, Mass.: MIT.

————. 1989a. *The New Conservatism: Cultural Criticism and the Historian's Debate*. Ed. S. W. Nicholsen. Trans. Shierry Weber Nicholsen. Cambridge, Mass.: MIT Press.

————. 1989b. "The Public Sphere: An Encyclopedia Article." In *Critical Theory and Society: A Reader*. Ed. S. E. Bronner and D. Kellner. New York: Routledge.

————. 1989c [1962]. *The Structural Transformation of the Public Sphere: An Inquiry into a Category of Bourgeois Society*. Trans. Thomas Burger. Cambridge, Mass.: MIT Press.

————. 1990a. "Justice and Solidarity: On the Discussion Concerning Stage 6." In *The Moral Domain: Essays in the Ongoing Discussion Between Philosophy and the Social Sciences*. Ed. T. E. Wren. Cambridge, Mass.: MIT Press.

————. 1990b. *Moral Consciousness and Communicative Action*. Trans. Christian Lenhardt and Shierry Weber Nicholsen. Cambridge, Mass.: MIT.

————. 1991a. "A Reply." In *Communicative Action: Essays on Jürgen Habermas's The Theory of Communicative Action*. Ed. A. Honneth and H. Joas. Cambridge, Mass.: MIT.

————. 1991b. "What Does Socialism Mean Today? The Revolutions of Recuperation and the Need for New Thinking." In *After the Fall: The Failure of Communism and the Future of Socialism*. Ed. R. Blackburn. London: Verso.

————. 1992a. "A Generation Apart from Adorno (an Interview)." *Philosophy and Social Criticism* 18 (2): 119–24.

————. 1992b. *Postmetaphysical Thinking: Philosophical Essays*. Trans. William Mark Hohengarten. Cambridge, Mass.: MIT.

————. 1993. *Faktizität und Geltung: Beiträge zur Diskurstheorie des Rechts und des demokratischen Rechtsstaats*. Frankfurt: Suhrkamp.

————. 1994a. *Justification and Application: Remarks on Discourse Ethics*. Trans. Ciaran P. Cronin. Cambridge, Mass.: MIT.

————. 1994b. "Struggles for Recognition in the Democratic Constitutional State." In *Multiculturalism and "The Politics of Recognition."* Ed. A. Gutman. Princeton N.J.: Princeton University Press.

————. 1996. *Between Facts and Norms: Contributions to a Discourse Theory of Law and Democracy*. Trans. William Rehg. Cambridge, Mass.: MIT.

————, and Niklas Luhmann. 1971. *Theorie der Gesellschaft oder Sozial-technologie— was leistet die Systemforschung?* Frankfurt: Suhrkamp.

Haraway, Donna J. 1985. "Manifesto for Cyborgs: Science, Technology, and Socialist Feminism in the 1980s." *Socialist Review* 80: 65–108.

Harvey, David. 1989. *The Condition of Postmodernity: An Enquiry into the Origins of Cultural Change*. Oxford: Basil Blackwell.

Hegel, G. W. F. 1967a. *The Phenomenology of Mind*. Trans. J. B. Baillie. New York: Harper and Row.

————. 1967b. *Philosophy of Right*. Trans. T. M. Knox. London: Oxford University Press.

Held, David. 1980. *Introduction to Critical Theory*. London: Hutchinson.

Heller, Agnes. 1982. "Habermas and Marxism." In *Habermas: Critical Debates*. Ed. J. B. Thompson and D. Held. London: Macmillan.

Hernnstein Smith, Barbara. 1997. *Belief and Resistance: Dynamics of Contemporary Intellectual Controversy*. Cambridge, Mass.: Harvard University Press.

Hohendahl, Peter Uwe. 1995. *Prismatic Thought: Theodor W. Adorno*. Lincoln: University of Nebraska Press.

Honneth, Axel. 1991 [1985]. *Critique of Power: Reflective Stages in a Critical Social Theory.* Trans. Kenneth Baynes. Cambridge, Mass.: MIT.

———. 1995a. *The Fragmented World of the Social: Essays in Social and Political Philosophy.* Ed. C. W. Wright. Albany: SUNY Press.

———. 1995b. "From Adorno to Habermas: On the Transformation of Critical Social Theory." In *The Fragmented World of the Social: Essays in Social and Political Philosophy.* Ed. C. W. Wright. Albany: SUNY Press.

Honneth, Axel, and Hans Joas, eds. 1991. *Communicative Action: Essays on Jürgen Habermas's The Theory of Communicative Action.* Cambridge, Mass.: MIT.

Honneth, Axel, Thomas McCarthy, Claus Offe, and Albrecht Wellmer, eds. 1992. *Philosophical Interventions in the Unfinished Project of Enlightenment.* Cambridge, Mass.: MIT Press.

Horkheimer, Max, and Theodor W. Adorno. 1969 [1947]. *Dialektik der Aufklärung: Philosophische Fragmente.* Frankfurt: Fischer.

———. 1972 [1947]. *Dialectic of Enlightenment.* Trans. John Cumming. New York: Continuum.Horkheimer, Max. 1947. *Eclipse of Reason.* New York: Continuum.

———. 1992. "Odysseus or Myth and Enlightenment." *New German Critique* 56 (Spring-Summer): 109–41.

Horkheimer, Max. 1972a. "The Latest Attack on Metaphysics." In *Critical Theory: Selected Essays.* Trans. Matthew J. O'Connell and others. New York: Continuum.

———. 1972b. "Materialism and Metaphysics." In *Critical Theory: Selected Essays.* Trans. Matthew J. O'Connell and others. New York: Continuum.

———. 1972c. "Traditional and Critical Theory (and Postscript)." In *Critical Theory: Selected Essays.* Trans. Matthew J. O'Connell and others. New York: Continuum.

———. 1989. "The State of Contemporary Philosophy and the Tasks of an Institute for Social Research." In *Critical Theory and Society: A Reader.* Ed. S. E. Bronner and D. M. Kellner. New York: Routledge.

———. 1993a. *Between Philosophy and Social Science: Selected Early Writings.* Trans. G. Frederick Hunter, Matthew S. Kramer, and John Torpey. Cambridge, Mass.: MIT.

———. 1993b. "A New Concept of Ideology?" In *Between Philosophy and Social Science: Selected Early Writings.* Trans. G. Frederick Hunter, Matthew S. Kramer, and John Torpey. Cambridge, Mass.: MIT.

Horowitz, Asher. 1994. "The Comedy of Enlightenment: Weber, Habermas, and the Critique of Reification." In *The Barbarism of Reason. Max Weber and the Twighlight of Enlightenment.* Ed. A. Horowitz and T. Maley. Toronto: University of Toronto Press.

Hoy, David Couzens. 1994. "Critical Theory and Critical History." In *Critical Theory*. D. C. Hoy and T. McCarthy, Cambridge, Mass.: Blackwell.

Huhn, Tom, and Lambert Zuidervaart, eds. 1997. *The Semblance of Subjectivity: Essays in Adorno's Aesthetics*. Cambridge, Mass: MIT Press.

Hullot-Kentor, Robert. 1989. "Back to Adorno." *Telos* 81 (Fall): 5–29.

Jameson, Fredric. 1981. *The Political Unconscious: Narrative as Socially Symbolic Act*. Ithaca, New York: Cornell University Press.

———. 1984. "Postmodernism, or The Cultural Logic of Late Capitalism." *New Left Review* 146 (July–August): 53–92.

———. 1988. "*History and Class Consciousness* as an 'Unfinished Project'." *Rethinking Marxism* 1 (1): 49–72.

———. 1990. *Late Marxism: Adorno, or, the Persistence of the Dialectic*. London: Verso.

———. 1991. *Postmodernism, or The Cultural Logic of Late Capitalism*. Durham: Duke University Press.

———. 1992. *The Geopolitical Aesthetic: Cinema and Space in the World System*. Bloomington: Indiana University Press.

Jameson, Fredric, and Masao Miyoshi, eds. 1998. *The Cultures of Globalization*. Durham, N.C.: Duke University Press.

Jarvis, Simon. 1998. *Adorno: A Critical Introduction*. New York: Routledge.

Jay, Martin. 1973. *The Dialectical Imagination: A History of the Frankfurt School and the Institute for Social Research, 1923–1950*. Boston: Little, Brown.

———. 1984. *Marxism and Totality: the Adventures of a Concept from Lukács to Habermas*. Oxford: Polity Press.

———. 1988. "Habermas and Postmodernism." In *Fin-de-Siècle Socialism*. London: Routledge and Kegan Paul.

———. 1992. "The Debate over Performative Contradiction: Habermas versus the Poststructuralists." In *Philosophical Interventions in the Unfinished Project of Enlightenment*. Ed. A. Honneth, T. McCarthy, C. Offe and A. Wellmer. Trans. William Rehg. Cambridge, Mass.: MIT Press.

———. 1993. *Force Fields: Between Intellectual History and Cultural Critique*. New York: Routledge.

Kellner, Douglas. 1989. *Critical Theory, Marxism and Modernity*. Baltimore: The Johns Hopkins University Press.

Knodt, Eva. 1994. "Toward a Non-Foundationalist Epistemology: the Habermas/ Luhmann Controversy Revisited." *New German Critique* 61 (Winter): 77–100.

Kolakowski, Leszek. 1978. *Main Currents of Marxism: the Breakdown*. Vol. 3. Oxford: Oxford University Press.

Kuhn, Thomas. 1970. *The Structure of Scientific Revolutions*. 2nd ed. Chicago: University of Chicago Press.

Kunnemann, Harry , and Hent de Vries, eds. 1989. *Die Aktualität der Dialektik der Aufklärung*. Frankfurt: Campus Verlag.

Laclau, Ernesto, and Chantal Mouffe. 1985. *Hegemony & Socialist Strategy: Towards a Radical Democratic Politics*. London: Verso.

Lohmann, Georg. 1980. "Gesellschaftskritik und normativer Maßstab." In *Artbeit, Handlung, Normitavitität*. Ed. A. Honneth and U. Jaeggi. Frankfurt: Suhrkamp.

Lukács, Georg. 1971. *History and Class Consciousness*. Trans. Rodney Livingstone. Cambridge, Mass.: MIT.

Lyotard, Jean-François. 1984. *The Postmodern Condition: A Report on Knowledge*. Minneapolis: University of Minnesota.

Mandel, Ernest. 1978 [1972]. *Late Capitalism*. Trans. Joris De Bres. London: Verso.

Mannheim, Karl. 1936. *Ideology and Utopia: An Introduction to the Sociology of Knowledge*. New York: Harcourt, Brace and World.

Marcuse, Herbert. 1955. *Eros and Civilization: A Philosophical Inquiry into Freud*. Boston: Beacon Press.

———. 1958. *Soviet Marxism*. New York: Columbia University Press.

———. 1965. "Repressive Tolerance." In *A Critique of Pure Tolerance*. Ed. R. P. Wolf, B. Moore Jr. and H. Marcuse. Boston: Beacon Press.

———. 1968a. "On Hedonism." In *Negations: Essays in Critical Theory*. Trans. Jeremy J. Shapiro. Boston: Beacon Press.

———. 1968b. "Philosophy and Critical Theory." In *Negations: Essays in Critical Theory*. Trans. Jeremy J. Shapiro. Boston: Beacon Press.

———. 1969. *An Essay on Liberation*. London: Penguin.

Marx, Karl. 1954 [1867]. *Capital*. Ed. F. Engels. Trans. Samuel Moore and Edward Aveling. 3 vols. Vol. 1. Moscow: Progress Publishers.

———. 1959 [1894]. *Capital*. Ed. F. Engels. 3 vols. Vol. 3. Moscow: Progress Publishers.

———. 1973 [1939]. *Grundrisse: Foundations of the Critique of Political Economy (Rough Draft)*. Trans. Martin Nicolaus. Hammondsworth: Penguin.

———. 1974a. "The Civil War in France." In *The First International and After: Political Writings Vol. 3*. Ed. D. Fernbach. Hammondsworth, Middlesex: Penguin/New Left Books.

———. 1974b. "The Eighteenth Brumaire of Lois Bonaparte." In *Surveys from Exile: Political Writings Vol. 3*. Ed. D. Fernbach. Hammondsworth, Middlesex: Penguin/New Left Books.

Marx, Karl, and Friedrich Engels. 1978. "Manifesto of the Communist Party." In *The Marx-Engels Reader*. Ed. R. Tucker. New York: W. W. Norton.

Matustík, Martin Joseph Beck. 1998. *Specters of Liberation: Great Refusals in the New World Order*. Albany: SUNY Press.

McCarthy, Thomas. 1978. *The Critical Theory of Jürgen Habermas*. London: Hutchinson.

———. 1985. "Complexity and Democracy, or the Seducements of Systems Theory." *New German Critique* 35 (Spring/Summer): 27–53.

———. 1994. "Philosophy and Critical Theory: A Reprise." In *Critical Theory*. D. C. Hoy and T. McCarthy, Cambridge, Mass.: Blackwell.

Misgeld, Dieter. 1977. "Critical Theory and Hermeneutics: The Debate Between Habermas and Gadamer." In *On Critical Theory*. Ed. J. O'Neill. New York: Seabury.

———. 1985. "Critical Hermeneutics Versus Neoparsonianism?" *New German Critique* 35 (Spring/Summer): 55–82.

Mitchell, W. J. T. 1986. *Iconology: Image, Text, Ideology*. Chicago: University of Chicago Press.

Nägele, Rainer. 1986. "The Scene of the Other: Theodor W. Adorno's Negative Dialectics in the Context of Poststructuralism." In *Postmodernism and Politics*. Ed. J. Arac. Minneapolis: University of Minnesota Press.

Negt, Oskar, and Alexander Kluge. 1993 [1972]. *Public Sphere and Experience: Toward an Analysis of the Bourgeois and Proletarian Public Sphere*. Trans. Peter Labanyi, Jamie Daniel, and Assenka Oksiloff. Minneapolis: University of Minnesota Press.

Nicholsen, Shierry Weber. 1997. *Exact Imagination, Late Work: On Adorno's Aesthetics*. Cambridge, Mass: MIT.

Niznik, Józef, and John T. Sanders, eds. 1996. *Debating the State of Philosophy*. Westport, Conn.: Praeger.

Offe, Claus. 1984. *Contradictions of the Welfare State*. Ed. J. Keane. London: Hutchinson.

Ollman, Bertell. 1993. *Dialectical Investigations*. New York: Routledge.

Panitch, Leo, and Colin Leys, eds. 1999. *The Socialist Register: Necessary and Unnecessary Utopias*. Rendlesham: Merlin Press.

Pensky, Max, ed. 1997. *The Actuality of Adorno: Critical Essays on Adorno and the Postmodern.* Albany: SUNY Press.

Phelan, Shane. 1993. "Interpretation & Domination: Adorno & the Habermas-Lyotard Debate." *Polity* XXV (4): 597–616.

Postone, Moishe. 1996. *Time, Labour, and Social Domination: A Reinterpretation of Marx's Critical Theory.* Cambridge: Cambridge University Press.

Reinhardt, Mark. 1997. *The Art of Being Free: Taking Liberties with Tocqueville, Marx, and Arendt.* Ithaca: Cornell University Press.

Rocco, Christopher. 1994. "Between Modernity and Postmodernity: Reading Dialectic of Enlightenment against the Grain." *Political Theory* 22 (1): 71–97.

———. 1995. "The Politics of Critical Theory: Argument, Structure, Critique in *Dialectic of Enlightenment.*" *Philosophy and Social Criticism* 21 (2): 107–33.

Rockmore, Tom. 1989. *Habermas on Historical Materialism.* Bloomington: Indiana University Press.

Rorty, Richard, ed. 1967. *The Linguistic Turn: Recent Essays in Philosophical Method.* Chicago: University of Chicago Press.

———. 1979. *Philosophy and the Mirror of Nature.* Princeton, N.J.: Princeton University Press.

Rose, Gillian. 1978. *The Melancholy Science: An Introduction to the Thought of Theodor W. Adorno.* London: Macmillan.

Rosen, Stanley. 1987. *Hermeneutics as Politics.* New York: Oxford University Press.

Rudolph, Werner. 1992. *Auf der Suche nach dem verlorenen Sinn: Die "Dialektik der Aufklarung" im System der Kritischen Theorie und ihr Verhaltnis zur philosophischen Tradition.* Berlin: Schelzky & Jeep.

Ryan, Michael. 1982. *Marxism and Deconstruction: A Critical Articulation.* Baltimore: Johns Hopkins Press.

Scheuerman, William E. 1994. *Between the Norm and the Exception: The Frankfurt School and the Rule of Law.* Cambridge, Mass.: MIT Press.

Schoolman, Morton. 1997. "Toward a Politics of Darkness: Individuality and its Politics in Adorno's Aesthetics." *Political Theory* 25 (1): 57–92.

Shapiro, Michael. 1989. "Politicizing Ulysses: Rationalistic, Critical, and Genealogical Commentaries." *Political Theory* 17 (February).

Sills, Chip, and George H. Jensen, eds. 1992. *The Philosophy of Discourse: the Rhetorical Turn in Twentieth-Century Thought.* 2 vols. Portsmouth, N.H.: Boynton/ Cook.

Sloterdijk, Peter. 1987. *Critique of Cynical Reason*. Minneapolis: University of Minnesota Press.

Sohn-Rethel, Alfred. 1978. *Intellectual and Manual Labour: A Critique of Epistemology*. Trans. Martin Sohn-Rethel. Atlantic Highlands, N.J.: Humanities Press.

Spivak, Gayatri Chakravorty. 1988. "Scattered Speculations on the Question of Value." In *In Other Worlds: Essays in Cultural Politics*. New York: Routledge.

Stone, Robert. 1992. *A Flag for Sunrise*. New York: Vintage.

Taylor, Charles. 1989. *Sources of the Self: The Making of the Modern Identity*. Cambridge, Mass.: Harvard University Press.

———. 1994. *Multiculturalism and "The Politics of Recognition."* Ed. A. Gutman. 2nd ed. Princeton N.J.: Princeton University Press.

———. 1995. "Cross-Purposes: The Liberal-Communitarian Debate." In *Philosophical Arguments*. Cambridge, Mass.: Harvard University Press.

Theunissen, Michael. 1980. *Sein und Schein: Die kritische Funktion der Hegelschen Logik*. Frankfurt: Suhrkamp.

van Reijen, Willem, and Gunzelin Schmid Noerr, eds. 1987. *Vierzig Jahre Flaschenpost: "Dialektik der Aufklarung," 1947–1987*. Frankfurt-Fischer.

Warren, Mark. 1988. *Nietzsche and Political Thought*. Cambridge, Mass.: MIT.

Weber, Shierry M. 1977. "Aesthetic Experience and Self-Reflection as Emancipatory Processes: Two Complementary Aspects of Critical Theory." In *On Critical Theory*. Ed. J. O'Neill. New York: Seabury.

Wellmer, Albrecht. 1985. "Reason, Utopia, and the Dialectic of Enlightenment." In *Habermas and Modernity*. Ed. R. J. Bernstein. Cambridge: Polity.

———. 1991. "Truth, Semblance, Reconciliation: Adorno's Aesthetic Redemption of Modernity." In *The Persistence of Modernity*. Cambridge, Mass.: MIT.

White, Stephen K. 1988. *The Recent Work of Jürgen Habermas*. Cambridge: Cambridge University Press.

———, ed. 1995. *The Cambridge Companion to Habermas*. Cambridge: Cambridge University Press.

Whitebook, Joel. 1988. "Reconciling the Unreconcilable? Utopianism after Habermas." *Praxis International* 8 (1): 73–90.

———. 1995. *Perversion and Utopia: a Study in Psychoanalysis and Critical Theory*. Cambridge, Mass.: MIT Press.

Wiggershaus, Rolf. 1994. *The Frankfurt School: Its History, Theories, and Political Significance*. Trans. Michael Robertson. Cambridge, Mass.: MIT.

Wilson, W. Daniel, and Robert C. Holub, eds. 1993. *Impure Reason: Dialectic of Enlightenment in Germany*. Detroit: Wayne State University Press.

Wolin, Sheldon S. 1960. *Politics and Vision: Continuity and Innovation in Western Political Thought*. Boston: Little, Brown and Company.

Young, Iris Marion. 1990. *Justice and the Politics of Difference*. Princeton, N.J.: Princeton University Press.

Zimmerman, Michael E. 1994. *Contesting Earth's Future: Radical Ecology and Postmodernity*. Berkeley: University of California Press.

Žižek, Slavoj. 1989. *The Sublime Object of Ideology*. London: Verso.

Zuckert, Catherine H. 1996. *Postmodern Platos: Nietzsche, Heidegger, Gadamer, Strauss, Derrida*. Chicago: University of Chicago Press.

Zuidervaart, Lambert. 1991. *Adorno's Aesthetic Theory: the Redemption of Illusion*. Cambridge, Mass.: MIT.

INDEX

237